James Attlee works in art publishing in London and is the co-author of *Gordon Matta-Clark: The Space Between*.

www.rbooks.co.uk

ISOLARION

A DIFFERENT OXFORD JOURNEY

JAMES ATTLEE

James Attlee

BLACK SWAN

TRANSWORLD PUBLISHERS
61–63 Uxbridge Road, London W5 5SA
A Random House Group Company
www.rbooks.co.uk

ISOLARION
A BLACK SWAN BOOK: 9780552775236

First published in the United States by the University of Chicago Press
First publication in Great Britain
Black Swan edition published 2009

Addresses for Random House Group Ltd companies outside the UK
can be found at: www.randomhouse.co.uk
The Random House Group Ltd Reg. No. 954009

The Random House Group Limited supports The Forest Stewardship
Council® (FSC®), the leading international forest-certification organisation.
Our books carrying the FSC label are printed on FSC®-certified paper.
FSC is the only forest-certification scheme supported by the leading
environmental organisations, including Greenpeace. Our
paper procurement policy can be found at
www.randomhouse.co.uk/environment

MIX
Paper from
responsible sources
FSC® C016897

Typeset in 11/15pt Giovanni Book by
Kestrel Data, Exeter, Devon.
Printed and bound in Great Britain by Clays Ltd, St Ives plc

4 6 8 10 9 7 5 3

For Charlotte

I myself have been tempted for a long time by the cloud-moving wind, filled with a strong desire to wander.
MATSUO BASHO, *The Narrow Road to the Deep North*

'Isolarion' is the term for the 15th-century maps that describe specific areas in detail, but that do not provide a clarifying overview of how these places are related to each other. FROM THE PUBLICITY FOR THE EXHIBITION ISOLARION BY SOPHIE TOTTIE, LUND KUNSTHALLE, SWEDEN, 2005

CONTENTS

SECOND PARTITION

Acknowledgements

I would like to thank collaborators and early readers of the manuscript whose advice and support have been invaluable, especially Wes Williams, Richard Milbank, Simon Mason, Anna Perring, Marian Pocock, and my editor at the University of Chicago Press, Susan Bielstein; Helena Attlee and Alex Ramsay, who first introduced me to the *Anatomy*; the librarians, archivists, and local historians on whose work I have depended; and the people of East Oxford for their time and their generosity of spirit.

Some names have been changed to protect the author.

INTRODUCTION

I

A time may come in your life when you feel the need to make a pilgrimage. A time when the pressure to return your staff pass, kiss your loved ones goodbye, and set out on a journey becomes too insistent to ignore.

The impulse that propels you may be religious or it may be secular. Perhaps the words of a preacher have ignited a fire in your heart; or perhaps the dusty volume you stumbled across on the shelves of a second-hand bookshop has awoken a thirst for distant shores that cannot be shaken. You may be sick at heart or in body, in need of counsel or immersion in healing waters. The passage of a birthday may have triggered the desire to seek out the birthplace of your ancestors or revisit a scene from your childhood.

The motivations of the pilgrim are as varied as their destinations. You may be headed for a holy city, a site of revelation or miracles, where a god has appeared or a prophet has spoken. You may wish to visit the place where a composer brooded, a poet walked, or the grave-yard where a singing voice lies buried. There may be a rite you must perform or a memory you need to lay to rest.

Jerusalem, Mecca, Rome, Graceland, Thebes, Varanasi, Bethlehem, Tepeyac, Père-Lachaise.

And so you consult an astrologer or a travel agent, close up your house, give instructions to your servants, smear your forehead with ashes, slit the throat of a quiescent herbivore, smash a coconut on the sidewalk, take up the flagellant's whip, board a train, a tourist coach, an aeroplane, or a leaking tramp-steamer, or simply put on or take off your shoes and walk, run, shuffle, dance, or crawl on your knees up holy mountains, rocky paths, marble steps, and glaciers, braving war zones, border guards, con men, rapacious hoteliers, foreign food, and (most of all) your fellow travellers.

Perhaps you wish to know your God better. Peraps it is yourself you wish to get to know. Whatever your intention, one thing is certain: that the end of the journey will not be as you imagined.

Medina, Lumbini, Gangotri, Bodhgaya, Santiago de Compostela, Shikoku, Valldemossa.

Certain, too, is that your singing, stamping, shouting, chanting, weeping, whirling, and prostrating; your basilicas, temples, grand hotels, and coach-parks; your tented cities and smoky campfires on the banks of great rivers all look much the same from space. Which is not to denigrate any of the traditions that set these journeys

14

in motion and give them structure, for they are clearly one of the things that mark us as human.

For we do not all migrate as the eel or the caribou, the swallow, the tern, or the salmon. Equally driven, our goals are less explicable, our needs more arcane. The journeys we undertake do not necessarily involve travelling large distances. Many of us are not free to set aside our responsibilities for an extended period; there are mouths to feed, bills to pay, deadlines to meet that keep us entangled in the present, anchored to our locations, and yet jerked here and there by the breeze from another place, like thistle-down caught in a web.

This was my situation. Yet gradually it dawned on me that the voyage I needed to make began in my own neighbourhood, within a few minutes' walk of my front door. It had been there all the time, under my nose, even as I made other abortive attempts to discover a starting point. This would be an urban, post-modern, fragmentary pilgrimage that could be dipped in and out of, freeze-framed, and re-run, visited between other commitments – and yet nonetheless a voyage of discovery for all that.

There is an old road in my neighbourhood that follows approximately the path that ran between the city walls of Oxford and the medieval leper hospital at Bartlemas, and beyond it to the village of Cowley. Until the beginning of the nineteenth century, farmers still grazed their flocks and made hay in the unenclosed meadows and marshland that lay outside the city wall. Cowley Road is now the main thoroughfare through East Oxford, connecting the academic and touristic heart of the city with the Cowley Works, the car factory that in its heyday in the 1960s employed over twenty thousand people and has been a magnet for immigrant workers since the 1920s. Its name is derived from the Anglo-Saxon, a combination of the word *lea*, a glade or clearing in the forest, and the name *Cofa* – Cofa's Glade. Today it is lined with businesses that seem to represent every nation on earth. Among them are Jamaican, Bangladeshi, Indian, Polish, Kurdish, Chinese, French, Italian, Thai, Japanese, and African restaurants; sari shops, cafés, fast-food outlets, electronics stores, a florist, a Ghanaian fishmonger, pubs, bars, three live-music venues, tattoo parlours, betting shops, a Russian supermarket, a community centre, a publisher, the headquarters of an international NGO, musical instrument vendors, butchers (halal and otherwise), three cycle shops, two video-rental stores, post offices, two mosques, three churches, a Chinese supermarket, a pawn shop, a police station, two record shops, two centres of alternative medicine, a late-night Tesco, an independent cinema, call centres, three sex shops, numerous grocers, letting agencies, a bingo hall, and a lap-dancing establishment that plies its trade on Sundays.

Why make a journey to the other side of the world when the world has come to you?

II

Have they not travelled within the land so that they should have hearts with which to understand, or ears with which to hear?

QUR'AN 22.46

I live in a famous city, a city that has been sold to you in a thousand ways. A myriad of writers have set their dramas upon its ancient streets, discoursed upon its architecture, and provided guides to its quads and colleges. Few even mention the Cowley Road, let alone the people who live and work there. Many of its inhabitants have made their own journeys from far away, under all kinds of circumstances. They have brought with them not only their cuisine, but also their beliefs, their values, their trades, their prejudices, the stories of their past, and their hopes for the future. This is the other Oxford, the one never written about. This city has dispatched anthropologists, explorers, scientists, authors, and poets to every nation represented on Cowley Road. Perhaps it is time to flip the coin and see ourselves through their eyes.

In 1994 the artist Francis Alys walked through the streets of Havana wearing a pair of specially constructed magnetic shoes. Three years previously he had taken a magnetised metal 'dog,' that he christened *The Collector*, for a walk through the streets of Mexico City. At the end of these 'strolls,' both the shoes and *The Collector* were covered in the metal detritus of the city. Somehow this accretion was redolent of the overheard conversations, snatches of music, smells, and other sensory impressions that one gathers on an urban walk.

I have no magnetic shoes. Instead I carry a notebook, a pen, and an old-fashioned cassette recorder loaded with magnetised tape, with which I intend to capture the sounds of the voices I encounter. One way in which to classify people is by which sense they primarily relate to the world. We can all think of friends who *consume* life; who, when they are not cooking or eating, are constantly picking at, shopping for, or reading about food. Others are dominated by the visual, sensitive to the coded messages of colour and design embedded in their habitat by nature and human ingenuity. Then there are the tactile ones, constantly reaching out to touch and stroke, sensitive to the fabric and texture of life. For yet another category, it is the sound of things that matters. As a child I progressed through the world testing the resonance of surfaces made of wood, plastic, metal, stone. I was constantly being told to stop tapping my feet, drumming my fingers, beating out a rhythm on whatever came to hand. Even today, in the middle of laying a table, I can become distracted by the ability of the 'give' in the blade of a knife to approximate the spring of a snare drum. Now it is my wife and children who beg me to desist, and I am genuinely surprised: *Can't they hear how great that sounds?* Given this predilection, it is only natural that I am interested in capturing the aural landscape of the road as well as its visual qualities and wafting odours. My analogue tape recorder will replace Alys's magnetic shoes. At those times when a recording device is inappropriate – in casual conversation, interacting with friends and neighbours – I will have to press a button in my head marked *Record*. Then, when I summon up the characters that I have met upon my journey in the eye of my imagination, I will run the conversation again and try to convey their words as exactly as I can.

It was Heraclitus, of course, who came up with the formulation that we are never able to step into the same river twice. If the Cowley Road is a river, the big fish lie hidden beneath the surface in the shadow of its banks: landlords, entrepreneurs, developers, local politicians, wheeler-dealers, import-export men.

The obverse of Heraclitus's maxim may be that one is never able to step out of the river the same, twice. A neuron in the brain is altered with every experience. The self, if it exists, must be a constantly evolving thing. Those coming to the banks of the Ganges or the Jordan to immerse themselves do not expect to leave the same as they arrive. Perhaps this will apply to me, also.

Because we are at war, I learn that Muslims are buried on their right shoulder, facing Mecca. I am astounded that I never knew this simple yet fundamental detail. People are living and dying all around me, the formative rituals of their lives as hidden as the rites of a people half a world away. Perhaps this is always so. In any case, it cannot hurt to attempt to lift a corner of the curtain.

I wind up my radio before hanging it on the corner of a radiator and stepping into the shower. In *The Wind-Up Bird Chronicle*, Haruki Murakami uses the song of the wind-up bird as a motif for the engine that keeps life going. For me it is the sound that the handle of my wind-up radio makes that starts the day. Two academics are having a discussion about transport problems as I apply the soap. 'A hyper-mobile society is an anonymous society,' one says. For seven years I have been getting up at an unholy hour to travel by train back to London, where I have lived for most of my adult life, to work. In many ways I still feel more rooted there than in Oxford. I was used to inhabiting a city abundant in space and spectacle, large enough to lose myself in. A hyper-mobile man, I have to learn to travel more thoughtfully, to slip beneath the surface and explore more deeply. Space is relative. One aim of my pilgrimage will be to connect me to the neighbourhood in which I live. At the same time, perhaps my journey will offer clues to a wider reality. Oxford is an untypical city, its centre preserved in aspic for the tourists, its biggest landlord an ancient institution that still owns an inordinate amount of its buildings. Much of the change and diversity in the city has therefore been concentrated into a small area, its visible expression squeezed like toothpaste from a tube along the length of Cowley Road. Paradoxically it is this place, often overlooked or omitted from the guidebooks, that is a barometer of the health of the nation. It is both unique and nothing special. It could be any number of streets in your town. For that reason alone, it seems as good a place as any from which to start a journey.

FIRST PARTITION

EMBARKATION

We should go forth on the shortest walk, perchance, in the spirit of undying adventure, never to return – prepared to send back our embalmed hearts only as relics to our desolate kingdoms.

HENRY DAVID THOREAU, 'Walking,' from *Excursions* (1862)

Our starting point is a red-brick pub built at the end of the nineteenth century. A road sign affixed to its wall points the direction of our journey: B480 Cowley. It projects like the prow of a ship, dividing the traffic into two streams flowing up Iffley and Cowley roads, so that sitting in the front of the bar, one can see out onto both streets simultaneously, as well as onto the Plain. The result of road improvements carried out in the 1770s, its position earned it the name 'The Cape of Good Hope.' This name has not survived into the new century; instead it has been rechristened 'The Pub, Oxford.'* The pub sign is a reproduction of the painting *The Scream* by Edvard Munch, after the version he painted in oils on cardboard rather than the later graphic versions he produced as

*Correct at the time of writing; the original name has subsequently been revived.

woodcuts. The sunset is there in lurid orange and the screaming female figure, with, in this version, strangely protuberant eyes. Two figures flutter in the background, black as crows. Along the pub frontage is emblazoned the slogan 'It's a Scream.' This pun on the Munch work provides the rationale for the décor, the key to the whole *concept*, I realise. Inside, the words are repeated in yellow on the black polo shirts of the staff. The Victorian interior has been transformed. Ceiling and window-frames are painted green, the walls a mustard yellow, and the radiators vermilion. A blue leather sofa sits on a raised dais surrounded by green iron railings. Beside it cluster cubes of red and blue vinyl seating, their primary colours reminiscent of the furnishings in a kindergarten.

Munch worked and reworked *The Scream*, as was his practice. His main sources of inspiration were his own journals, albums, and previous works. 'I have always worked best with my paintings around me,' he said. 'When they were placed together a sound went through them right away and they became quite different than when they were separate. They became a symphony.' All his works were part of a series, 'a poem on life, love and death.' He first expressed the intense anxiety he felt one evening at sunset in words, only later portraying the emotion visually in *Despair* and *The Scream*. Writing was as important to him as the visual arts. The first commandment of the Kristiania bohemian group that he belonged to, which was led by the anarchist novelist

Hans Jaeger, was 'Thou Shalt Write Thine Own Life.'

This he did. Sitting in a library, I jot down Munch's differing accounts of the intense experience that inspired the numerous versions he created of the famous image:

I walked along the road with two friends
Then the sun went down

The sky suddenly became blood and I felt the
Great scream in nature . . .

I walked along the road with two friends
Then the sun went down

And I felt as if a breath of sadness
(A sucking pain beneath the heart)

I stopped – leaned against the railing
Tired to death

Over the blue-black fjord and city
Lay blood and tongues of fire

Over the blue-black fjord and city lay
Clouds of dripping steaming blood

My friends walked on and I was left in
Fear with an open wound in my breast

My friends walked on and I was left
Trembling with fear
And I felt a big, unending scream go through nature

Inside the Pub, a giant screen shows MTV videos, dancing figures rendered spectral by the late-afternoon sunlight spilling in the open door – as spectral as the voices of the long-dead African-American singers sampled by the dance DJs whose rhythms animate the shaking, snaking bodies. Oil drums, sawn in half lengthways, containing one clear and one yellow bulb, hang from the ceiling. This is not an environment designed to be seen when sober or empty of the crowds that will flow in as the evening progresses. To arrive early like this is an embarrassment, like being the first one at a party. Only a lost tourist or a dedicated alcoholic would choose to drink here in the afternoon. Slot machines pulse with multicoloured lights. A young man with a bunch of keys hanging from his belt roams the room, rearranging the position of plastic menus that advertise *'The Scream Burger – It's the Double-Decker Daddy of the burger world!'* And coffee: *'We don't do Decaff – No Caffeine, No Point.'* He tells me the Pub is part of a 92-strong chain, mostly in university towns. Did he know what the inspiration was behind the use of Munch's image? 'Oh, *The Scream*? I couldn't tell you. To be honest, I think we might have to stop using it; I don't think we have permission. Or perhaps we did have and we don't any more. Anyway, I'm not climbing up a ladder to take it down!'

The figure from Munch's picture has been rendered as an inflatable, on T-shirts, calendars, posters, postcards, and mugs. These are versions that the Norwegian artist could not have predicted. I am not sure why the image has exerted such a lasting fascination that it has been possible to sell and resell it in this manner, particularly to the young. Does the feeling of existential angst that Munch portrays strike a chord? Or have people taken it to mean something quite different; an expression of frustration, perhaps, or the combination of fear and exhilaration that is the drug of choice of the young male? Has nature's howl of pain become the whoop of the teenager on the roller coaster or the rictus of fear on the face of the young man charging downhill in a shopping trolley for the TV cameras?

The Pub lies at another border; the ancient one between town and gown. Clearly designed to appeal to students, it attracts another clientele as well, young men preparing for a night out in the city. Until fairly recently, foreign students were advised not to cross Magdalen Bridge; the sons of ambassadors and the daughters of American presidents are more often to be seen in the West End of London than on the Cowley Road. Of course, many of the students and those that teach them now make their homes in what residents sometimes call the Independent Republic of East Oxford. Both the ancient, original Oxford University and the newcomer Oxford Brookes University are building more and more student accommodation in an area already under pressure in terms of affordable housing. Yet a trip to the Cowley Road for many students is still an encounter with 'the other.' Sometimes that encounter is harsh and unexpected. Three students lived next door to us for a year or so; quiet, unassuming boys studying something to do with science or mathematics. They went for a drink at the pub at the beginning of Cowley Road one night (it was then under different management). As they left, they were assaulted – punched in the face and relieved of their watches and wallets. When they returned from the Accident and Emergency Department of the hospital with their cuts and bruises tended to, they found that their shared house had been burgled and that their laptops, inscribed with the precious research for their PhDs, had all vanished. In the way that one does, all three had failed to back up their work. On the other side of a one-brick thick Victorian wall, we had not heard a sound.

The starting points of journeys are often brash, unattractive places. Ferry terminals, stations, airports, the transit ships in *Star Wars*. Loads are shunted, lorries backed up, tanks filled, decks sluiced down, straps tightened, windscreens washed, luggage X-rayed, stowaways and contraband smuggled on board. These are not places to seek out haute cuisine; the Scream Burger is the national dish of the itinerant. Munch's painting could be incorporated into the flag of those who find themselves stateless, unable to go back but unable to progress either, caught in a web of bureaucracy without rights or a discernible future. 'The past life of émigrés is, as we know, annulled,' writes Theodor Adorno. Walter

Benjamin was such a one, caught on the border of Vichy France and Spain, clutching the briefcase that contained a manuscript, the survival of which he repeatedly told his travelling companions was more important than his own. Overcome by thirst on the journey through the mountains, he knelt to lap water from a puddle like a dog. What is the worst that can happen, he asked his guide, who remonstrated with him; in a couple of days I may be dead of typhus, but I will have crossed the border and my manuscript will be safe. He wanted it to reach Adorno in New York. At the border the Spanish refused to let the travellers through, and Benjamin, fully aware that he was too weak to go any further, took cyanide in his hotel room. What of the manuscript? It disappeared without a trace, sucked into the vortex of *The Scream*, the drag of its undertow etched in the swirling lines of sea and sky.

PURIFICATION

When devout Hindus travel to make puja at a temple, their heads are shaved. Our Tamil friends from London, Sri Lankan refugees from the civil war who first arrived in Britain hidden under blankets in the back of a lorry, have won their British citizenship after waiting over a decade. They now feel secure enough in their status to take their children to visit the temples of South India for the first time. Their sons, dressed in sportswear and keen Tottenham Hotspur supporters, grumble good-naturedly at the extreme coiffure they will have to undergo.

Almost opposite the Pub, at number 7, is a barber, a somewhat glamorous establishment with a varnished wooden floor, across which hair drifts like the iron filings in an Etch A Sketch. Black-and-white photographs by Herb Ritts and Ruth Orkin and reproductions of Klimt paintings decorate the walls. The rhythm of the techno that bubbles from the speakers is overlaid with swathes of sound that seem to be synchronised with the movement of the electric clippers across the head of a customer having a number-two cut. To entrust your head to the scissors of an unknown barber is a frightening thing, but I enter the brightly lit interior in the humble spirit of one embarking on a pilgrimage. I am not seeking a ritual haircut; I am looking for the same one I have always looked for, a haircut that improves your appearance without making you look as though you just had a haircut. This is the hardest one to find.

When I worked as a musician in London, I had an acquaintance, a second-generation Clerkenwell Italian also in the business. Through him I found myself a regular at a barber's on Wardour Street, run by an Italian named Gino. Gino's was down some steps in a tiny basement; he was the only barber on the premises, a small, dark-skinned man with gold chains around his neck, what appeared to be a gold watch around his wrist, and the beginnings of a pot-belly beneath his white T-shirt. He travelled into the West End every day from a southern suburb of the city; returning home in the evening, he would call his house from the phone-box outside the station, letting it ring two or three times and then replacing the receiver. This was the signal for his wife to put the water on to boil for his pasta, he told me, so that it would be ready when he walked through the door.

The man cutting my hair today seems to have a lot on his mind; we do not speak. This is fine with me. I am assessing him in the mirror, deciding whether we are to embark on the relationship of trust that should exist between a man and his barber. At Gino's, conversation was obligatory. It was an intensely male environment, where the normal hierarchies were laid aside and policemen and Soho criminals alike could find temporary sanctuary from the street. Many were the confessions that Gino received, in the quiet afternoons. There was something about him that inspired men to unburden themselves; and, I was to discover, if you played him right, he could be persuaded to pass on what he had heard, like a corrupt priest who had lost respect for his vows. This was how I learnt that my acquaintance was allegedly involved in some serious financial misdealing. To be more precise, Gino suggested he was printing money (the speciality *de la maison* being obscure currencies) in the little print-works in which he had an interest and had bought his house (where I had eaten Sunday lunch beneath a portrait of the pope, along with his silent, ancient mother) with wads of the stuff. The best thing about it was that his wife suspected nothing! In Gino's eyes, this was quintessentially Italian. If you had no secrets from your wife, what kind of life was it?

Sometimes barbers give you too much information. Aged twenty-two, I was foolish enough to find associating with petty criminals in some way glamorous. This was the result of personal immaturity and a rural childhood, and later led to a lot of pointless trouble. Today's barber plays his cards close to his chest, and I like him the better for it. However, he does not deliver the haircut

I am looking for and penalises me for requiring the use of scissors – they do not fit the soundtrack apparently. I leave more of my hair and more of my money than I had bargained for behind me – a common state for a pilgrim – and head off up the Cowley Road.

OF MUSIC AND CANNIBALISM

Migrations. The flight from tedious states. Against urban scleroses. Against conservatives and speculative boredom.

OSWALD DE ANDRADE, 'Cannibal Manifesto' (1928)

At number 33 lies Galeria Brasil, a tiny commercial gallery dedicated to the folk art and crafts of Brazil. At the front it displays a selection of ceramics, jewellery, sculpture, and clothes, including a wide selection of Havaianas, Brazilian flip-flops that are all the rage this summer. I am more interested in what one can find towards the back of the shop. Here they offer a selection of the popular prints created to illustrate the poems of the street poets of the Brazilian North-East. For many years these troubadours have declaimed their poetry on the streets, hanging their pamphlets, or *folhetos*, for display on a *cordel* (string). For many of the rural poor, the *folhetos* were the only kind of literature they came into contact with, brought back from the local market town to the village, passed around and read out loud by the literate to gatherings of appreciative listeners. In the heyday of *folheto* production, local presses turned out thousands every week. The pamphlets are illustrated by dramatic woodcuts, in some cases executed by the poets themselves (as in the case of one of the best known living *cordelistas*, Jota Borges), in others by artists commissioned by the presses that produce the pamphlets. As the journeying of the *cordelistas* has been restricted by the changes overtaking modern Brazil and the *folhetos* have had to compete with other forms of entertainment, their illustrators have started to produce their work in larger formats, to take advantage of interest from galleries and collectors who have become aware of the vibrancy of the popular culture of the North-East. The woodcuts, known as *xilogravuras*, have some of the immediacy and angularity of German expressionist prints, but their subject matter is purely Brazilian – an apocalyptic cocktail of myth, politics, and religion. Saints battle the devil; a young couple rides through the air on a peacock; people are turned into animals as payment for their sins; the rural poor rise up, demanding their rights.

I visit on a Saturday afternoon; the shop is constantly busy with customers, particularly young women attracted by the jewellery in the window. Brazilian friends of the gallery owner, Celine, drop by to show her their photographs and share news from home. In between these comings and goings, I ask her how she came to open Galeria Brasil on Cowley Road. Her voice on my tape is backed by the Brazilian music that is a continuous accompaniment to the activity in the gallery.

'Since I was a child, I have adored north-eastern ceramics. I used to play with little figures when I was a child, and I have always loved them. When I came to England for the second time, I decided to set up a shop where I could trade on a fair basis with the producers and the artists in Brazil. I had worked for Oxfam in Brazil, mainly with battered women, helping them to empower themselves in the Trade Union movement – it was really in the backlands of the North-East. I am not connected to any fair-trade organization, but I interact with the artists and I pay the price they ask, and if I think that it is too cheap, I tell them, "Look, you are charging too little." I bring things over on a very small scale. I love doing it. I cannot survive just on the big pieces and the sculpture and so on, so I decided that I needed to have the bread and butter, and also I wanted to promote these small clothes designers from the North-East of Brazil; I bring these very crazy things for the young people and also the fashion jewellery that is doing very well. That is what I sell most. What I like best are the prints and the sculptures, but everything I sell reflects Brazilian culture – like some of the clothes, the old style of how grandmothers make bedspreads is in that top there . . .' She points towards a blouse hanging on a rail and then breaks off as she notices some customers hovering near the window. 'Do you want help with the flip-flops? What size are you?'

When she returns after a successful sale and sits down

at her desk, I ask her to tell me a little about the art of the *cordelistas*.

'Listening to the *cordelista* is very *roots* for me; I grew up going to the market with my mother and hearing them, so it is something very familiar, the naivety and the simplicity of the rhymes is very beautiful; I don't know how to describe it . . . Nowadays you don't get it in most of the big cities any more, although in Rio there is a huge north-eastern community. Because of the drought in the North-East, people migrate south to the city to search for a better life, and there they try to recreate the culture they have abandoned . . . They have a north-eastern market in Rio where you can still hear these people singing . . .'

Cowley Road is another place in which people ply trades learnt in distant lands. Almost anyone can find something here to remind themselves of home; at the same time, there is always something to transport you to a different world.

'Cowley Road is a very special street,' Celine continues. 'All the restaurants and the little greengrocers' shops and the little boutiques. Have you noticed how many businesses at this end of Cowley Road are owned by women? There is my Galeria Brasil and Bridget Wheatley, the jeweller. There is Bead Games, Eau-de-Vie, the health centre, that is owned by two women. Uniikki, the boutique, is owned by Raija; I think she is Finnish. And there is a woman who owns an Indian restaurant, the Mirch Masala . . . Many people from South America and the Caribbean go to the Pakistani grocers because you find similar types of vegetables to the ones we get at home. Mangoes, papayas, and coriander. Those beautiful mangoes that they only sell by the box come in June when it is the mango harvest in Pakistan; June, July, half of August . . . I love the Moroccan shop. Do you eat meat? Have you eaten the *merguez* sausage they make? It is Moroccan lamb sausage; they have a spicy one and a non-spicy one, and it is cheap and delicious. I usually grill them. You ought to try . . .'

Celine, who lives locally, has made something of a study of her neighbourhood. 'Although East Oxford is very multicultural, it has a very English character of its own; very tolerant, easygoing . . . There are a lot of professional liberals, doctors, and people working for NGOs in London . . . The other side [of town] is more snobbish, more boring. I lived in Summertown, and on Saturdays sometimes you didn't see a single black person on the street . . . But I am always arguing with the council, because sometimes my street is so dirty. I ring the council, and they say it is too many people from outside and they throw rubbish, and I say I don't care . . . if that is the case, you have to have a strategy to keep it clean. If you go to North Oxford, it is spotless. I think if you drop a matchbox on the floor there, the guys will come to pick it up . . .'

This belief that they are discriminated against in terms of services – regarded as less important than inhabitants of the more affluent parts of the city – is characteristic of residents of East Oxford. I emerged from my house one day to find the Victorian kerbstones that edged the pavement being removed by council workers. Weathered and uneven, these were the only original pieces of street furniture remaining in the vicinity. As they were levered out of position, they were replaced with uniform concrete slabs. I have a particular connection with these kerbstones. On millennium eve, to celebrate the turning of the century, we had a huge party in our street, starting at five in the afternoon and carrying on until three in the morning. While countless thousands of others travelled to exotic locations or crowded to the centre of cities, we had decided that we would bring the millennium home and party where we lived. After games for the children in the afternoon and a communal meal, accompanied by music from a barrel organ played by an elderly resident, the bacchanal began. Aided by copious amounts of alcohol, a couple of hundred people danced in a tent erected in the middle of the street to music spun by local DJs. As each DJ arrived, often from previous engagements in the city, they had to push their way through the crowd to the decks, cheered and back-slapped like boxers climbing into the ring. Champagne, beer, vodka, tequila, and lethal Cuban rum flowed in an apocalyptic mix.

The music tent got more and more crowded as the evening progressed. At a certain point, stepping back-wards to give space to another dancer, I tripped on an up-ended bench stored at the edge of the dance floor, fell backwards, and hit my head on one of those Victorian kerbstones. For a few moments I lost consciousness, vanishing as completely as though I had fallen down a hole in history, a gap between the centuries. Seconds later I had got to my feet and returned to the mêlée on the dance floor as though nothing had happened (although onlookers told me later that I appeared to be dancing in slow motion). Looking around at my family, friends, and neighbours, I remember feeling an almost transcendent happiness that did not all originate in a bottle; the sensation felt by the traveller, returning home after a long journey. The next day, gently touching the lump on the back of my head, I realised that my life could have ended at that moment; people die in such absurd and unexpected ways. If it wasn't for the people that I would have left behind, I cannot think of a better way to go. A month or so after the kerbstones were removed, along with their historic patina created by cracked heads, cartwheels, children's feet, car tyres, horses' hooves, and the imprint of a century of human lives, they reappeared in the genteel and scenic Thames-side suburb of Iffley Village. Rumour had it that the villagers, fiercely proud of the Cotswold charm of their neighbourhood, had bought them from the council. If true, our history had been, quite literally, sold down the river.

Some months later a local councillor tells me that in fact the kerbstones were first removed to a council store of antiquated street furnishings and re-deployed in Iffley when street repairs needed to be undertaken. The picturesque beauty of an area like Iffley Village, with its thatched roofs and Saxon church, is far easier to defend from despoilment than the workaday streets of East Oxford, no less historically authentic, yet regarded as largely disposable. On Cowley Road, Celine is concerned by the way in which remaining housing stock is being taken over. 'Most of the houses that still exist are rented to students and that is fair enough, but what I oppose is building large buildings to accommodate students in this neighbourhood. The university is very powerful; they could easily build their student accommodation in the outskirts – the students can use buses and bicycles – not around here. You know the gas station behind the Kazbar they knocked down – they are going to put up a big block for students there. And Brookes University is building a huge student accommodation in Southfield Road; it will have an impact on the traffic and the character of the area. That is just my opinion, my observation . . .' Where a critical mass of students gather, Starbucks and the Gap will follow, for these entrepreneurs believe that today's students no longer want to be Che Guevara; they want to be Ross from *Friends*, sipping cappuccino on a sofa in their preppy clothes, in an artificial neighbourhood shipped out from Seattle.

The culture of the North-East region that Galeria Brasil promotes has played an important part in renewing the arts in many areas of Brazilian life. In the late 1960s, it was two musicians from Bahia, Gilberto Gil and Caetano Veloso, who spearheaded the musical movement Tropicalia that shockingly combined traditional music from Recife with outrageous costumes and psychedelic rock music from the West. It both satirised and scandalised the repressive, conservative society that was Brazil under military dictatorship, equally uncomfortable with the subversive currents in Western rock music and the rawer elements of its own indigenous culture. Both Gil and Veloso experienced imprisonment and exile and, later, a triumphant return to their homeland. Gil became Brazil's minister of culture and Veloso a national institution. Veloso gave the movement its intellectual rationale, taking inspiration from the 'Cannibal Manifesto' written by the Brazilian poet and philosopher Oswald de Andrade in 1928. In it, Andrade evokes the example of the Tupi Indians, a Brazilian tribe that practised cannibalism and famously ate a bishop whom they disapproved of. 'Only cannibalism unites us. Socially. Economically. Philosophically . . . Tupi or not Tupi,' he writes. The 'Manifesto' has been endlessly revisited by succeeding generations of Brazilian artists, holding as it does a key to utilising foreign influences without being colonised by them. Any cultural manifestation, it implies, can be eaten, digested, and then spat out as something else, a methodology exemplified by the Tropicalistes. Cannibalism is defined as 'absorption of the sacred enemy,' the turning of the taboo into a totem. Far from being dominated by European powers, Brazil and the Americas hold the real power in the colonial relationship as eventually it is they who will eat and digest the Old World; the Spanish and Portuguese colonists credited with 'discovering' South America, far from being conquistadors, were in reality mere refugees, fleeing their inevitable fate.

Is this the hidden strength of the Cowley Road? It has a history of soaking up the culture of incomers, re-deploying it most obviously as the various mutant versions of national cuisines it offers up for sale along its extent. In the greater struggle against being overwhelmed by larger cultural forces – the universities with their ever-expanding populations, the retail chains, and the city planners – it looks more vulnerable. Perhaps we can only grasp at the hope offered in Andrade's 'Manifesto,' that the road will absorb even these encroachments, gaining strength as it adds them to itself, before turning like a Brazilian python and swallowing its invaders whole.

DOING MY PART

Let's talk it over, let's get it straight
Don't let the situation escalate
You know there's always problems when a man is wrapped up in his art
But don't you worry, baby, you can count on me to do my part

You wash the dishes, I gotta run
You know that nightlife ain't such fun
Now don't wait up for me 'cause I know you need your rest, sweetheart
But don't you worry, baby, you can count on me to do my part

MOSE ALLISON, 'You Can Count on Me'*

I live in a small Victorian terraced house that would
have originally been a two-up, two-down with a tin bath
in the parlour. Cunning internal division of its spaces
today allows the accommodation of an impressive
number of books and human beings of varying ages
while still leaving room for a whippet and a 1970s
Hammond organ, as well as various musical instruments
and items of electronic equipment. To describe it as a

---

*Mose Allison, 'You Can Count on Me to Do My Part,' from *Wild Man on the Loose*,
  courtesy of Mose Allison/Audre Mae Music Co. BMI, 1993 (Renewed).

hive of activity would for once be apposite. With its interconnecting spaces, each cell-like in size and lined with its occupant's belongings, it hums with a constant background soundtrack of music, laughter, television shows, late-night conversations, arguments, and sudden squalls of tears. We exist in intense communion, like meerkats in a burrow or a colony of gannets on a rock, treading on each other's toes even in our dreams.

To keep this particular colony fed means long hours doing what a character in one of Murakami's stories describes as 'shovelling snow.' And so I ride the steel rails through the dreaming fields and the red-tiled streets of West London, past the factories, the canals, and the gold dome of the temple at Neasden, disembarking inside Brunel's cathedral of a station, to put in time at a culture palace by the river. Why is this not enough, an often fascinating job, love, human proximity? When I look back, I see that the things that have interested me, aside from the people I care about, have always been ones that took me *away*. Somewhere along the line, the idea took hold that for life to mean anything, you can't just be feeding your kids; you also have to feed your notebook. Unlike with kids, it doesn't matter much with what. And then gradually, as you glance back at the pages you have filled, you may begin to discern a direction, an indication of what is calling you and where you might go. When that happens, you have no choice but to follow. Yet however understanding the response of those you leave behind, every departure is a negotiation tinged with guilt, given an added intensity by the sense that time spent on your solitary journey is time borrowed, duty evaded. In this way, we create the rods with which we chastise ourselves. Or to put it another way, you can climb over the pram in the hall, but don't be surprised if it follows you down the street. It is only much later you realise that people don't mind if sometimes you have to be gone, as long as when you *are* at home you are not acting like you were somewhere else.

THE MELANCHOLY PILGRIM

I write of melancholy, by being busy to avoid melancholy . . . [and] make an
antidote out of what was the prime cause of my disease.

ROBERT BURTON, *The Anatomy of Melancholy* (1621)

The therapeutic benefits of setting out on a journey
have long been recognised. Robert Burton writes in *The
Anatomy of Melancholy* that there was 'no better physic
for a melancholy man than change of air, and variety of
places, to travel abroad and see fashions.' For, he goes on,
'peregrination charms our senses with such unspeakable
and sweet variety that some count him unhappy that
never travelled, and pity his case, that from his cradle to
his old age beholds the same still; still, still the same, the
same.' Pleasant views are especially good for the spirits;
'to have a free prospect all over the city at once, as at
Granada in Spain, and Fez in Africa,' is recommended,
as is climbing a tower in Greenwich or St. Mark's steeple
in Venice. Neapolitans and the inhabitants of Genoa
are blessed with the ability 'to see the ships, boats and
passengers go by, out of their windows, their whole cities

being situated on the side of a hill.' However, unlike the travel correspondents of Sunday newspapers today, Burton seems to have been aware that such destinations were beyond the means of many. Those seeking to take the physic of travel must be prepared to start closer to home; perhaps even in their own neighbourhood. 'Some are especially affected with such objects as be near, to see passengers go by in some great roadway, or boats in a river . . . to oversee a fair, a marketplace or out of a pleasant window into some thoroughfare street, to behold a continual concourse, a promiscuous rout, coming and going, or a multitude of spectators at a theatre, a mask, or some such like show,' he writes, describing fairly nearly the experience of the pilgrim on Cowley Road.

The book kept Burton busy throughout his life, subject as it was to constant revision, and ran into eight editions between 1621 and 1676. Burton himself suffered greatly from melancholy and hoped by his researches both to cure himself and to provide a way out for others from the mental labyrinths that had ensnared him over so many years. In this he was not entirely successful. In the 'Note on the Author' added at the beginning of the edition I possess, a Victorian reprint published by William Tegg and Company in 1857, a Mr Granger is quoted as saying that Burton wrote 'with a view of relieving his own melancholy, but increased it to such a degree, that nothing could make him laugh, but going to the bridge-foot and hearing the ribaldry of the bargemen, which

rarely failed to throw him into a violent fit of laughter.'*
(This is not the only literary reference to the linguistic
skills of Oxford bargemen, incidentally. In *Vanity Fair*,
Thackeray describes the discomfort of a tongue-tied
minor character, the Oxford student and rake James
Crawley, a 'modest boy who could not face the gentlest
of [the female] sex . . . when she began to talk to him, but
put him at Iffley Lock and he could out-slang the boldest
bargeman.') With the ribaldry of bargemen on the city's
waterways replaced by the screams of unsteady tourists
in punts and the slap of the oars of college eights, I like
to believe that if he were alive today, the same desire for
colourful diversion would attract Burton to the bustle
of the Cowley Road. For despite the melancholic's
propensity for lone introspection, there is no antidote
as effective for the dark humour as the everyday human
interactions that take place in the small shops that line
its extent.

For the reader, there is a poignant subtext to the
Anatomy; as one learns of the personal characteristics
that make a person susceptible to melancholy and
the circumstances that foster the development of the
evil humour, one seems to be reading a portrait of the
author himself. By his own admission, he lived a 'silent,
sedentary, solitary, private life . . . penned up most part
in my study.' Elsewhere he warns in the strongest terms

---

* This anecdote is more usually attributed to Bishop White Kennett.

against solitude and excessive learning and lists at great length the illnesses that accrue from the sedentary pursuit of knowledge. 'Contemplation . . . dries the brain and extinguishes natural heat,' he writes. 'For whilst the spirits are intent to meditation above in the head, the stomach and liver are left destitute, and thence come black blood and crudities by defect of concoction, and for want of exercise the superfluous vapours cannot exhale.' The worst climate for provoking melancholy, he asserts, is 'thick, cloudy, misty, foggy air, or such as comes from fens, moorish grounds, lakes, muckhills, draughts, sinks, where any carcase or carrion lies, or from whence any stinking fulsome smell comes.' Many cities and districts are accused of having such an atmosphere, including Durazzo in Albania, Pisa, Ferrara, Romney Marsh, the fens in Lincolnshire, Bruges, Amsterdam, Stockholm, and Hull. At the same time, with the typically melancholic compulsion to see many sides to every issue, a compulsion that at best leads to indecision and at worst to stasis, he mentions that foggy air is thought by some to be an aid to the memory and cites Cambridge in this respect. The reader is left wondering whether it was his loyalty to his alma mater that precludes a mention of Oxford in his catalogue of sickly towns, lying as it does in a river valley surrounded by bogs and water meadows, and famous for its fogbound winter climate. In the light of his researches, it would seem the worst location for one of his mental disposition, a vivid memory not being the most desirable attribute for an obsessive introvert. He could hardly have failed to come to the same conclusion himself. Did he therefore take his own advice and travel, in search of better air? 'I never travelled, but in map or card, in which my unconfined thoughts have freely expiated,' he confesses. The only journeys he made were mental ones with the aid of John Rouse, the librarian at the Bodleian, soaring like an eagle from his eyrie among the college towers, his wanderings recorded in the pages of the book that was his own epic pilgrimage.

It is impossible to know whether he frequented Cowley Road; there would have been little to attract him there, unless it was an historical interest in the site of the well at Bartlemas (although generally he detested stories of papist miracles) or the opportunity to gather plants for his researches. In his day the road was known as Berrye Lane and built on a causeway across the treacherous and frequently flooded Cowley Marsh. Peat was cut from the marsh in spring, dried over the summer, and sold for fuel to supplement firewood in the winter. Peat is of course the embodiment of the earth's past, a sedimentary layer cake that still supports complex life at its surface; it is possible Burton's rooms at Christ Church were heated with hissing, smoking slabs of the stuff, a fitting fumigation for his dreams. To give him his due, he never attempted to present himself as immune from the disease he studied with such devotion. 'I confess it again,' he writes in the *Anatomy*, 'I am as foolish, as mad as anyone.' He died in his room at Christ Church on 25 January 1640, sufficiently close to the date he had calculated for his own death in his horoscope for some of his students to mutter that he may have ensured his reputation as an astrologer with the aid of a length of rope. The *Anatomy* edition of 1651–2 has a note appended by the publisher to the reader, in which we are informed that 'since the last impression, the ingenuous author of it is deceased, leaving a Copy of it exactly corrected, with several considerable Additions by his own hand; this Copy he committed to my care and custody, with directions to have those Additions inserted into the next Edition; which in order to his command, and the Publicke Good, is faithfully performed in this last impression.'

In Burton's day, when medicine was still heavily reliant on classical theories, melancholy was thought to arise from an excess of black bile. A person's health was determined by the balance within them of the four humours; each individual was seen as being predominantly phlegmatic, sanguine, choleric, or melancholy. An excess of any one of the humours could lead to ill health. At a deterministic level, today we might say that an individual's disposition depends on the levels of certain chemicals within the neural circuits of their brain and the efficiency of the functions responsible for delivering and retaining optimum quantities of these magical substances. The awareness of the centrality of this neural soup to our being is not as new as we might think. Laurence Sterne poked fun at the concept in *Tristram Shandy* (1760), a work itself considerably influenced, to comic effect, by the obsessive digressions of the *Anatomy*. 'As for that certain, very thin, subtle and very fragrant juice,' Sterne writes, 'which *Coglionissimo Borri*, the great *Milaneze* physician, affirms, in a letter to *Bartholine*, to have discovered in the cellulae of the occipital parts of the cerebellum, and which he likewise affirms to be the principal seat of the reasonable soul . . . my father could never subscribe to it by any means; the very idea of so noble, so refined, so immaterial, and so exalted a being as the *Anima*, or even the *Animus*, taking up her residence, and sitting dabbling, like a tadpole, all day long, both summer and winter, in a puddle – or in a liquid of any kind, how thick or thin soever, he would say, shocked his imagination; he would scarce give the doctrine a hearing.'

Medics in Burton's day understood that melancholy was not without its benefits, unlike modern doctors, eager to medicate away every bump in life's highway. Melancholy people were imaginative, the best wits, often poets, capable of profound study and deep meditation. The philosopher A. C. Grayling, writing in the twenty-first century, would appear to agree, when he describes melancholy as a state 'in which it is possible to feel and understand things not available in other moods – for our moods are like tunings on the wireless, picking up truths at different frequencies, so that if we don't know the gamut of human feelings, neither can we know the gamut of human truth.'* He would have agreed with Burton, however, that once the dark humour predominates, problems arise. 'The mind itself by those dark, obscure, gross fumes, ascending from black humours, is in continual darkness, fear and sorrow,' Burton writes. 'Obscured as the sun by a cloud.' The melancholy carry darkness around inside them; this explains why they are not afraid of being abroad at nightfall. 'Many melancholy men,' Burton explains, 'dare boldly be, continue and walk in the dark, and delight in it.'

While the four humours theory of medicine, on which Burton based his understanding of melancholy, has long since disappeared from medical textbooks, and none of the alternative medical practitioners on Cowley Road offer it as a therapy (now *there's* a business idea), the condition itself has not. Depression may not be an exact synonym for melancholy; and the lives of sufferers in the sixteenth and twenty-first centuries are of course markedly different. People, arguably, are not. As Burton writes, ''Tis not to be denied, the world changes every day . . . We change language, habits, customs, manners, but not vices, not diseases, not the symptoms of folly and madness, they are still the same . . .' This is the conclusion we come to when navigating the literature of past ages, experiencing that spark of empathy between

---

* A. C. Grayling, *The Meaning of Things: Applying Philosophy to Life* (London: Weidenfeld & Nicolson, 2001), 98.

author and reader that can jump the centuries. In his *London Journal*, Boswell complained to Doctor Johnson that he was 'much afflicted by melancholy, which was hereditary in my family.' Johnson confessed that he also 'had inherited a vile melancholy from my father.' He was 'greatly distressed by it, and for that reason [was] obliged to fly from study and meditation to the dissipating variety of life.' His first serious attack was in 1729, when he left Oxford and had what would probably be called today a nervous breakdown. Johnson studied Burton well; he famously said that *The Anatomy of Melancholy* 'was the only book that ever took him out of bed two hours earlier than he wanted to rise.' As he was a notorious lie-a-bed, this was a literary achievement indeed. The key things in combating melancholy, he told Boswell, were to have 'a constant occupation of mind, to take a great deal of exercise and to live life moderately; especially to shun drinking at night.' The wisdom of this concise advice has not faded with age, but is in accord with the latest thinking on depression in our own times.

Boswell was right in saying that melancholy can run in families; the latest research indicates that genetic predisposition is a significant, perhaps the most significant, factor in depression. Conventional medication is a blunt instrument; sufferers in the twenty-first century are as keen to find a herbal cure as Burton's readers were in the seventeenth century. Burton would have echoed John Gerard, the author of the famous

Herball, in his belief in the efficacy and the divine source of remedies based on plants (he left a treasured copy of Gerard's *Herball* in his will). 'Wise men hath made their whole life as a pilgrimage to attaine to the knowledge of them,' Gerard had written, 'by the which they have gained the hearts of all, and opened the minds of many, in commendation of those rare virtues which are contained in these terrestrial creatures.' In the *Anatomy*, Burton recommended borage and bugloss, black hellebore as a purge, melissa balm, marigold, wormwood, pennyroyal, endive, dandelion, rosemary, and hop. 'It rarefies and cleanseth,' he wrote of the latter. '[W]e use it to this purpose in our ordinary beer which before was thick and fulsome.' Hence it might clear the blood of the black bile that produces melancholy. He had been early in citing the efficacy of St John's wort (*Hypericum perforatum*), the current favourite among herbal remedies, although it came rather far down the pecking order in his list of cures (Gerard had recommended it principally as a salve for wounds). The plant's linkage with mental afflictions survived into the early nineteenth century. Robert John Thornton, in his *Family Herbal* of 1810, probably drawing and expanding on Burton, writes that 'formerly it was supposed, and not without reason, that madmen were possessed of the devil, and this plant was found so successful in that disorder that it had the title *Fuga Daemonum*, as curing daemoniacs.' So the perforate herb enjoyed a brief moment in the spotlight in early modern times, before returning to obscurity for a century or more. By which digression I at once emulate Burton, include a coded recommendation, and hope to provide an example of the cyclical, as opposed to linear, advance of knowledge.

Burton does not confine his examination of the effect of diet on the mind to plants. He also writes of fish (warning particularly against the flesh of those that dwell in muddy ponds) and different meats. Perhaps with his tongue in his cheek and perhaps not (there is often a discernible twinkle in his eye as he solemnly signposts yet another digression), he cites authors that recommend 'an old cock, a ram's head, a wolfe's heart borne or eaten.'

What has all this to do with our journey down Cowley Road? Why would I choose an eccentric seventeenth-century cleric as a travelling companion? For me, as for Burton, writing is both a way of escaping melancholy and a cause of it. Writers and artists will tell you that when they are engaged with a project, they experience the everyday as if saturated with significance. News reports half-heard on the radio, an article in a discarded newspaper, a chance conversation with a stranger on a train – all seem to relate to and be connected with the work in progress. Obviously, at its most intense, this state is one step away from psychosis and is no guarantee of the production of anything worthwhile. The alternative, however, is worse. Creative activity for some is a kind of glue that cements life together. Without it, the tectonic plates begin to shift, the cold wind of the abyss blows between the gaps, and the black humour infiltrates, like a miasma, every area of waking life. And yet the cure itself can become the problem. Depressives are urged not to lead lives dominated by impossible ideals – but what more unobtainable dream is there than to find the time to write, when everything conspires against it? Yet withdrawing from the world to seek the space to think is also fraught with perils. As Fernando Pessoa writes in *The Book of Disquiet*, the fragmentary near-novel that can be read as a classic study of the melancholic mind: 'Solitude torments me; company oppresses me. The presence of another person distracts me from my thoughts.' Melancholy, at first a sweet muse, can lead the traveller into the middle of a forest and abandon him there. Burton understood all this and had the courage to face the monster down, stare the Black Dog in the eye, here in the city where I live. I find the nature of his project inspirational. I believe, like him, that there need be no conflict between an interest in the latest advances in science and technology and a fascination with the past; the voice of a character in an old book can speak as clearly as one in the street.

Did Burton kill himself? We will never know. Even if in the end he lost the battle, if the legend is correct, his suicide should be read more as the completion of a scholarly thesis than as a defeat. And although his book is a work of extraordinary erudition and originality, his struggle with the business of surviving everyday life makes him one of us. The years that separate his age from ours are of little consequence. For as he himself wrote, 'We are of the same humours and inclinations as our predecessors were; you shall find us all alike, much at one, we and our sons . . . And so shall our posterity continue to the last.'

BREAD AND CIRCUSES

And then there was that strange element in the evolution of so many towns: the drive to the West which so often leaves the eastern part of the town in poverty and dereliction. It may be merely the expression of that cosmic rhythm which has possessed mankind from the earliest times and springs from the unconscious realisation that to move with the sun is positive and to move against it is negative; the one stands for order and the other disorder.

CLAUDE LÉVI-STRAUSS, *Tristes Tropiques*

An important part of the character of East Oxford comes from the nature of its development. In the 1860s, thousands of plots of land were laid out by land societies on the previously unenclosed Cowley Field, the marshy meadow to the south-east of the Plain. They were bought by developers, a mixture of small investors and local builders, and built on over an extended period, resulting in a variety in the building styles selected and the occasional quirk in road layout. Every street had its shops: general stores, bakeries, laundries, fish-and-chip sellers, and the like. Most have disappeared, converted into houses, their previous use apparent from their rectangular bay windows, while commercial activity is largely confined to the main arteries; only Magdalen Road still retains its own butcher and ironmonger. One local bakery survives, on Hertford Street. Generations of children going to St Mary and St John First School have begun the day by buying Diane's warm bread rolls or a few pennyworth of sweets in a paper bag from the bakery opposite the school gates. She makes less than half a dozen different kinds of bread: our favourite is Cotswold Crunch, a chewy, satisfying brown loaf with a firm crust. As soon as all the loaves are gone from the shelves – often shortly after midday – the shop closes. A few years back, she had problems with her brick-lined baking oven and spoke about closing for good. The local community was deeply shocked. Customers pledged their undying support. Shamelessly manipulative parents deployed tearful infants, pushing them through the door to plead with the soft-hearted Diane not to shut up shop. Eventually she and her husband relented, if only to clear the premises of weeping children.

The fame of the bakery extends throughout the city, as if the aroma from its oven had drifted down Cowley Road, across the barnacled towers of the university, to the leafy enclaves of North Oxford. I am approached at the end of a three-day publishing event in London by a colleague who makes his home there.

'Look at this,' he says, showing me a book he has acquired from another publisher's stand, in exchange for one of his own. 'This is the only freebie I've picked up during the whole fair – what does that say about me?'

It is a book on bread-making, its cover featuring a pin-up of a tantalisingly moist loaf, fresh from the baking tin, pornography for the amateur baker. I make appropriate sounds of admiration.

'Is that baker still going around your way?' he asks, suddenly serious. I tell him that it is.

'Do they do croissants,' he asks, 'pastries, tarts, or rye bread?'

'No, they just make a few different types of bread and some rolls. It's a baker's shop, not a patisserie.'

'I'm thinking of buying it when I leave this publishing game,' he says. 'Then we'll give you a real bakery; sourdough bread, the lot!' He smiles triumphantly, awaiting my approval.

To my own surprise, I feel passionately defensive. I am not on my journey now; I have no tape recorder in my hand; yet suddenly I am there, despite my geographical displacement, as vividly as if I were standing outside the bakery.

'We don't need a new bakery; we are fine with the one we've got,' I say, rather stiffly. I sound, even to myself, like a country yokel telling an incomer, 'We don't want any of your fancy city ways around here.' What has happened to me?

'Oh, come on, you can't resist change,' he replies with a laugh. 'Your area will move upmarket whether you want it to or not. Anyway, I'd better get on.' And he is gone, supervising the packing up of his stand.

I am tired, I realise, with a tiredness that follows events like these, but which doesn't seem to affect my entrepreneurial colleague. I admire his energy and vision, the fact that he is planning the next stage in his life. But still I resent this threatened incursion into our neighbourhood and his certainty that we will succumb to his menu of improvement and move 'upmarket'. Where does this reaction come from? Since I started writing about these streets, it is as though I have possessed them for the first time. I have walked them physically and brooded over them in my imagination, trying to read their meaning, as though their layout was the key to an encrypted manuscript. I have digested them as thoroughly as the baker's bread, and now they are at work from within, changing my attitudes, giving rise to new and sometimes irrational emotions. These changes are, I can see, part of my journey and, although a little alarming, to be expected. After all, what is the point of travelling, if you return the same as you set out?

As is always the case, there is a coded history in the street names of East Oxford. Circus Street is the first side street after the Plain on the south side of Cowley Road. Charles Parker, a surgeon from Shrivenham who purchased the lot in 1858, named it after Newsome's Alhambra Circus, a highly acclaimed travelling show that plied its trade on that spot, its Moorish name giving it an added glamour, before building commenced in the early 1860s. In Parker's day, Islamic rule in southern Spain was a distant memory, preserved only in the romantic ruins of its architectural legacy, and Muslims had largely disappeared from Western Europe. Victorian scholars, however – contemporaries of the men who built much of East Oxford – had come to recognise the contribution that Arab learning had made to Western civilisation. In the twelfth century, European scholars flocked to Spain to forage through its extensive libraries. Arabic translations of Plato, Aristotle, and other classical philosophers were translated once more, this time into Latin, and re-entered the European canon. Over nine hundred English words are derived from the Arabic. For a period at least, Al-Andalus was a model of religious tolerance, a place where Islamic and Jewish philosophers and theologians were able to exchange ideas freely and Christian scholars were able to gather the materials that fuelled the European Renaissance. After all, the faithful are instructed by the Qur'an, 'Do not argue with the followers of earlier revelations otherwise than in the most kindly manner, unless it be with such of them that are set on evil doing – and say: We believe in that which has been bestowed upon us, as well as that which has been bestowed upon you: for our God and your God is one and the same and it is to him that we surrender ourselves.'

In the Museum of the History of Science in Oxford, I come across a brass astrolabe, made in 1081 in the

Spanish city of Guadalajara, by one Muhammad ibn Sa'id as-Sabban, who was also known as the Astrolabe Maker of Saragossa. Constructed from cast and sheet brass, it is engraved with a celestial map, a two-dimensional model of the heavens in relation to the horizon, with a sighting device attached to the back by a central pin. Its intricacy and craftsmanship speak volumes about the civilisation that produced it. In 1886, in his elegiac history *The Story of the Moors in Spain*, Stanley Lane-Poole wrote: 'For centuries, Spain had been the centre of civilisation, the seat of arts and sciences, of learning and every sort of refined enlightenment. The Moors were banished; for a while Christian Spain shone like the moon, with a borrowed light; then came the eclipse, and in that darkness Spain has grovelled ever since.'

This romantic tone transferred into the popular realm with the appropriation of Moorish names and motifs wherever an aura of exoticism was required. The Alhambra Palace at Granada, a popular destination for adventurous English travellers, gave its name to places of entertainment from Brighton to Bradford. This Orientalist fascination with Moorish motifs has survived into the twenty-first century on Cowley Road. On the opposite side of the street from where the circus would have pitched, and within a stone's throw of Boucherie Chatar, a popular café-bar called the Kazbar serves Mediterranean tapas. Its architecture is designed to evoke a North African souk, with yellow walls and Islamic-inspired metal grilles in the windows. Inside, the walls and tables are decorated with turquoise and aquamarine tiles. On summer evenings, a retractable roof is rolled back so that one can dine beneath the sky, accompanied by the screams of swifts as they swoop for insects in the warm updrafts of the city streets. The traveller down Cowley Road is therefore presented with a choice between the real North African encounter at the little supermarket across the street and this idealised but nonetheless enjoyable fiction.

Today the circuses that visit Oxford set up in South Park or on the bleak expanse of grass behind the ice rink, rather than in the vicinity of Cowley Road. I have been a fairly frequent visitor. I believe that lessons learnt under the Big Top as a child remain useful for the rest of our lives. For instance: clowns are seldom funny and often frightening; there's no point paying for expensive seats at the front because sooner or later someone will come and pour a bucket of water over your head; and, most importantly, people are not always what they seem. The surly Cockney girl in nylon overalls serving candyfloss may reappear minutes later as a beautiful Mongolian or Italian trapeze artist, her smile almost as dazzling as the sequins that sparkle on her costume as she revolves slowly beneath the spotlight, twenty feet above your head. These insights have been impressed upon me at circuses ranging from the magnificent to the humble; from the camp show-business glamour of Billy Smart's to a tiny circus in a Portuguese village entirely manned by one family. The charm of the circus for me as a child did not wholly lie in the potency of its illusions. It was the smells that played as much of a part as the sound of the band and the visual spectacle in creating its special atmosphere. The acrid reek of the big cats overlaid with the sweetness of popcorn; the aroma of an alien world that came wafting from the trailers, the realm inhabited by the sorry specimens of tropical fauna that travelled with the circus in those days. Of course, the cruelty involved in condemning such creatures to the circus life was obvious to me from an early age. Seeing large, wild animals in captivity, whether in zoos or circuses, was always an intense experience; awe-inspiring, yet almost unbearably sad. This feeling is not confined to childhood. I experience similar conflicting sensations as I regard a rural landscape through the window of a car; we cherish what we destroy. It may be that this will become the dominant human emotion as our century advances, the zeitgeist of our times.

When I was twelve or thirteen years old, I worked for a day in a small circus, in exchange for free admission to the evening performance. I spent the afternoon clearing out animal pens; the thing that struck me most was the size of the elephant droppings, their perfect spherical shape, and the ease with which they could be flicked across the ground with a broom. Some years later I was making my living selling the catalogues of exhibitions by a new breed of British artists. One of them, Chris Ofili, was also struck by the potential of elephant dung. Dried, coated with varnish, and sometimes decorated with sequins, elephant droppings played an important structural as well as symbolic role in his swirling, intricate, Afro-centric, technicolor paintings, sometimes attached to the canvas and sometimes acting as feet supporting the frame. When they were exhibited at the Brooklyn Museum of Art in New York in 1999 as part of the Sensation exhibition, the combination of this natural material and an image of the Virgin Mary enraged Mayor Rudolph Giuliani to such an extent that he called for the show to be banned, to prevent offence to the faithful. His intervention, still spoken of with hushed and grateful reverence by museum staff, turned the exhibition into a huge success overnight. Successful politicians need enemies; perhaps Giuliani was still searching for a suitably challenging foe, unaware that one was waiting in the wings, only too eager to enter battle on religious principles. One other thing was obvious; despite his proven abilities as a master of ceremonies, he had never worked in a circus.

BOUCHERIE CHATAR

Everything that happens in the world we live in, happens in us. Anything that ceases to exist in the world we see around us, ceases to exist in us. Everything that was, assuming we noticed it was there, is torn from us when it leaves.

FERNANDO PESSOA, *The Book of Disquiet*

Naturally, when Celine urged me to sample the *merguez* sausages from Boucherie Chatar, I needed little persuading. They are long, thin, and orange-coloured, mottled with blotches, and they release a powerful aroma of fresh coriander and cumin when cooked. I can honestly say they are the best I have ever tasted. Such discoveries, passed on by word of mouth, lighten the path of the traveller. To survive, shops like this cannot depend solely on the North African community but need a wider local customer base, open to new culinary experiences not available in their local supermarket. This is something the area seems to provide. East Oxford grew up populated by college servants, artisans, labourers, and those described in 1893 as 'a residuum of the thriftless, careless, lazy, ne'er-do-well sort whose nomadic instincts prevent them from settling to anything.' Those of this group not driven out through the colonisation of the neighbourhood by middle-class arrivistes are still resident, along with a huge variety of others, in the triangle of narrow streets bounded by the twin tributaries of the Cowley and Iffley roads. The gentrification of the area continues apace; houses triple in value in the space of a few brief summers. At the same time, the uniformity and density of the terraced housing-stock means that well-heeled owner-occupiers rub shoulders with those in rented and social housing, students living in shared accommodation, refugees staying in hostels, mental-health users of halfway houses, and bed-sit dwellers.

Boucherie Chatar stands between the Kashmir Tandoori Halal Restaurant and the Hi-Lo Jamaican Eating House ('*From a Penny to a Thousand Pounds*') and opposite the Bangladeshi Islamic Education Centre and Mosque. Their sausages are sold from the halal butcher's counter at the rear of the shop, spotlessly clean and decorated with a colour poster of Mecca. Opposite the counter is a shelf bearing vats of different kinds of olives from which you can spoon your choice into polythene bags for weighing. The shelves in the front of the shop are packed with foodstuffs as well as less expected items like ornate teapots for the mint tea that the proprietors sometimes take with their friends at a small pavement table in the summer months. Tucked beneath the counter in the window, you will find hookah pipes and beautifully embroidered Moroccan slippers. Fresh baguettes in paper wrappers are delivered daily and stand in a barrel. They are chewy, completely unlike the crusty, salty 'French bread' sold in British stores. At the till they bend them in half to fit in your plastic bag, confident that they won't break. They don't. The three young North African men who work in the shop rib each other in a mixture of Arabic, French, and English. Over the Christmas period, I have made enough last-minute late-night dashes for supplies for my presence to register. 'Hello, boss, good to see you, man,' I am greeted as I enter.

'Your *merguez* sausages are famous,' I tell him. In fact they had been the topic of conversation at an East Oxford dinner the previous evening, along with French philosophy, Leyton Orient's defeat by Oxford United at the Kassam Stadium, and the death of a friend's father. 'It is because it is North African food,' he replies modestly. 'Most people in England don't know North African food; it is very tasty and good, lots of spices. Fifty-five per cent of my customers are North African. They are not just coming from Oxford; they come from Bicester and Banbury, lots of cities, all of Oxfordshire. All the Moroccans from Witney is coming here – we have a lot of families coming from Witney. We have a lot of French things here too, like yoghurt, drink, cheese, so we have a lot of French people coming.'

'Where do you get your wonderful bread?' I ask.

'Oh, the stick bread, that is coming from a Frenchman;

he does deliveries to the restaurants. He is from Nice, this man, and he lives in Oxford for about twenty years.'

The thing about urban voyages of exploration is that your discoveries often melt away, like snowflakes on a slide, even as you make them. A year or so after I first encountered his produce, the mysterious Frenchman ceased his deliveries to Boucherie Chatar; whether he went out of business, retired, or returned to his homeland I do not know, but his absence changed our lives in a way that only someone who wasn't French would consider insignificant. My consolation is the usual one I offer myself in such circumstances: if I had not noted his presence, I would not be mourning his passing.

DESIGNATED DESIRE-LINES
Planning a New Road

The city itself is a form of literature in which streets are the lines of a book that can never be completed.

PETER ACKROYD*

I have never been keen on local politics – it can appear to share many of the characteristics of an amateur dramatic production, displaying an excess of intensity and ambition on too small a stage. However, sooner or later, anyone who hangs around the edge of a battlefield is going to get drafted. The Cowley Road is not to be allowed to continue existing unassisted; it pushes too many of the alarm buttons that draw the notice of local and national bodies dedicated to controlling our cities. Business failure, litter, street crime, traffic congestion, drug and alcohol use, a multi-ethnic demographic. List these factors and release them in the wind, and they act like pheromones, stimulating and exciting

*From an essay in the catalogue for the exhibition Richard Wentworth/Eugene Atget: Faux Amis, at the Photographers Gallery, London.

all those with a mission to improve and regulate the urban environment. Especially, it has to be said, in such a thoroughly marketed and controlled city as Oxford. Here, a street that would not raise an eyebrow in Brooklyn or South London becomes a symbol of otherness, eligible for all kinds of funding. Wherever there is funding there will be those whose career it is to write proposals on how to spend that funding. To justify their salaries, they must come up with all kinds of activities and functions that will bring 'improvements' to the locality; in this way, entirely innocently, an engine of change is created, driven by its own circular internal logic, which once set in motion is not always easy to control.

As I have expressed an interest in the future of the road, I am invited to participate as a delegate in two 'planning days' with other members of the public and the consultants hired to re-design the road. These meetings are part of the public consultation taking place on the needs of different road users; the whole process is funded by the Department of Transport and is the first of its kind. It is hoped that it can serve as a model for schemes elsewhere in the country.

The venue for the first meeting is the Asian Cultural Centre, located in the converted chapel that originally served the Oxford workhouse. It is my son's birthday and I arrive late, half-paralysed by guilt and conflicting commitments. I follow the signs and climb the stairs to a room beneath the rafters. There we are to hang in a space formerly inhabited by the hymns and prayers of the undeserving poor, suspended on a false floor of our own self-belief. On my arrival, I find that delegates have already been divided up into interest groups. A facilitator suggests I join the pedestrians' group, which seems appropriate for a pilgrim. A good representation of vocal cyclists are already present, and other groups represent the interests of car users and bus passengers. The road is an accident black spot; maps pinned to the walls are statistical cluster bombs of information, peppered with incident sites. Illegally parked vehicles on the kerb cause buses to swerve out and collide with oncoming traffic. The doors of stationary cars are suddenly opened, swiping cyclists from the saddle. Mothers with push-chairs scurry halfway across the road to the pedestrian 'refuge' in the middle, only to find their precarious perch too small, their offspring projecting dangerously into the traffic. Pedestrians, not finding regulated crossings on their preferred route, take their chances with disastrous consequences.

All day we are immersed in the minutiae of bus stop clear-ways, kerb build-outs, and pedestrian desire-lines. We learn the natural history of pedestrian crossings: Pelican crossings are the standard push-button type; puffins are more 'intelligent' and react when a pedestrian is still on the crossing, giving them more 'green-man time'; toucans incorporate crossings for cyclists; zebras, their retro road-stripes marked only by flashing Belisha beacons, are stupid but cheap. The internal dynamics of our group emerge; people contribute because they believe passionately in their position or because they seek to gain approval. They wish to change our minds or make us laugh. Several find it hard to summarise their thoughts or to avoid the temptation of restating points already made by others in their own words. Their dedication, however, is impressive; they have traded in their Saturday to come here and debate the ideal position of bus stops and the requisite road width required for the safe passage of a bus and a bicycle. We look at the road from every angle, discussing how we use it, where we wish to cross it, and how it can be made safer. The first signs emerge of differing views among the delegates; this, after all, is direct democracy, in the classic early communist style. No detail is too small for examination; the width of a kerb or the positioning of a tree has the potential of provoking endless debate. As with all such experiments, the challenge comes in responding even-handedly to the views expressed, however out of tune with our own they might be.

'I can't stand the way those Asian grocers clutter up the pavement with their boxes of fruit,' exclaims one friendly and humorous middle-aged lady, her manner one of bustling efficiency. 'And the disgusting rubbish they pile up there,' exclaims a young woman, her mouth twisted with revulsion at the thought. 'They shouldn't be allowed to get away with it.' There is no malice in their words; just a desire for order, hygiene, adherence to a certain model of shopkeeping they have grown up with and that for them forms a Platonic ideal. I am genuinely surprised that anyone could think this way. To me the parade of shops they are referring to provide one of my favourite pedestrian experiences in the city.

The shopkeepers generally operate two styles of business from the same premises. Inside, dry goods are stacked on shelves. On the pavement, fresh fruit and vegetables are piled high in colourful displays, constantly replenished by deliveries throughout the day. Teetering towers of boxes, either wooden or cardboard, bear the distinctive artwork of their country of origin, whether it be Pakistan, Ghana, Spain, Italy, Morocco, Kenya, or Brazil. Displays change with the ebb and flow of supply; one day there is a huge delivery of oranges, and the gold of their skins dazzles in the morning sun. On others the stalls are awash with greens and purples; bunches of coriander, plantain, okra, avocados, cauliflower, aubergine, red cabbage. During Ramadan, there are always bunches of fresh yellow dates, traditionally the food with which Muslims break their fast at sundown. Other less well-known delicacies are available: tinda, a round, green vegetable that looks as though it could belong to the pumpkin family; quodo, a type of pale green squash; and vegetables looking like prickly cucumbers, known as bitter gourds, that live up to their name however long they stay in the pot. Sacks of onions in metal-cage trolleys remain on the kerb until they are needed. In the morning, it is true, the pedestrian has to pause as boxes are carried back and forth from shop entrances. In the evening, groups of men cluster for conversation in the doorways of flats between the shops; others speak on mobile phones, walking up and down and gesticulating as if they were in their own home. A lorry draws up outside the halal butcher's, and a bearded man in a bloodstained white coat jumps down from the cab and opens the back doors to reveal whole sides of mutton and beef hanging on hooks. Selection and negotiation on price are completed at the kerbside before the meat is carried into the shops over the lorry-driver's shoulder. At the weekend, school-age boys help out at the fruit and vegetable stands, as adept at clinching a sale as any cockney market trader. The youngest must be ten or eleven years old, chubby and smiling, already with a proprietor's swagger. He catches me eyeing a display of sugar cane, cut into easy chewing lengths. 'I already tried that – it's good,' he tells me. I decide to buy some for my kids; to my knowledge, they have never experienced this organic, stringy form of candy. He hands me a bag, and I scoop up a generous handful. Inside the shop, I am served with the same politeness as the previous customer, who has filled several carriers. My purchase comes to a few pence.

'Should a pavement be like a motorway?' I ask the

pedestrians' group, knowing that I sound eccentric, contrary. 'Isn't it more interesting, more stimulating to have to negotiate your way along a footway, to move from side to side occasionally as you pass through a city, rather than always straight ahead, even if you are using a wheelchair?' There is embarrassment, shrugging of shoulders. An older man decides to speak his mind. 'It makes me really angry,' he says, 'the way they just put their rubbish on the pavement. The police ought to enforce the law.' It is clear he would be happier if the shops operated in a manner less like market stalls and more like the gleaming supermarket that dominates the central section of the road. Markets are the only equivalent of this kind of trading in north European culture. Traditionally our shops are as sealed off as our houses, entered through a door that must be opened by hand and that triggers the ringing of a bell or other alarm signal. Inside is inside; outside is outside – two separate kingdoms with boundaries that are clearly defined, never blurred. The pavement belongs to this outside kingdom; it is reserved for walking along, providing swift and safe passage for pedestrians to and from their destinations. To pause here is to loiter, to dawdle, to obstruct the flow of human traffic. To extend the activities carried out indoors to the pavement is anathema to English culture. Yet in Naples, I have seen the residents of back-streets move their kitchen chairs out to the pavement to enjoy the cool of the evening. In Ghanaian cities, cooking takes place communally in the compound, in full view and with the collaboration of the neighbours. On urban Indian streets, scribes set up their offices on the pavement, with typewriters at the ready to compose letters for the illiterate. And on Willesden Lane in northwest London, one long, hot summer, televisions appeared on the pavement during the sweltering nights, their blue glow spilling across the asphalt and illuminating the ankles of passers-by.

An article in the *Oxford Times* takes up the theme of the despicable litter created by the grocers' shops. Under the headline 'Horrified by Visit to City Streets,' they report the impressions of a city centre resident visiting the Cowley Road. 'It was bad when I visited five years ago and it's got worse. I went down to Cowley Road looking for a restaurant and all I found was a dirty rundown place,' he told the reporter. 'The shops are filthy, there's food and rubbish lying around outside ... I'm very concerned and quite horrified.' His address is given as a bland new development of the kind that is springing up along the banks of the canal. I have walked through a similar estate, built on the flood plain next to Port Meadow. A pink-and-yellow brick confection of faux Georgian squares, houses built from scratch to look like stable blocks converted into houses, bell towers without any bells, weather vanes without any weather. A plethora of notices warned against speeding, littering, and running into the road. Not a dog barked or child cried out. The whole place was eerily silent, wrapped in a veil of river mist; although we were the ones outside, it was as though we viewed the settlement through net curtains.

In contrast to the paper's correspondent, I have to confess to being quite interested in what people leave lying around on the street. One man's trash is another man's treasure, as the saying has it. When I walk home late after a night out, I sometimes examine the fruit boxes stacked up waiting collection. The wooden crates are stapled with colourful labels; a Spanish orange crate carries a depiction of a disturbingly coquettish baby in a diaper, holding a bag of fruit, casting a mischievous glance back over its shoulder as it toddles away. Packaging from the Indian subcontinent is characterised by bold graphics and a poetic use of language. 'Roshan Mangoes – The World's Choicest Fruit,' claims one box. 'Most Delicious and Aromatic – Fresh by Air!' A box of radishes bears the stamp of the Azienda Agricola San Michele, in Lazio. Somehow the monster of globalism is tamed when you know the name of the farm where the food you are eating was grown.

At seven o'clock on the evening before the planning meeting, I go on an emergency mission to buy coriander on Cowley Road. We have just discovered that the bunch of greenery we had purchased that afternoon was in fact a type of long-stalked, flat-leaf parsley sold in the grocers' shops in the area, and we have guests arriving within the hour. I cycle down to Naz Oriental Grocers, one of my favourite local stores. I am always impressed by the way the proprietors cater to the requirements of the local community of all ethnic backgrounds, from sweet potatoes and yams for the Afro-Caribbeans to French honey for the white bourgeoisie. The latest offers are written up in the window. 'Paratha: FROZEN, 0.99p a box. Chicken Legs, £12.00 a box, or 0.99p a kilo. SHAHZADA Pakistani Basmati Rice 20 kg £14.99, 10 kg £8.99, 5 kg £4.99.' As I arrive they are packing up, moving boxes of aubergines and oranges from the pavement back into the store. I find a box of coriander and pinch the leaves to confirm my identification, releasing the herb's unmistakable pungent scent. At the counter I notice more leaves, rolled into tubes and wrapped in cling film. 'What are these?' I ask the young man behind the counter. 'We call them *patra*,' he replies. 'They are like banana leaves – you can use them for a plate to eat your meal off. They are very popular with our Cambodian and Gujarati customers.' There is no charge for this insight into the culinary habits of two such distinct cultures with a shared affection for eating off a plate that grows on a tree. So a trip to the grocer's becomes a voyage of discovery and, as always on the Cowley Road, a need identified is a need supplied. Isn't this worth a few boxes stacked on the pavement?

I cannot help noticing as I look around the room that the faces of the assembled delegates are 100 per cent white;

Asian shopkeepers are completely unrepresented. While we sit and discuss their business, they are busy trading, as they do every day, unloading lorries, stacking boxes on the pavement, and supplying the many and varied needs of the community they serve. Meanwhile, unknown to them, the session in the Asian Cultural Centre draws to an end. The consultants are taking away our findings to try and put the conflicting demands of the different interest groups into a workable plan, to be presented at the second planning day in three weeks' time.

FURTHER PURIFICATION OF
THE PILGRIM

My ritual immersion as a pilgrim takes place at the Eau-de-Vie Flotation Centre at number 34 Cowley Road, near the beginning of the old road to Bartlemas. While the centre offers other therapies, 'flotation' is the one they choose to flag up on their masthead, and I am intrigued to find out more. I learn from their leaflets that the float will take place in a tank filled with warm water heavily impregnated with Epsom salts, so that the body is supported in the manner experienced by bathers in the Dead Sea. I have always wondered what this feels like, and the opportunity to try it so near home, without travelling to a war zone to bathe surrounded by bobbing elderly tourists, is attractive. What interests me more is that the process takes place in a sealed tank, in silence and in darkness. 'The only thing in touch with the millions of sensitive nerve endings that cover the skin is silky, skin-temperature water,' the literature promises. 'Gravity creates 90% of the brain's workload. It has to constantly calculate and compensate for the effects that gravity has on the body. The flotation tank alleviates this work, releasing the brain and triggering a natural chain reaction . . .' I have never understood quite what people meant by meditation, but I do know that emptying the mind of thoughts – or at least slowing down the constant chatter of internal dialogue – leads to a feeling of renewal and refreshment. I have experienced this both on my own in rare moments and at a Quaker meeting that I attended some years ago. To sit in silence by common consent with a group of people is a remarkable experience. Silence within, it seems obvious, may be easier achieved through silence without.

Composer and artist John Cage, best known to the general public as the creator of the piece 4'33" that comprises four minutes thirty-three seconds of silence, first became fascinated by the subject in the late 1940s. 'I found out by experiment (I entered the anechoic chamber at Harvard University) that silence is not acoustic,' he writes. 'It is a change of mind, a turning around. I devoted my music to it.' In another account of his experience, he tells us that he 'discovered that silence was not the absence of sound but the unintended operation of my nervous system and the circulation of my blood. It was this experience and the white paintings of Rauschenberg that led me to compose 4'33" . . .' Cage's words are on my mind as I arrive for my flotation session, carrying a towel in a rucksack as though on a trip to the beach and without having consumed my usual half pint of coffee at breakfast. The reception area is small; two women are seated behind a counter, one of whom, with short blonde hair and an open smile, I already know is the co-owner of the centre. Her colleague is refilling the perfumed oil in a candle-holder made of pottery. Candles burning in bright daylight, I find, are a sure-fire signal that you are entering an area that designates itself as alternative. A middle-aged man in a white cotton costume and bare feet, presumably one of the 'highly trained and qualified practitioners' I have read about in the leaflet, enters and sits on a couch looking somewhat moodily out of the window, awaiting a client. Such environments make me uneasy, I have to confess. I know that my lifestyle would be off their scale in terms of stress, irony, and caffeine intake. Are they able to tell all this at a glance? Presumably so, if any of them are Reiki therapists, trained to detect movements of the 'universal life force energy' in a 'gentle yet powerful exchange . . . at a deep soul level.'

'Have you brought a towel?' I am asked brightly. The dark-haired woman takes my credit card and passes it to the owner, who runs it through the machine. She passes the slip back to the first woman, who passes it to me for signature. I sign and pass it back, and she passes it to the owner to place in the till. She smiles, looking up. 'This overstaffing is ridiculous,' she says. 'It makes you think of a joke,' I reply, a little nervously. 'How many alternative therapists does it take to process a credit card?'

'Totally,' she replies, laughing. So that's all right; humour is allowed within the temple. I am shown along a narrow corridor to the flotation room that lies behind a stripped pine door. The room contains a shower, pleasantly tiled in white and blue in vaguely Portuguese style. Half of the space is taken up by the flotation tank, a large blue plastic object that emits an aqueous gurgling sound. A pair of earplugs in a cellophane wrapper lies on a table. My guide lifts the lid of the tank. The space inside looks remarkably small for one over six foot long when floating, but perhaps this is an illusion. The water is churning.

'Oh no, we have never had a complaint from any one that it is too short,' I am reassured. 'The water is being filtered at the moment. Once you have showered, you should climb in and close the lid. These two buttons here are for the internal light and for the alarm. There are earplugs here if you want to use them – we recommend that you put them in while you shower. You can have the light on or off as you choose. Don't worry, if you press the alarm by mistake, you can just press it again to turn it off. After a little while, the filter will stop. The overhead light will dim. For the first ten minutes, you will hear music, then that will fade into silence. Ten minutes before the end of the session, the music will start again, to bring you back. The best thing to do is spread out like a starfish to get centred. Then you can put your hands behind your head like this' – she demonstrates, reaching her arms up into the air so that they hover above her head – 'that's very good for releasing the back if you have back problems. Try not to rub your eyes or touch your face too much when you are in the water. You have short hair, so you won't be trying to get that out of your eyes' (she lifts up a tress of her own long brown hair, and I have a distracting image of it uncoiling in the water). 'If you do have to, try and shake your hands first, like this.' She makes a quick, flicking movement of her fingers that I am sure I have seen elsewhere – perhaps in a documentary on spirit possession in South-East Asia? 'Enjoy your float.'

And she is gone. The room is oppressively warm and humid, and my clothes stick to my skin. Swiftly I lock the door and undress. I am, I note, *anxious* to begin my *relaxation* – a classic conflict. After all, every two minutes is costing me a pound – not a sensation, I imagine, experienced by the anchorite in their cell or the yogi in their Himalayan cave. I consider the earplugs and decide against them; I have always found them an overly distracting presence. I am a little concerned by the mention of music; in an ideal world, the music one hears should be a matter of personal choice. When it arrives through a neighbour's wall in the middle of the night or over a garden fence on a sunny afternoon, it is almost always an intrusion. The thought of having music prescribed for one and piped into an enclosed space, from which there is no escape, is alarming. However, I am not the expert here on flotation, or indeed on relaxation, and I put these worries aside. I shower quickly, although I am already clean; this part of the ritual must be for the benefit of those with whom I will be sharing the dense, heavily salted water. Presumably the filters cannot remove traces of perfume, deodorant, hair gel, and the other chemicals with which we anoint our bodies, like modern-day Pharaohs ready for the tomb.

I lift the lid and climb into my cell. The water is warm; the body temperature of an athlete that just ran 1,000 metres. The filters are still pumping it around the confined space. As I sink back into its embrace, the skin of my face stings viciously – shaving before a float is clearly not a good idea. I turn off the internal light. The sensation of buoyancy is extraordinary; I feel like a balloon on the end of a string. While the filters remain on, this is not exactly relaxing, as the movement of the water gently bounces my suddenly light body off the vinyl walls. Gradually the turbulence subsides. Then the music starts. It is exactly what I feared: generic, new age relaxation music. A synthesised wash is punctuated by an occasional, ponderous, bell-like 'bong' in the same key. After what seems an eternity, another note a minor third above is introduced. The composition is immediately and completely predictable. With flesh-crawling dread, I anticipate the shift to a major key, an indictable crime in a piece like this, at the same time wondering, with the reflex jealousy of the ex-musician, what somebody got paid to write this tosh. It seems to be designed to penetrate water, a kind of moronic sonar. For stupid dolphins, perhaps? I put up with it as long as I can – possibly two minutes, but time stretches like gum stuck to the sole of my shoe – then decide to use the earplugs after all. I leave my isolation chamber, to which I had been getting accustomed, and get back in the shower. I try inserting the earplugs, but soon realise that if I do, I will be conscious of their presence the whole time I am in the tank. I am very aware of my precious, expensive relaxation time gurgling down the drain with the shower water, and this, I realise, is making me stressed. I decide to return and face the music, just as it begins to fade. The overhead light, visible through little portholes in the roof of the tank, also begins to dim, like the lights at a cinema before the beginning of a movie. The water is still, oily. I make like a starfish, as instructed.

Like Cage, I am impressed by the noises made by my own body. At first I notice the hammering of a pulse behind my ears. Then the heart, labouring away in my chest, which is riding bizarrely high above the surface of the artificially supportive water. Surely I can calm that down. I breathe slowly and deeply, as the literature I was handed as a first-time floater had advised. This is more like it. I push away from one wall as gently as I can, trying to find a space where I can float without being aware of the limits of my confinement.

From somewhere I hear a persistent knocking and a

voice calling: it sounds like 'The power is off.' That's not very peaceful, I think to myself. It must be coming from next door. If there has been a power cut, I won't know about it until the water cools down. I resolve to ignore the intrusion. After about half a minute, the banging ceases. A little later I notice that my heart has quietened, although I am not sure that it has slowed down. Is this possible? The pulse behind my ears has gone, replaced by a rushing sound, like water. I wait twelve beats between each breath and concentrate on trying to empty my head of the thoughts that continue to flicker across my internal screen. This isn't so easy; I haven't tried anything like it for years. Even then I didn't try it very much. I switch my attention to relaxing my body, working my way up from the toes. Soon I feel relaxed all over, apart from my left shoulder, which starts to ache. This is the shoulder that I hunch unconsciously when I concentrate, type, drive a car, or play the guitar. OK, that's a result, I think. All my stress seems to manifest itself in one physical location, surely an easy target for a highly qualified and trained practitioner. I bob there quite happily with my aching shoulder, the short-wave static of my thoughts ever more fitful and inconsequential. I even smile when the underwater orchestra emits its first 'bong.'

On leaving the tank, I realise with acute embarrassment that in my hurry to get back in after my failed attempt with the earplugs, I had forgotten to turn the shower off. This was the cause of the muffled shouts I had heard through the door, and the sound like rushing water. How could I have done this? Perhaps I have drained the centre's hot-water tank, condemning their clients to chilly therapy sessions? Is massage oil removable from the hands with cold water? The room is even more humid than it was before. My clothes feel clammy and insufferably hot. I can't help feeling that the smiles in the reception area seem a little forced as I emerge, mumbling an apology, but they are generous in their forgiveness. 'Don't worry about it,' the owner tells me. 'It must have been like floating near a waterfall in the jungle.' I step out into the cool air. 'You leave your float session with a sense of clarity, focus and both physical and mental renewal,' the leaflet has promised. I wander into the Boucherie Chatar, where I stand contemplating a remarkable offer on tins of chickpeas, without the will to come to a purchasing decision. It is as if I am still floating, adrift in the shallows of the Cowley Road. It is there, by chance, that I meet my wife. We go into Joe's café; I decline a coffee, which has the appeal at that moment of a free jump-start from a defibrillator, and drink a yoghurt and fruit concoction called a berry cola. I notice as we talk together that I am laughing easily, at the smallest thing. The conversation of my four-year-old son is suddenly fascinating. I am, in fact, uncharacteristically relaxed. It is my wife who looks nervous.

ENROBED

Look at that host all dressed in white
(Wade in the water)
Look like the children of the Israelite
(Wade in the water)
Look at that host all dressed in Red
(Wade in the water)
Look like the children that Moses led
(Wade in the water)

TRADITIONAL (GOSPEL SONG)

From the earliest times, clothing has done more than shelter us from the extremes of weather; it has also denoted the trade and signified the rank of the person wearing it. For certain professions, it has a ritual significance, physically manifesting an authority vested in its wearer by God, an institution, or the state. From the necklace of bear's teeth around the shaman's neck to an archbishop's vestments, from the sheriff's badge pinned on a dusty shirtfront to the finery of the High Court judge, clothing alerts us to the fact that the figure we are looking at does not stand alone, but is part of a larger body, whether temporal or spiritual.

Taylor's the Robemakers stands next to a kebab house
and a games supplier, its dignified maroon frontage, with
its name spelt out in gold, striking an unusual note on
Cowley Road. It is not a shop that invites the casual passer-
by to enter; those peering into its windows through the
protective metal grille will see tailors' manikins clothed in
the vestments of a priest or judge; silk ties and waistcoats,
cuff-links, wigs, wing-collars, spotted handkerchiefs,
and all the other paraphernalia of the well-turned-out
cleric, academic, or court official. Inside, the shop has
the atmosphere of a gentleman's tailor; wooden drawers
line the walls behind the glass-fronted counter. In a
small room beyond the main shop are work-benches,
an ironing board, and robes on further manikins cut
out and awaiting a fitting. The proprietor is in his fifties,
slim and wiry with a grey beard and the slightly stooped
posture of the tailor. A quiet-spoken man, he is at first
understandably reticent at my sudden intrusion into his
working day, but his fascination with his own craft soon
takes over as we speak. His involvement with the trade
stretches back generations.

'My father was in the business and his father before
him. Before that we were stonemasons – but always based
in Oxford. My dad grew up in Jericho. They used to cut
everything on a Sunday, have Monday off, and work the
rest of the week. The big houses down there were all bustling with this and that in those days. I grew up aware
of the business, but I didn't help out when I was young.

My dad showed me how to make the academic and the legal robes; he was making them for a company – not the clerical stuff, that's new.'

'It seems a very specialised profession. How many people in the UK are still making robes?' I ask.

'There's a few. I'm the only one in the country who can do all of it. There's big companies that concentrate solely on clerical and two main companies that concentrate on academic and legal, but I'm probably the only one who can order, cut, and make myself. I can't think of anyone else who can do that.'

'Are the tailoring skills involved being lost?'

'It's just been destroyed. Eade and Ravenscroft used to have a factory in Stockport, but they lost a lot of their workers to the biscuit factory. It's wages – at the end of the day, it doesn't matter if it's interesting or not, it's the money. That's what drove them to look abroad in the end; if you can't recruit those sort of people in Manchester, you're not going to get them anywhere in England. It's like the building industry – that's a prime example; they're crying out for people to learn the trades. When these ten countries join the EEC, they'll get all the building workers they want then. It won't be our lads going over to Germany; it'll be all the Poles and that lot coming over here . . .'

'Who are the main customers for the robes you make?'

'I don't do so much of the academic robes now – it's

too complicated and the big makers make it as hard as possible for other people to get in on it. I stick mostly to legal and clerical. At Oxford there are lots of colleges aimed specifically at ecclesiastics, and all the colleges have got ordained people in them. St Stephen's House, just over the road, is one of the biggest Anglo-Catholic colleges in the country. When they're training they just wear cassocks, but once they're ordained, they need everything. Then there's Catholic clergy, Methodists . . . . I'll make for anybody who wants them, I'm not proud!'

'It's interesting that both church and judicial robes give the wearer their identity in terms of their profession,' I say.

He nods. 'With the legal clothes, you tell who's who by what they are wearing. There are specific gowns for the High Court, the Crown Court, the District Court, and the judges; then you've got the barristers, the solicitors, and the clerks. The QCs* have been knocked on the head, which is a bit of a shame. This government seems to want to adopt the American system; they're being very successful in destroying traditional things. It started with civil stuff, and now it's progressed to the legal. Fortunately they can't touch the clerical. It's funny because the Americans want to come back to our system. We get so many of them over who would like to buy wigs and gowns.'

---

*QC: acronym for Queen's Counsel.

'Why is that?'

'It's because it's not just dress as such; it gives the individual anonymity. If they're up against some chap in court who is very intimidating, they don't want him recognising them in the street two months later. It's amazing how a wig and gown changes a person's appearance.'

'Doesn't it also give them authority in the way that a priest's vestments are supposed to do?'

'That's right. When priests put on their vestments, you are dealing not with them but with a representative. When you see a dog collar, you know what it represents. When you see vestments of a certain colour, you know what season or saint's day it is. Every colour has its significance; everything has a point or a history to it.'

'It must be a language that you have to learn in your profession.'

'Yes. You pick it up quickly, you have to – but there are still bits and pieces it takes ages to get right. Some of the Catholic colours are different to the Anglican colours, and it can be a bit confusing working out which is which.'

'Is there a danger you'll get it wrong and cause offence?'

'Oh, that's too bad really! But it's not like it was thirty or forty years ago when they were more pompous about it; all that's gone out the window. You don't get vicars and clerics ordering golf jackets now or different types of dinner jackets. They still want frock coats, but you don't get all the different kinds of frock coats you got fifty years ago. Mind you, they can't afford it nowadays. Fifty years ago they all came from well-off backgrounds; it was a good career . . .'

Taylor's is a fairly recent arrival, having moved here from a more central location in the city. I wondered how a robe-maker felt about the road. 'Do you feel like a fish out of water here?'

'Oh, no, it's a great road to be on, with all the diversity of cuisine and everything else. It's easy for people to get to me. The parking is better; people don't want to go into town. People can drive in from Bristol, Reading, or Buckingham; they can park round the corner, and they're nice and close. It's a good location. I don't get passing trade. You get one or two coming in that shouldn't, but you put up with that. I've known Cowley Road for forty years, and it's always been different, diverse. It's always had its own character.'

OF LOVE AND JEWELS

Lovers and madmen have such seething brains,
Such shaping fantasies, that apprehend
More than cool reason ever comprehends.

WILLIAM SHAKESPEARE, A Midsummer Night's Dream

Few events can change the course of a person's life as dramatically as falling in love. Shakespeare wasn't the first or the last to notice that in the early stages of infatuation, lovers display behavioural symptoms very similar to those of psychotics; among them are elation, sleeplessness, loss of appetite, reckless use of money, daydreaming, and monomania. Indeed, strong attraction when thwarted leads to the deepest despair and is often cited as a trigger for mental breakdown. It is no surprise that Burton deals extensively with Love-Melancholy in his *Anatomy*. 'The symptoms of the mind in lovers are almost infinite,' he writes, 'and so diverse that no art can comprehend them; though they be merry sometimes, and rapt beyond themselves for joy: yet most part love is a plague, a torture, a hell, a bitter-sweet passion at last . . . For in a word, the Spanish Inquisition is not comparable to it.' Those fortunate enough to come safely through these turbulent waters to the calm haven of a happy and settled relationship find themselves in a different country, where new customs are observed and new responsibilities taken on. Life is never the same again.

Much of what passes between lovers is private. However, there are certain romantic conspiracies that require accomplices, the modern equivalents of Juliet's nurse. One of those confidants is the jeweller, commissioned to give solid form to the lover's mental yearnings. I ask Bridget Wheatley, who has a jeweller's shop on Cowley Road, whether she sees much love-related behaviour on the Cowley Road.

Bridget is one of those people who sell things by *not* selling them. Softly spoken, with large eyes and long, light brown hair, it is obvious, despite her politeness, that she would rather be bent over her workbench, where the real business of the jeweller is done, than extolling the virtues of her merchandise. Her very reticence, an unfeigned attribute of her character, inspires trust and makes those who frequent her shop even more eager to secure their purchases.

'Yes,' she tells me, 'Valentine's Day and Christmas are amazing, with men buying what they think their ladies will like. You get a few things coming back, but I'm usually happy to put them back into stock. I had one young man who was Australian who was going back home. He wanted to take a ring back with him – red gold with diamonds. I bought the gold and he paid his deposit, but the next day he rang to say the relationship was off. I gave him a refund. Now I have some red gold in my collection.'

To be at the mercy of the progress of other people's romantic lives must present its challenges as a business model, but Bridget seems to face such uncertainties with equanimity, much as a seafarer learns to face storms or a farmer unseasonal weather. Her shop is a space in which to make as well as to sell, a workshop as well as a show-case. Around a third of what she sells she makes herself, with the rest sourced from designers whose work she admires. The shop interior has a bright, modern feel with jewellery arranged in glass cases around the walls and in the centre of the room. She shows me the space behind the counter where most of the work gets done; there are two workbenches, each with its own lamp, with tools neatly arranged on shelves around them. 'I have a second bench so that someone else can work at the same time as me, but it's a bit tight. I'm on my own today, so I've spread myself out. I've been buying more tools recently to complete my workshop. I've got oxyacetylene now, which I use for patterning and high-temperature work. Out the back I do the etching – it's difficult when you're handling nasty chemicals and you have to keep an eye on the shop.'

I ask her to explain a little about the etching process, and she hands me a piece of silver that is scored with intricate patterns. Then she shows me a similar sized piece that is covered on both sides with a dark coating. 'This, on the front, is a mixture of pitch and beeswax; it's soft and you can draw the design straight into it. On the back here is a layer of lacquer for protection, to prevent the acid from eating right through. Before Christmas I had a commission from a Welsh girl called Myfanwy who wanted an ear-cuff. It had to have a Welsh love spoon on it. It worked really well.'

'So your commissions can be very individual?' I ask.

'Oh yes. People want stuff made by me for them personally. And they want to see me when they come in the shop, which can make it difficult for the people who cover for me when I'm not here.'

A man enters with a musical peal from the chimes above the door and a broad smile; when I listen back to my recording, it sounds as though a magical character has just arrived on the stage of a theatrical production. The first thing I notice about him is the large silver ring with a blue stone that he wears on his right hand. He needs another box for the earrings he has just given to his wife; no, no, she loves them but she had been cooking and had put the box down in a 'nasty, oily mess.' Bridget hands him a replacement box, and he leaves with the look of a satisfied customer. 'You can see he likes jewellery from that ring he was wearing,' I say.

'I made that,' Bridget replies.

'My eyes were drawn to it straightaway,' I tell her. 'You are creating his image, the impression he makes on people, just as much as if you were designing his clothes.'

'I suppose I am,' she says. 'He's a good customer. He wanted something solid for his ring, not hollow; but he's still not completely satisfied – he wants me to file it down, but I think it's right as it is. Some people are incredibly fussy.' But she says it with an indulgent smile.

I ask her how good a location she found Cowley Road for a jewellery business. One day we had met in the city centre, and she had complained that she felt the area's reputation dissuaded potential customers from visiting. 'Well, more and more people are coming. Places like Coco's and the Kazbar are raising the profile of Cowley Road. I have started to use gold and diamonds, quite a departure from what I was doing before. It will be interesting to see what reaction that gets. My average price is creeping up from when I opened the shop – it has to if this is going to work. I have had more precious commissions recently, so that is changing. I suppose the overall image of Cowley Road is still a bit downbeat, but we will see . . .'

She echoes the fears expressed by others about the pressure on properties on the road. The building that includes the shop has been the subject of an eternally delayed rent review, mired in bureaucracy for the past three years, and she fears the council may be getting ready to evict her and its other tenants. 'There's people around here who would make an offer for this building. In two years the lease is up for renewal again. I'm very frustrated. We're good for the local economy; I'm training two people here who have never worked in jewellery before. There are ten other people working in the businesses in the building altogether; another jeweller, two computer guys, and a picture framer out the back. It's a service to the community and a refreshing change from the estate agents and eating places elsewhere along the road.'

The chimes peal once more, and a young man strides up to the counter, come to collect a commission. Bridget hands him a ring, and he breaks into a relieved smile. 'Oh, I'm very happy with that, thank you. She'd better be happy with that too!' We admire the ring, made of silver with rubies and diamonds, all of equal size, set around its circumference. His rapt attention and look of expectation have a timeless quality; he obviously has complete faith in the power of his ring to bind him forever to his lover. Robert Burton has more than one story of the efficacy of rings as magical tokens of love. He writes of a young gentleman of Rome who, on the day he was married, went to play a game of tennis and, finding himself encumbered, put his newly minted wedding ring for safe keeping on the finger of a brass statue of Venus that stood by the court. Having finished his game, the bridegroom tried to retrieve the ring, only to find that the statue had crooked her finger, making it impossible to remove. Eager to return to his wedding feast, he decided to fetch the ring the next day and rushed home. That night, however, as he lay next to his bride, Venus came to his bed chamber and inserted herself between the lovers, declaring that she was now his lawfully betrothed wife . . .

In another tale that Burton took from Petrarch, he relates how the emperor Charlemagne foolishly doted on a common and apparently charmless woman, to the chagrin of his friends and followers, and was so besotted that when she died, he embraced her corpse and couldn't be parted from her coffin, but had it carried with him everywhere. A bishop prayed to God that the meaning of this extraordinary behaviour be revealed and was told that the cause of the emperor's mad love lay beneath the dead woman's tongue. On investigation the bishop found a small ring there, which he removed. The king's affection immediately transferred to the bishop, who he now would not allow out of his sight. In consternation the bishop threw the ring into a deep lake, whereupon the king built a house on its shore in the midst of a marsh 'to his infinite expense' and a temple nearby, in which he was eventually buried. Such are the forces subject to the jeweller's art.

The young suitor turns over the ring; he would doubtless be happy if it had the powers described in Petrarch's legend. 'It's different, not having one big rock.

You remember her grandma's ring I brought in? That had rubies too.' He had surreptitiously borrowed the ring so that Bridget could size the new one; part of the regular collusion between jeweller and client. He obviously enjoys such clandestine activities. 'Actually, I'm taking her to Barcelona on Friday, and she doesn't know it. I'm working abroad next week and coming home on Thursday evening. We fly at eight o'clock on Friday morning, and I'm not going to tell her where we are going until we get to Heathrow.' He is exhibiting classic lover's behaviour, familiar to jewellers everywhere and a foundation of their business: extravagance, lack of inhibition, and elation. We wish him luck as he leaves, and he gruffly declares that he doesn't need it; as far as he is concerned, his destiny is set as firmly as the jewels in the ring he grips in his palm. I watch him walk off down the street, his smile a beacon in the gloom of a winter afternoon.

BEHIND THE BLUE DOOR
(INSIDE THE PRIVATE SHOP)

The windows of the premises on the corner are boarded up and painted blue, like the rest of the shop front, so that it presents blind eyes to the street. This is the traditional design for such places since time immemorial; discreet, anxious not to attract the attention of the law by giving offence to the public. In an age when billboard advertisements have brought the visual language of pornography to the high street, the approach now seems a little old-fashioned. It is certainly a design that discourages all but the most determined visitor. Its exterior is so unreadable, so private indeed, that its door takes on the quality of a gateway to another dimension. However, it has been a feature of the road for at least the last two decades, and I decide that whatever goes on behind its shutters is part of the area's economy and merits investigation. In its doorway, which I have never seen opened, the dust of the street – comprised of the pollen of trees, mud from car tyres, the shredded filters of cigarettes, fragments of atomised newsprint, chewing gum, and scraps of discarded foodstuffs and packaging, all sifted and pounded by the wheels of traffic and dyed a uniform grey by its gasoline breath – is piled in an exhausted heap. It is situated opposite a bus stop. Whenever I pass and think about entering, the queue waiting for a bus appears inordinately long and made up almost exclusively of people known to me. They stare glumly across the road, as though their sole function in life is to monitor who goes in and out of the blue door. As each bus pulls up, the queue is replaced within seconds by an equally serious and watchful line. At a casual glance, it is hard to tell whether the premises are open for business or closed. I decide not to push at the door in full view of the bus stop, perhaps to find myself caught up in a ludicrous and very public struggle when it won't open, but to return another time. 'Exactly what reputation are you trying to maintain?' my wife asks me, when she requests a report on my afternoon's activities; 'just get on with it.'

My children come to the rescue. 'The entrance is round the back,' they say; the front door is locked. They just know, that's all – it is part of the street knowledge of the area that is passed on from generation to generation, in playgrounds and pub car parks.

Once through the entrance and having read the notices warning me that I may be confronted by imagery I deem offensive, I enter a room that is brightly illuminated with fluorescent tubes, as though in overcompensation for the lack of natural light. The walls are lined with shelves holding hundreds of pornographic videos and DVDS, presenting a frieze of writhing bodies as intricately entwined with each other as a ball of worms in a compost heap. Men have been enraptured by nakedness since the world was young. 'The one stimulus that evokes human seed from the human body is the human form,' writes the Roman poet Lucretius, who was claimed by Saint Jerome to have taken his own life after being driven mad by a love philtre, half a century before the birth of Christ. 'As soon as this seed is dislodged from its resting place, it travels through every member of the body, concentrating at certain reservoirs in the loins, and promptly acts on the generative organs. These organs are stimulated and swollen by the seed. Hence follows the will to eject it in the direction in which tyrannical lust is tugging . . . So, when a man is pierced by the shafts of Venus, whether they are launched by a lad with womanish limbs or a woman radiating love from her whole body, he strives towards the source of the wound and craves to be united with it.'

My arrival must have been monitored on CCTV, for a man enters quickly from behind a partition, greeting me and taking up a position behind the counter. He is pale, young, with dark, thinning hair. I can't help noticing as he walks across the room that his brown trousers are too short and leave his ankles exposed, the kind of detail easily overlooked in a world without windows. After a short time, I am joined by another customer, a smartly dressed man of about thirty, who starts to browse the DVD selection. I take a look around. A selection of dildos, varying in size and in the number of prongs and attachments they feature, are racked at one end of the room, like Kalashnikovs for sale on an Afghan market stall. At the other end, inflatable sex dolls in packets and a few straps, harnesses, and other costumes hang rather forlornly from hooks in the wall. But these are a distraction from what the shop is really about, which is moving images of people having sex.

Many of the cases of the DVDs on offer feature piles of naked bodies. Typically, in these compositions, a central female figure lies on her back, often attended by one or two female companions who bend over her, manipulating her to create a more effective display. The presence of men is signified by their sexual organs, which jut into the picture from off-screen. Sometimes they merely point, like fingers emphasising the action. At others they are gripped in fists or inserted in mouths or other orifices. One cover features a close-up of the cheerful, smiling face of a young woman who appears to have had an accident with a bucket of wallpaper paste.

Of course, I know that this fictional smile, and others like it, may be hiding all kinds of other stories; real stories of coercion, addiction, and desperation. Of people who set out on journeys to a new land, only to find themselves

112

forced into this kind of work against their will. Of women who fall into the hands of debt collectors and end up as 'bonded workers' in a brothel – as well as the much smaller number who have chosen this as their career path for their own reasons. I lived for a couple of years in an area of London well known as a centre for prostitution. When I moved into my flat, a welcoming committee paid me a visit and explained that if I kept my nose out of their business, I could look forward to a long and happy life. I took their advice. At about seven o'clock one morning, I was walking down the street to work, past the group of young women who stood shivering in a line on the corner. There were three or four white girls standing there, their thin, bare legs whipped pink by the raw wind – flamingo legs, as I used to think of them – and one black girl with a big Afro, shifting from foot to foot to keep warm, her hands deep in the pockets of her fake fur jacket. Something made me glance across at her again, and our eyes met; we recognised each other. She was a friend I hadn't seen for a year or so, a young single mother with a little blond-haired son born with a cleft palate. We lived in the same building for a while, until we all had to move on, drank in the same pubs; she had a crush on the singer in our band, so she often used to show up when we played.

The shame of certain moments stays with you for life. I wish I could say that when I saw her I crossed the road, gave her a hug, asked how she was doing, and exchanged numbers so that perhaps I could have found out why she was selling her body on the street where I lived. But the surprise of seeing her there, the earliness of the hour, and what I can only describe, shamefacedly, as embarrassment rendered me unable to utter more than a one-word greeting that was entirely neutral in tone and meant nothing. She replied in kind. For some reason, I remember her so clearly, although we weren't close; her perfectly plucked eyebrows (she was embarrassed at the vigour with which they grew); the blue, self-inflicted tattoo on her forearm, done with biro ink; her brave, sardonic smile, with her mouth turned down at the corners. Always in my mind's eye, she is holding the hand of her little son; I wondered whether she was there because of him, to put clothes on his back, or because they had taken him away, and she had then descended into whatever addiction it was she was financing by standing there. I never found out. She wasn't there the next morning, or the next.

Robert Burton relied on the accounts of travellers to the New World of encounters with tribes that dwelt entirely without clothes to argue that nakedness was less alluring than a gentlewoman arrayed in all her finery. However, no sooner had he made this claim than reference to the Bible forced him to acknowledge that David was seduced by seeing Bathsheba at her bath, as were the elders on seeing Susanna. His case was further undermined by classical authorities. 'Apelles was enamoured of Campaspe when he was to paint her naked,' he admits. 'Amongst the Babylonians it was the custom of some lascivious queans to dance frisking in that fashion . . . The Tuscans at some set banquets had naked women to attend upon them . . . Nero would have filthy pictures still hanging in his chamber, which is too commonly used in our times.' Voyeurism, erotic dancing, topless waitresses, pornography. Plus ça change.

A whole range of videos on the shelves chronicle the exploits of a plucky band of British women travellers. With titles like *English Girls Pissing in Berlin* and *English Girls Pissing in Los Angeles*, their covers feature squatting figures doing just that. There is a militaristic tone to the theme, as though a squad of crack troops has been sent out on operations overseas. There is something predictable about what is on offer, because sexual appetites are, in the end, rather predictable. *Anal Adventures, Big Boobs, I Love Asian Babes* – most of what I see seems squarely aimed at the male heterosexual market; none of Lucretius's 'lads with womanish limbs' here. More diverse material may be available, but I hesitate to ask. Perhaps wrongly, I don't expect the owner of the shop to want to discuss his trade with me. After all, its watchword is discretion.

The other customer expresses approval at the DVDs on offer. 'Oh yes, we're licensed to sell hard-core material; they're completely uncensored,' he is assured. 'Just let me know what you're looking for.'

'Which are good?' the man asks, scanning the racks,

in the manner of a diner consulting with a waiter in a restaurant.

A handful are taken down and offered for closer perusal. 'We sell a lot of these private films, like *Private Student House* or *Private Pool Party*. It tells you on the back what they are about . . .'

I leave them to strike a deal and walk out into the light of day, my reappearance unobserved, as far as I can tell. In the window of the newsagent a few doors down, an advert catches my eye. Although written in strangely mutated English, its message is clear.

THE WAY TO BE A LOVER

DO YOU WANT TO BE AN ACTRESS OR LOVE ACTOR
AND BE PART OF A GLAMOUR ENVIRONMENT?

LEARN HOW TO ENJOY YOUR LOVE LIFE AND
FEEL YOUR WAY TO BE A LOVER

WANTED, GIRLS OR GUYS, NEW FACES,
BETWEEN THE AGES OF 20 AND 28

EXCHANGE YOUR EXPERIENCE AND GIVE AN EFFORT
TO WHAT YOU ALREADY KNOW . . .

I wonder if anyone will reply to the advertisement, either through curiosity or need, and what kind of journey they will embark on if they do.

FROM THE LITERAL TO THE
ALLEGORICAL AND BACK

I have met with but one or two persons in the course of my life who understood the art of Walking, that is, of taking walks – who had a genius, so to speak, for sauntering, which word is beautifully derived 'from idle people who roved about the country, in the Middle Ages, and asked charity, under pretense of going à la Sainte Terre,' to the Holy Land, till the children exclaimed, 'There goes a *Sainte-Terrer*,' a Saunterer – a Holy-Lander.

HENRY DAVID THOREAU, 'Walking,' from *Excursions* (1862)

I have come to the Globe Café at number 92 Cowley Road to seek some advice before travelling any further along my route. I have arranged to meet my friend Wes Williams, who has written a book on the pilgrimages made to Jerusalem by sixteenth-century French priests and the narratives that their travels generated. His own journey to being an expert in the subject is an interesting one; his parents were missionaries in the Salvation Army, a tradition that has little time for the concept of ritual or holy places. I arrive late on my bicycle and see Wes already sitting with a coffee at the window. With his long, dark hair tied back in a ponytail and his full beard, he looks as much like a medieval pilgrim himself as an Oxford don. I fumble with the lock anxiously; Wes is a busy man at the best of times and today is Christmas Eve.

The Globe is a strange, hybrid kind of place, designed to cater to the student market like other café-bars at this end of the road. The tables are made of translucent imitation glass, the milky-green colour of glacier water. A board on the wall advertises the drinks available: 'shooters' include Kamikaze, Bubble-Gum, Slippery Nipple, Brain Hemmerage [sic], Red Maxican [sic], Man O' War, and Melon Ball. At ten thirty in the morning, customers for shooters are thin on the ground, even on this legendarily bibulous street. We have the place to ourselves, although my interview tape is awash with ambient noise created by coffee machines, clinking glasses, and mobile phones. The two men who staff the place seem determined to create an atmosphere of business on their own by deploying all the gadgets at their disposal.

We begin by talking about the different meaning pilgrimage has in religious traditions. 'In most religions a place is set that you need to reach,' Wes explains. 'What matters is not the journey you make to that place or what it takes to get there; strictly speaking, the journey is a non-space and the encounters you may have on the way are unimportant. All that matters is being in that place – having an encounter with God or standing in the footsteps of a saint or a holy person. That is one form of the journey. But as soon as it is narrated, it is nearly always cut across by the sense of the journey as training or as an initiatory structure, whereby all the encounters you have and all the places you visit on the way are preparing you for your arrival.'

'So when you get there, you're ready,' I say.

'Exactly. The sixteenth-century priests I studied knew that getting to Jerusalem was the thing. But they couldn't help writing up an encounter with a man with an axe in a forest as an allegorical training in overcoming passion. Or else they portrayed it as a providential moment – just as they were about to be hacked to pieces, the voice of an angel would sound and make the man run away, proving that God wanted to preserve them for Jerusalem.'

'So the pilgrimage is both allegorical and physical.'

'This is where we get into the difference between the Protestant and non-Protestant approaches. The Protestant tradition allegorises the whole thing so that Jerusalem is death, your final destination. It's not about a particular place any more, so the whole of life becomes a pilgrimage. In the Catholic and also in the Muslim and Hindu traditions, you take time out of your normal routine to make the pilgrimage – you wear different clothes, have a different haircut, give up eating meat, or abstain from sex for a month. There are holy trees; there are holy wells; there are places where you cross over into another world. You have to be there for it to happen, whereas for the Protestant, revelation could take place in a coffee shop.'

He pauses briefly and looks around, as though checking on the likelihood of it happening in the Globe Café.

'Of course, this is an *après coup* explanation; both types of interpretation of pilgrimage existed in the church before the Reformation, but the Protestant tradition took up and emphasised the allegorical dimension over the other. It's tied in with the Protestant work ethic and the Industrial Revolution as well. The agricultural labourer's activities were bound to certain rhythms and seasons of the year – times of intense work and times of relative freedom where there might be a space to go off and spend time on some ritualised activity. For the factory labourer, every moment spent away from the factory is an opportunity cost to the employer. The machine needs feeding with workers. Our experience in this country is not so much about feasts and festivals as it is about bank holidays. Instead of a pilgrimage, we got the occasional day-trip to the seaside, and Protestant theology reflects this. To summarise, and to oversimplify somewhat, the Catholic is in a separate space as a pilgrim, whereas the Protestant is on a permanent pilgrimage. The reward for this is that every minute matters; but that is within a Protestant accountancy of time, when any moment may be that of your salvation or damnation.'

'I suppose Bunyan is the best example of that kind of account.'

'Yes, *Pilgrim's Progress* is the ultimate Protestant

pilgrimage text. The Protestant model of writing is that everything is connected and everything is meaningful; this can be both liberating and oppressive.'

'That kind of mind-set can also be a symptom of melancholia. Internalised, withdrawn, brooding on the meaning of life, the sense that what is real is what is going on in your head rather than out in the world . . .'

'Yes. Travel writers – if you can call them that – often fall into one of the two camps. I would argue that W. G. Sebald in *The Rings of Saturn* is a very Protestant author. He wanders around East Anglia having an internal dialogue, and the actual places he visits don't matter as places, only as symbols or as ways of achieving some kind of self-revelation.'

In fact, Sebald was from intensely Catholic, rural Bavaria; from a village, as he told an interviewer, 'of about a thousand inhabitants, in a valley covered with snow for five months of the year. It was a silent place.' However, we are not about to allow a detail like this to spoil our thesis. We agree that many of the walk-on characters that appear in his travelogues are very rarefied; either academics, like Sebald himself, or archetypal eccentrics. The books seem to exist in another time. Though written in a unique voice and full of arcane information on a range of subjects, they are saturated in melancholy, permeated with a sense of loss and of things coming to an end.

'If there are two ways of approaching pilgrimage, I feel there are also two ways of relating to literature and poetry and art,' Wes continues. 'One approach sees literature, power and politics, ideology, and the way people think as all completely intertwined and interdependent. This is something like the first position of Edward Said, when he maintained that you cannot separate *Mansfield Park* from the slave trade that provided the gold to pay for the house and fuel the society that surrounded it. Some academics stop there and say that their job is simply to explain cultural production within its historical context. But Said also made clear that that's not enough. He talks about the specificity and transcendence of literature, at least the importance of the gesture of trying to make it so. I would argue that a political poem by Mayakovsky, say, even though ostensibly it comes from a desire to see revolutionary change, is different from a political pamphlet. It is not finally subject to all the languages that politics is subject to.'

'Isn't an interest in the rituals and sacred places of pilgrimage rather remote from the tradition that you grew up in?'

'Oh, absolutely. I was brought up in the Low Church. Spending time in India as a child, where my parents were missionaries, pilgrimage was everywhere. We used to go out and watch when they dragged the huge chariots through town, the processions with painted and decorated elephants and so on. I think I was encouraged then to think of it all as a spectacle, but also as a mistake, a misreading, a far too literal understanding of the journey of life. Even now I do sometimes wonder whether taking time out from the daily rhythms to discover something is valid. Don't we believe that if something is worth knowing, it is has to be integrated into our daily lives? It is the pastoral question . . . If we go off into the forest to learn lessons, are the things we learn there applicable to life in the city, or are they just forest lessons?'

We agree that a poem, or a piece of art, can be an attempt to bring back something of that forest experience, to fashion it into something that can exist back in the city. Like a stone picked up on the forest floor and brought back in your pocket, I think to myself, in a far too literal fashion. Ruskin, teaching his clerks and shopkeepers to sketch and observe at the Working Men's College in Camden, aimed to give them a resource that they could draw on in their daily lives as they recollected those moments of intense engagement with nature. These ideas have their genesis in the nineteenth century, I realise; cultural edifices that still inform our thinking were being constructed at the same time as the streets that surround us, brick by brick.

Wes picks up his coffee cup and glances out of the window. I feel I can detain him no longer; I know he is travelling to the West Country to spend time with family over Christmas and needs to pick up gifts on the way. As we stand and gather our belongings, he adds, 'Of course, writing a book is a kind of pilgrimage too . . .'

WITTGENSTEIN'S LION AND A CAPPUCCINO SEA

I suspect that with regard to Wittgenstein, the world is divided into two camps: those who fully understand his ideas, a select group that may only number a few hundred; and those who are seduced by the poetic compression of his statements and intrigued by the extraordinary charisma of his personality. At the risk of provoking the ridicule and contempt of my readers, I happily confess to pitching my tent in the second, much larger encampment. Naturally, admiring Wittgenstein for his language is about as great a misunderstanding of his intentions as it is possible to make, akin to admiring the architecture of industrial buildings designed with purely functional purposes in mind. Wittgenstein blamed the limitations of language for causing most of the philosophical dead ends that had entrapped thinkers down the ages. Philosophy itself was nothing more than the struggle to resist the bewitchment of the mind caused by the inexactitude of our use of words and our deeply ingrained linguistic habits. Philosophical problems arise, he maintained, when language goes on holiday. Furthermore, our concepts of truth, meaning, reality, and knowledge only exist in as far as they are accepted by those in the same conceptual community as ourselves, at a particular moment in history. Even though we may learn the language of an Amazonian tribesman, therefore, we can never truly share his perception of the world. The same must be true of Chaucer, say, or of Aristotle. If a lion could speak, Wittgenstein famously wrote in the *Philosophical Investigations*, we would not be able to understand him. Yet Wittgenstein's ideas are very current here on Cowley Road; indeed, the area could be seen as a laboratory in which some of his central propositions are put to the test. If he was right, the inhabitants of East Oxford live in a soup of mutual incomprehension and misunderstanding, our lives parallel universes of opposing cultural values and belief systems. Yet somehow interactions of every sort occur daily in a society that would have seemed to him unimaginably cosmopolitan, despite the fact that he was raised in pre-war Vienna, itself a bubbling stew of German, Magyar, Slav, Jewish, Polish, and French cultural influences.

The headquarters of Blackwell, the famous Oxford publisher and the first to publish Wittgenstein's *Philosophical Investigations* in English, stand on the

Cowley Road;* (during the philosopher's lifetime, they were located above the famous bookshop on Broad Street.) Although Wittgenstein taught at Cambridge, it was Oxford that became the centre of Wittgenstein studies after the Second World War, thanks largely to one of his Austrian disciples. Friedrich Waismann worked with Wittgenstein in Vienna, acting as his personal assistant and often taking dictation from him. He came of humbler stock than Wittgenstein, who was the son of a fabulously wealthy Jewish industrialist, and as a young man he seemed content with his supporting role. After years of loyal service, he could be forgiven for expecting a warm reception in Cambridge, where he arrived with his family as a penniless refugee in 1937. Wittgenstein was not pleased to be reminded of his former connection with the Vienna Circle, with whom he had broken. He refused to cede any opportunities to Waismann, even warning students against attending his lectures. He was ruthless in his treatment of those he disagreed with; perhaps there was also an element of personal vanity in his determination that his reputation should not be tainted through association with the ideas he had once espoused. Great men write their own history; there is no one they fear more than the unauthorised biographer. Waismann found Cambridge as closed to him as an ex-

---

*At least they did when these lines were written; they have subsequently moved to new premises in Cowley.

colleague of Wittgenstein as Vienna had been to him as a Jew; he had fled one dictator only to encounter another. After two barren years, Waismann moved to Oxford, where he was given a post as reader in the philosophy of mathematics. Here he could breathe again and make a life; although he complained about the lack of cafés. As the old Viennese proverb has it, the Jew belongs in the coffee house.

It goes without saying that Wittgenstein was not the only celebrated author on Blackwell Publishing's list. A friend of mine worked in a temporary cabin at the back of their Cowley Road premises during the 1980s. Engaged in a search for an elusive file, he pulled open a drawer and found himself looking at the original artwork to one of Enid Blyton's Famous Five adventures. Blyton, for those unaware of her literary legacy, was a fabulously successful children's author of the first half of the twentieth century, whose facile but gripping tales were peopled by a cast of gender and racial stereotypes. Her stories were loved by children and loathed by liberals and educationalists with equal fervour; my friend, the son of two teachers, had been forbidden to read them as a child. In the scene portrayed on the cover he held in his hands, evil is abroad in the shires. The children, in the foreground, bound together in a prepubescent, asexual gang by their loyalty to each other and their ideals, point upwards to a mysterious fire on a hillside. They appear galvanized by a mixture of fear and a sense of patriotic duty. These stories portrayed an England very different from the one outside the main entrance to the publisher's offices; one that was exclusively white, predominantly rural, and where any foreign interloper was a possible spy and not to be trusted. Today, especially in the city, it is hard to recognise the island that Blyton wrote of as the same one we inhabit; occasionally, however, it seems one can hear an echo of longing for her creation in the voices of those stricken with nostalgia for a society where every man knew his place and every man was an Englishman.

Cafés have arrived with a vengeance in Oxford. Waismann could have drunk his fill of coffee in the city today, though he would have regarded most of it as swill compared to the almost infinite permutations of the Viennese mélange served in the coffee houses of his youth. In these establishments, the cream of the intelligentsia took refuge from their cold, high-ceilinged apartments, gathering at their habitual tables; these served as a combination of office and drawing-room, where they looked after business, heard the latest gossip, and received their mail. There is a legend concerning the arrival of coffee in Vienna that is inseparably entwined with the history of Europe's relationship with Islam. In mid-August 1683, Vienna lay under siege. Turkish forces completely surrounded the city, and supplies were running low. Georg Franz Kolchitsky, a diplomat returning from a mission to Constantinople, is said to have adopted a disguise and passed through the Turkish lines; the letters he delivered to Charles VI from the head of the relieving army encouraged the embattled commander to hold out. Not much is known of Kolchitsky's origins. Some claim he was a Pole, others a Slav, a Ukrainian, or an Armenian, his indeterminate ethnicity making him an ideal representative of one of Europe's most culturally diverse cities. True to his word, the Duke of Lorraine arrived with his army, and the Turkish forces were driven back on 11 September of that same year; an event long seen as an historic blow to Islam. It has never been established whether the fact that this event shares a date in the calendar with the destruction of the Twin Towers in New York over three centuries later is anything more than a bizarre historical coincidence.

After the city's liberation, the story goes that Kolchitsky was given the sacks of coffee beans left behind by the fleeing Turks as a reward, in addition to a property near St Stephen's Square. There he was said to have opened the city's first coffee house and hit upon the addition of sugar and milk to lessen the bitterness of the beans, thus inventing Vienna's signature concoction. The reality appears to have been somewhat different. History records the presence of a Turkish delegation that held court as early as 1663 in Leopoldstadt, Vienna's new 'Turkish quarter'. There the Pasha's two highly skilled coffee-makers, or *rahveci*, Mehmed and Ibrahim, served

129

coffee and sherbet to Viennese guests. Perhaps Kolchitsky attended one of these soirees and, recognising a business opportunity, decided to buy the franchise.

Oxford's first coffee house, which is often cited as the first in England, was opened more than two decades earlier than Kolchitsky's, in 1651, not by a Turk but by a Jew called Jacob, underlining the fact that new customs and ideas can sometimes arrive in outlying, maritime islands before they penetrate to the heart of a continent. Jacob's establishment is thought to have been the first business registered by a Jew in Oxford since the Middle Ages. After the blood-libel and pogroms of the twelfth century and their banishment by Edward I in 1290, Jews were only officially allowed back into England to conduct lawful business by Cromwell in 1655.

Within fifty years of Jacob's establishment opening its doors, there were two thousand coffee houses in London alone; Doctor Johnson's favourite, on Fleet Street, was named the Turk's Head. Robert Burton, whose penetrating gaze swept the world from his eyrie in the Bodleian Library, wrote of the Turkish predilection for coffee drinking in *The Anatomy of Melancholy*, over thirty years before Jacob served his first customers. 'The Turks have a drink called coffee (for they use no wine) so named of a berry as black as soot, and as bitter (like that black drink which was in use amongst the Lacedaemonians, and perhaps the same), which they sip still of, and sup as warm as they can suffer. They spend much time in those coffee houses, which are somewhat like our ale-houses, or taverns, and there they sit chatting and drinking to drive away the time and to be merry together, because they find by experience that kind of drink, so used, helps digestion and procureth alacrity.'

Strange that it takes a seventeenth-century author to explain so succinctly what I am doing when I buy my cup of coffee before boarding the morning train: *procuring alacrity*.

Today coffee drinking is no longer widely perceived in the West as having originated in the Levant, Turkey, or even in Italy or France; the café culture that is such a feature of our cities is based on the American model, rolled out from Manhattan or Seattle. In the dystopian future portrayed by David Mitchell in his novel *Cloud Atlas*, in which corporations have taken over the world, no one asks for a coffee any more, they ask for a starbucks. The artist Richard Wentworth once claimed in a public lecture about Trafalgar Square that London was in danger of drowning in a sea of cappuccino; Oxford is close to sharing the same fate. Today, as in seventeenth-century Vienna, the people who serve us the now ubiquitous refreshment come from distant climes; students earning their way through college (would-be barristers doing their time as *barristas*, trainee engineers working the levers of the coffee machines); young travellers on working holidays; refugees gaining a first foothold in their adopted country; and illegals sending money home.

The fate of nations hangs on the stock market value of the coffee-bean; and there is always room for new arrivals in a service economy in which the indigenous population no longer care to serve.

VIRTUAL STREETS AND GATEWAYS
The Plans Revisited

Only the local is universal.
WILLIAM CARLOS WILLIAMS, *The Autobiography of William Carlos Williams*

I arrive for the second planning day, this time in a church hall, in plenty of time. Once again I am impressed by the number of people who have turned out on a weekend, helping themselves to coffee from flasks and taking their places at tables for a day's work. Representatives of East Oxford Action, the consultants, and the city council mingle with the delegates. Wes had pointed out to me that the Cowley Road has become, in Foucault's words, a discursive object. It is true that it has taken on another life in these meetings. When we agree, it seems to exist as if by common consent, a figment of our collaborative imagining. When we don't, it becomes territory to be fought over, an ideological battleground with both a physical and theoretical dimension. A virtual Cowley Road is again on display in the form of photographs around the walls, showing each and every building along

133

the length of street that we are examining; and in maps showing proposals made on the first day.

'Vision: A Cowley Road that is safe and pleasant,' declares a whiteboard at the front of the room. Why do the words 'safe' and 'pleasant,' used in conjunction, create in me a feeling of constriction and unease? I realise that this reaction reveals an aspect of my character that probably renders me unsuited for a public consultation exercise. But I, too, am a member of the public, a tax-paying citizen. As such, I have the right to have my say; and, somewhat to my surprise, I find I am determined to do so.

It was only at the end of the first planning day that I learnt that there had been a group of delegates dedicated to the aesthetic appearance of the road – the so-called character issues group. This, I realise, is the group I should have belonged to from the start. Meanwhile, they have made some proposals that I find I am in complete disagreement with.

I manage to get hold of the convenor of the meeting during a coffee break and explain that it is these 'character issues' that I am most interested in, and that I feel that it is here that I can be of most use. I am humbled by some of the other delegates' knowledge of bus widths and kerb surfaces. On the other hand, it so happens I have spent some time thinking about and researching issues around urbanism and public art; perhaps I could make a more useful contribution in this area. A slightly glazed look

comes to her eye. It is essential to the schedule of the
consultation that the meeting agrees on a plan regarding
the redesign of Cowley Road within a certain deadline.
The proposal is then to be put on display for a few days
in the empty shop on Cowley Road that is serving as a
showroom for the project, allowing the public a final say.
Their brief states they have to deliver a scheme that has
been thoroughly vetted by the public by a certain date,
so that work can commence. Clearly, in her view, my
concerns should not be allowed to hold things up. I can't
help sympathising with her predicament. However you
look at it, someone like me emerging from the woodwork
at this stage, and talking this kind of language, can only
mean trouble. 'I don't think we will have much time to
discuss these points today,' she says briskly, 'but there
will be opportunity to discuss them at a later stage.
Perhaps you would like to go home and wait until then.'
She approaches one of the planners and asks them for a
sheaf of papers, which she then hands me in the hope
that I will take them away and study them at my leisure.
Unfortunately for her, what I see makes me determined
to stay. Line drawings depict the road after the addition
of proposed 'gateways' at either end. This is the first I
have heard of such plans. In one drawing, metal poles
with hanging banners, a feature of so many city centres
redesigned in the 1990s, are shown alongside the road.
Generic children play and cyclists ride in this skilfully
homogenised environment, eerily free of traffic and

appearing as if sandblasted clean of character. My reaction to these images is the reverse of love at first sight.

I rejoin the pedestrians' group. We seem to have newly discovered skills in functioning as a team. We move at speed along our map of the road, coming to final decisions on the placement of crossings, bus stops, and car parking in record time. Contrary to expectations, we therefore have some time available to discuss the suggestions that have arisen regarding the aesthetic appearance of the road. The first is that the type of street furniture used in the park at Manzil Way is extended right along the road, to achieve a 'coherent' design. I dislike this slavish subjection to the concept of coherence; in my view, it has often been the blight of British planning, responsible for driving out creativity and innovation. If a new building is to be put up next to a Victorian warehouse or a Georgian town house, what is demanded is something that looks a bit like a Victorian warehouse or Georgian town house, with the result that our island is crowded with rows and rows of the worst kind of architectural pastiche, a Disney-esque replay of our history, while architects who attempt to leave something original as a marker of their generation face the worst kind of difficulties in achieving their goal.

I point out to the group that the design of the metal benches in the park, with their high armrests and curved surfaces, was originally selected to prevent their use by alcoholics and rough sleepers as surrogate beds. While they may have a cheerfully contemporary appearance, seen in another light, they are little more than instruments of social exclusion. Unfortunately the discomfort they generate is not confined to the indigent or the inebriated; freezing cold in winter and scalding hot in summer, they are also too high off the ground for comfortable use by children, as their feet don't touch the ground. As I am acutely aware of the shortness of time and the importance of making my point, my words have a compressed, staccato intensity that takes the group aback, I can tell. 'I bet you feel better for getting that off your chest,' someone says kindly.

The other feature of the design of the park are the 'concrete cannon-balls' that have been part of the portfolio of every town planner since the 1990s. They are used to delineate space, permitting pedestrian access and frustrating skateboarders and off-road cyclists. It is not so much their appearance that I object to as their ubiquity. Travel to cities around Britain and you will come across them again and again, as though they marked the passage of a giant concrete rabbit. The night after they were installed in the Manzil Way Park, a local was unable to resist the challenge they presented and a couple of the smaller ones were rolled away, never to reappear. I am relieved to hear that the design consultants are not too keen themselves on either the concrete balls or the metal benches. Perhaps we are to be spared 'coherence' on this occasion.

My chief worry is the 'gateways'. By this, the planners, they assure us, don't mean actual, physical gateways spanning the road, but some sort of signage at each end to designate Cowley Road a 'special' area, rather as if it were Oxford's Chinatown. Within these borders, they seem to say, people live lives slightly different from the norm. We are prepared to allow this, as long as it remains controllable and confined within this strictly defined area; if we consider it potentially lucrative, we might even promote it. I suppose we should not be surprised at this line of reasoning. This is, after all, a very cheap way in which to regenerate an area: rebrand it, put up some pretty signage, perhaps even give it a new name, and the middle classes will flock in, along with businesses catering to their needs. The market will do the rest. Who will regret the passing of what was there before?

Cities are criss-crossed with invisible lines of demarcation, discernible to strollers, pilgrims, and other explorers. They signal changes in demographics, atmosphere, building style, climate, and a host of other subtle variations in the urban fabric. They are there for those with eyes to see them; they should never be made explicit, institutionalised, fixed in stone, metal, or any other material. As Walter Benjamin writes in *The Arcades Project*, 'Nowhere, except perhaps in dreams, can the phenomenon of the boundary be experienced in a more originary way than in cities. To know them means to understand those lines that, running alongside railroad crossings and across privately owned lots, within the park and along the riverbank, function as limits . . . A new precinct begins like a step into the void – as though one had unexpectedly cleared a low step on a flight of stairs.' It is precisely the kind of unexpected psychic lurch that Benjamin is describing that would be eradicated by the erection of so-called 'gateways'.

The last chance for registering opinions regarding the proposed improvements is fast approaching. Three weekdays and a Saturday are specified as times when members of the public can come to the temporary office and register their views, all times when I cannot attend. Submissions are also invited in writing, so I decide to put my thoughts on paper as soon as I get home. My first attempt, scrawled in a notebook, takes the form of a declaration of resistance:

'Hands off!' Our lives are not for sale.
We do not wish to appear on your reality TV shows
Or have the area in which we live labelled a site of special tourist
* interest.*
We refuse to be penned into your reservations.
By paying our taxes, we do not give you permission to 'style'
* our environment*
Or impose your aesthetic on our neighbourhood –
We regard all such activities as cultural terrorism . . .

On reflection, it is not entirely clear to whom this diatribe is addressed: the design consultants, the co-ordinators of the consultation, or local government officials. Even as I write, I know that such language will win me few friends. I start again, working on a letter that I revise over a few days on the train, addressing it to the representative of East Oxford Action who is managing the consultation. I begin by thanking her for allowing me to take part in the design days and underlining my support for the work they have done in the area over the past couple of years. I then attempt to put into words my objections to the gateways and other features that have been suggested.

I feel that it is very dangerous to allow issues relating to the character of the road to slip through un-scrutinised. We worked hard on all the questions regarding road width, bus stop and crossing placements, and so on during the planning days, and the results of the consultation will undoubtedly bring benefits to users of the road. Unfortunately, if the inexorable rise of traffic continues, these benefits will be eroded over time and will have to be revisited. Changes made to the 'character' of the neighbourhood, on the other hand, can have a lasting impact that is not so easily adjusted at a later stage. I am writing to you to register some of my concerns.

The first and chief of these is over the introduction of what the design consultants term 'gateways' at either end of the Cowley Road. This urban planners' habit of labelling areas in a city became popular in the 1980s; there is now widely held unease about it for a number of reasons.

Firstly, what does such a sign say? Far more than that you are now entering a traffic-controlled area. It can be an indicator of a particular ethnic make-up of local residents; one thinks of Banglatown in East London or Korean Town in New York. Other examples allude to the dominant economic activity pursued in the area: the Jewellery Quarter in Birmingham is a good example.

To examine the effect of such signage in our city, we have to ask the question what does Cowley Road – and by extension, East Oxford – mean to residents of other parts of Oxford? If the answer is that the area is perceived as having a different socio-economic and ethnic background to the rest of the city – which I believe it is – such signage can be construed as both patronising and offensive. While ostensibly 'celebrating' an area's character, in effect what it does is package it for tourism. It creates a clearly defined 'reservation' where diverse elements are allowed to exist, at the same time marketing them to non-residents as a tourist attraction.

It is understandable that such an approach should be suggested in Oxford. Selling ourselves to outsiders is one of the city's chief industries. Parts of the city centre are preserved in aspic as a stage set for tourists to wander around while museums, guides, and tour buses provide explanations of our past and fast-food outlets and chain stores (the same that grace every high street up and down the country) provide sustenance and shopping opportunities.

Part of the attraction of East Oxford for its residents is that it is an area not obviously dominated either by the university or by the tourist industry. It has developed gradually since the 1860s, shaped by a number of different factors, including commercial activity and patterns of immigration. At present it resists the commercial and

141

planning pressures that have brought about the homogenisation of so many of our city centres throughout the nation. To stamp an identity on Cowley Road through the introduction of 'gateways' or other items of public art would be to distort, rather than enhance, the unique character of this sensitive area.

What, after all, is the aim of urban regeneration? Not, I am sure you would agree, to rob an area of its individual character; nor to 'soften it up' for the entrance of big commercial players that have so far restricted their activities to Cornmarket and Queen Street. Neither should it be to place artificial borders around a particular area, reinforcing notions of division between different sectors of the city's population.

At the second planning day, it had also been suggested that public art projects be commissioned for the Cowley Road. Public art is probably one of the most contested and divisive areas of cultural production. On the one hand, you have avant-garde pieces that are imposed on the public and provoke such a hostile reaction that they have to be removed. (Richard Serra's *Tilted Arc* in New York was a good example.) On the other hand, you have a proliferation of second-rate pieces that are really nearer to street furniture than art; often made by local craftsmen, they typically make clumsy allusions to industries in the neighbourhood and speak a kind of artistic shorthand, known in the trade as 'imitation in pursuit of distinctiveness.' (Although these projects ostensibly set out to enhance the unique character of a particular neighbourhood, they do so by imitating supposedly 'successful' models undertaken in other parts of the country, leading to a proliferation of similar looking projects.) Joseph Beuys's famous dictum that everyone is an artist has come horribly true. Local councillors, responding to the zeitgeist, volunteer themselves as curators of the public arena, even though their expertise lies in other fields. Aware that such objections can easily be dismissed as elitist, or mistaken for small-minded 'nimbyism,'* I attempt to tackle them in my letter.

While the rationale of 'inclusive' public art is that in many cases it is in some way democratic, the reality is that only a small percentage of the population respond to consultation or participate in the creation of such works. The resulting art is often mediocre and rarely adds to the ambience of a locality. The fact that those who have participated may feel some 'ownership' of the piece – the mantra behind many such projects – does not excuse these often aesthetically disastrous interventions in the local environment. Cowley Road has no need of any further public art. It is in itself an interesting and vital space that offers plenty of visual stimulation arising from the everyday activities that carry on there. Once again, it does not need rebranding or redecorating. One of the most important aesthetic judgements to be made by any artist is to know when to leave well alone.

Finally, I expressed my opposition to the proposal to

---

*NIMBY – acronym for 'Not in My Back Yard.'

roll out the design of street furniture in the park for the extent of the road and tried to explain my fear that the proposals would rob the area of its specific identity.

I have seen the kind of street banners depicted in one of the design consultants' drawings circulated at the second planning day, in cities from Manchester to Glasgow, from New York to Los Angeles. What function can such features play here, apart from to make 'here' more like everywhere else?

Would my protest have any effect? I could only wait and see.

COSMONAUTS AND COLESLAW

The Russian Fairytale supermarket at number 88 Cowley Road is a distinctive presence, with its name spelt out in both red Cyrillic lettering and Roman characters on a pale green signboard. Inside, the shelves are packed with delicacies. Deep-salted, preserved cherries; peeled and pickled garlic; four kinds of coleslaw in jars; tins of beef goulash; bilberries in syrup. The chilled compartment is stocked with a wide variety of salamis. A sign on the wall advertises the availability of the Yugoslav preserved fish speciality *imamo bakalor*, at £27 per kilo. Russian books and CDs, candlesticks, birch-bark hair slides, and the inevitable *matreshka* Russian dolls compete for space with the foodstuffs. A notice board carries advertisements for a Russian school, Russian-language classes, touring details of a Russian ballet company, and hand-written personal ads in Russian. Behind the counter, the shelves hold a bewildering variety of vodkas.

Raissa is a handsome woman with a broad smile and something of the resolute air of a figure from a

Soviet-era poster, her blonde hair pulled back tight into a bun at the back of her head. It is not always easy approaching people to interview them about their lives on the road. Understandably, some are suspicious; others uncomprehending. I knew that it would not be a problem persuading Raissa to talk. She has a strong entrepreneurial spirit that combines with her sense of hospitality to always make a visit to the shop a memorable encounter. She reacts with no surprise to my request and does not flinch at the sight of my tape recorder.

'I am from the centre of Siberia,' she tells me, 'if you heard about Lake Baikal, from there. It was ten years ago I came to England. It was regarding my daughter's education, because she finished high school in Moscow and we decided she needed a university degree somewhere, so why not here, in England?'

'Why did you choose to come and live in Oxford?' I ask.

'I have no idea! Possibly the first place I came to when I came to England. Actually I had been living in London and it reminded me of Moscow, very noisy and busy. Oxford is more peaceful, but with its student community, always very alive. When the first wave of Russians who came here wanted to do some business, we decided to open a Russian food shop.'

Before opening she must have done her market research to establish that there was a demand for Russian food in the area. 'What percentage of your customers are Russian?'

'About fifty and fifty, I can say; fifty per cent are Russian speakers. We have a lot of customers from the former Russian republics. There is one Slovenian shop in Oxford already, but I have Polish customers, Czech customers, Yugoslav, Greek, some Ukrainian, Baltic republics – it's all over, you see! We also have Turkish, Italian people, and we have African people . . .'

'What is it that draws people from such different backgrounds to the shop? What are they looking for?'

Raissa considers for a moment, as though struggling to account for such widespread popularity. 'We have very interesting mushrooms, Russian mushrooms. We have Russian rye bread. You can find gherkins here, but how they are preserved is a different way. We don't use vinegar; they are pickled in salt and spices.

'Why English people come here is for Russian famous soup called borscht. Sometimes I make it, home-made here, or in jars so people just have to add the same amount of water and boil together for two minutes and it is ready! And we have *pelmeni*, meat dumplings; this is a frozen food, similar to the ravioli way.

'And, of course' – and she lowers her voice suggestively – 'people come because Russia is linked to vodka!'

Ah yes, the vodka. We had eaten the previous night at the house of a Polish friend, and the evening had started with glasses of extremely cold Zubrowka, the Polish vodka flavoured with a strand of bison grass floating in the clear, slightly oily liquid. I had decided to come and buy a bottle. Raissa takes me on a tour of her selection, pointing at each in turn. 'We have Polish vodkas: blackcurrant, chilli, cranberry; Polish Spiritu, that one is 79.9 per cent; Goldwasser, with gold flakes in it – they are edible! Potato vodka, honey vodka, pineapple; Russian Gzhelka; we have Siberian, Old Kiev, Georgian vodka, Chechen . . . Usually in Russia we keep it chilled two or three hours in freezer before we drink it; when it's cold, you feel the fragrance. We also have Russian beer, Moldavian and Georgian wine.'

She pauses, her list of turbulent and warring republics complete, their fiery essences distilled and lined up peacefully on her shelves. 'But where will it appear, this thing you are writing?' I tell her that it is to be a book, not a newspaper article.

'Then I must tell you the most important thing. We are going to open a travel agency, based here' – she points to a storeroom through a door beside the counter – 'this will be the office. Of course, it will change inside the shop; we will change the window. We will have holidays very far north, close to Japan, on the Kamchatka Peninsula in Siberia. This is active holiday; it is not seaside. People will prefer if they want real nice, rough holiday, even with mountain climbing, volcanic, anything whichever they like. They can even go to the North Pole, but that is very expensive, at least ten thousand . . .'

'Would they travel through the Russian Arctic?'

'Yes, they start in Moscow, then St Petersburg, then Murmansk, and then to the North Pole. Then if you have heard about cosmonauts, astronauts – before they go to space, they have to train. Now people who would like to can do that! Working with a very famous Russian astronaut . . .'

I am glad that the heroes of the Soviet space programme are to find new employment in our altered world. I had been moved by the photographs an artist friend brought back from Russia: of a once-busy, green-lit spacesuit factory; of the ghostly shadow of an abandoned Soviet-era rocket on a wall and another sawn in half and turned into a children's playground ride. Perhaps visitors to Kamchatka from Cowley Road can capture something of the vanished spirit of those pioneering times by sharing in the cosmonauts' routines, living in the same places they lived. Who did Raissa think would buy these holidays?

'Well, trading here now for more than three years, I have met a lot of English people who have been in Russia, who have been in Kazakhstan, Uzbekistan, even further, in Siberia, and they just admire and want to go back there – possibly because the people are different; the hospitality is different. You can say it is the territory, because England is very small, and there you can drive

and drive, the wild forest around you, for days and days!'
She makes a sweeping gesture with her hands that seems
to encapsulate the vastness of the Siberian forest, the
mountains, and beyond them space itself.

Of course, it was from Kamchatka that Yuri Gagarin
blasted off to circle the earth in a space capsule. This
shop, too, will be a launching point, a portal offering
access to a place very different to the multilayered,
crowded environment of Cowley Road – a place in
which to commune with cosmonauts and to feel the wild
forest around you. While the connections being forged
between Siberia and East Oxford seem extraordinary,
they are in keeping with today's world. A journey to the
farthest limits of the globe begins at the travel agent in
the local shopping centre, while much of the exploration
remaining to be done is in our own backyard.

ST EDMUND'S WELL AND
A FADED WARNING

Pilgrimage, said Imlac, like many other acts of piety, may be reasonable or
superstitious, according to the principles on which it is performed. Long
journeys in search of truth are not commanded. Truth, such is necessary to
the regulation of life, is always found where it is honestly sought . . . [B]ut
that some places may operate on our own minds in an uncommon manner
is an opinion that hourly experience will justify.

SAMUEL JOHNSON, *The History of Rasselas*

When I had been with Wes at the Globe Café, he had
spoken of places 'where you cross over into another
world.' Although I didn't know it at the time, just such
a place existed in a previous age, a few hundred yards
from where we had been sitting. In the thirteenth century,
pilgrims came here to partake of the miraculous waters
of St Edmund's Well. It lay to the south of St Clement's
Church, on what is now known as the Plain, next to a ford
called Cowley Mill or Cowley Ford and at the entrance
to the unenclosed pasture of Cowley Mede. Its waters,
whether taken internally or applied to the body, were
thought to be very effective in curing sickness, healing

wounds, and 'working miracles on the vulgar.' The well took its name from Edmund Rich of Abingdon, the humble Oxford scholar who eventually rose to become Archbishop of Canterbury and was canonised in 1247. While Edmund was still a student at Oxford, 'courted by the greatest schollers of that age both for his piety and learning,' he would wander in the meadows around the periphery of the city in order to 'convers in privat with God.' It is thought that during one such tryst, Christ appeared to him, causing a spring to burst forth out of the ground on the spot. This spring was the source that fed the well.

In his day Edmund often walked the path along the Thames between Abingdon and Oxford, as I do today. Some of the meadows on the outskirts of the city are little changed, excepting the occasional pylon or burnt out joyrider's vehicle, the sound of bird-song accompanied by the distant rumble of the ring road; grazed by cows in summer, flooded in winter, graced by the exotic snake's head fritillary in spring. If through some slippage in time we were to meet beside the water, would he glance up at the man and his dog that approached along the riverbank? Would he be too engrossed in his meditations even to notice that he had inadvertently stepped onto the pages of a twenty-first-century narrative? He would certainly have recognised my walking companion as a hunting dog, mistaken it as a greyhound pup perhaps, although the whippet evolved some five centuries later in the industrial north, when scholar saints had all but disappeared.

Where is the well now, you ask. Why do the pedestrians on the pavements of Cowley Road not include foot-sore pilgrims, come to seek refreshment from its healing waters? To the English, an excess of devotion is always a flirtation with heresy. The well fell victim to its own popularity. It came to the attention of Oliver Sutton, Bishop of Lincoln, 'how strangely the people were besotted with a fond imagination of [the well's] vertues and holinesse, and that they did neglect to serve the true God by hankering after and worshipping this well.' Indeed, on Saint Edmund's Day (latterly removed from the Church of England calendar), the populace would come to the well and divert themselves with cakes and ale, music and dancing. This was uncomfortably close to the pagan traditions of the ancient Britons, who like the Germans and Saxons were prone to grant such places undue reverence. In 1291 the bishop sent an edict to the Archdeacon of Oxford, classifying such activities as the vilest error and superstition and threatening any that resorted to the well with instant excommunication. It was promptly filled in. The memory of Saint Edmund was best served by the French; his body can still be seen, entombed in a glass case, in a church at Pontigny in Burgundy. However, the Oxford College that bears his name still makes a nod to his miraculous powers. As part of its efforts to capture the conference and rental trade, the unremarkable Junior Common Room at St Edmund's Hall was renamed the Pontigny Room. Saint Edmund was known to have the healing touch, particularly with women who wanted to conceive. The Pontigny Room is frequently hired out for wedding receptions.

The Plain today is a busy traffic island. St Clement's Church has been relocated to Marston Road, its previous existence marked only by a stone on the roundabout, recording the position of the former graveyard; the Toll Gate that stood at this entrance to the city has vanished, along with the house beside it that famously had two entrances to its driveway, so that its owner never had to pay the toll. The peace stone erected in 1814 to mark Napoleon's first defeat (prior to his escape from Elba) has disappeared. One relatively ancient monument remains; next to the municipal roundabout stands the Victoria Drinking Fountain, inaugurated by Princess Louise on 25 May 1899. The fountain, like the well, has long ceased dispensing water. Beneath a conical, tiled roof topped with a clock and supported by stone pillars, four basins stand beneath decorative scallop shells, the scallop the symbol incidentally of pilgrimage along the Way of St James to Santiago. The brass spouts are silent; the basins contain a few dry leaves and two empty plastic Merrydown cider bottles. The fountain's inscription tells us that it was sponsored by Mr and Mrs Morrell, the local brewing barons, formerly of Headington Hill Hall. Their names are obscured by algae and a century of pollution;

as is often the case, the traces of this relatively recent age seem as distant and as indecipherable as those of ancient Egypt. Around the roof, however, a Latin inscription is picked out in gold, still clearly legible to those with the education to decipher it. The fact is that few (and I include myself) can now easily read the cryptic messages left by previous generations on so many buildings in our cities. Presumably within half a century, their import will be almost entirely lost. The first difficulty with this one is to decide where it starts and where it finishes: each word is picked out on a different face of the roof's octagonal support. I circle the building several times before making my decision: *Lympha gadit ruit hora sagax bibe carpe fugacem*. A locally published guidebook I find in the library provides a translation: 'The water drips, the hours go by; be warned, drink, catch them ere they fly.' These representatives of the great local brewing family, dispensers of narcotic forgetfulness, their beer both the solace and the undoing of the Victorian working man, counsel constant vigilance and attention to the present moment. Most evenings on the Cowley Road, I would judge the locals more interested in absorbing the Morrells' product than their moral advice, but I aim to bear it in mind. I hear a rumour that the fountain is to be restored to working order. Anyone wishing to drink will have to play toreador with the traffic; there is no crossing connecting the fountain with the pavement. There is a little door in the fountain's side that is unlocked; I open it, exposing the disused pipework inside. Once repaired, will it bring water pumped from the mains, or might it reach deep into the earth, through the stones and rubble that choke the mouth of St Edmund's Well?

Of course, this would have been the logical point for the beginning of my journey; a miraculous well rather than a misappropriated Munch painting. But I had no idea when I set out that the well had ever existed, that any pilgrim before me had taken this route. I did not plan to become enmeshed in religion; my pilgrimage was to be a secular one. What is more, the Plain, despite its commanding position at the gates of the city, is unprepossessing, it is so beset, so overrun with traffic. From a distance Victoria Fountain, beneath its conical hat, looks like the spindle of a roulette wheel. It spins and the buses, cars, vans, and bicycles ricochet up St Clement's towards London, down the Iffley Road towards Rose Hill, over Magdalen Bridge into the city centre, or down Cowley Road, dusting the pilgrim with carbon monoxide and diesel particulates, contributing to the twenty-first-century background hum that drowns out the drip, drip of the passing hours.

SECOND PARTITION

MAKING DO AND GETTING BY

On a Wednesday evening in May, I make the journey from London to Oxford by car, driven by the artist Richard Wentworth. It is a trip he makes several times a week to fulfil his commitments as the director of the Ruskin School of Drawing and Fine Art. I want to talk to Richard about the photographs he has made over the past twenty years or so, that he has collected under the loose title *Making Do and Getting By*; photographs taken on the street, many on the Caledonian Road near his London home, others snatched on his travels around the world. The subjects of the photographs are almost always things, not people; but things manipulated, positioned, or abandoned *by* people. Resilient gestures, he calls them. A catalogue of overlooked events.

So accustomed is he to driving the route that we seem to glide, as if drawn along on the thread of our conversation. In his late fifties, Richard is still wiry, his grey hair cropped short. He dresses conservatively, the only touch of flamboyance in his appearance an oversize pair of tortoise-shell spectacles, as if a cartoonist wanted to emphasise that this is a man whose job is to look. In fact, to be with him is to notice things; he is constantly glancing around and commenting, as if the paraphernalia of the present moment were laid out for his enjoyment, merely awaiting his arrival. He is the kind of artist who loves to talk; about work, about the art world, and about life. It's a chance to get ideas out there, to expose them to the light and see if they float, taking those that do and feeding them back into the process. Our conversation ranges back and forward in time and across the globe, from a dinner he has recently had with a Jesuit priest at the Vatican to the junk shops of the Caledonian Road in London. After more than two decades of exhibiting internationally, he appears to know everyone and to have been everywhere and is generous with his connections. When he suggests introducing me to a writer of his acquaintance, I own up to a slight unease; I haven't read the man's book, but from a reference elsewhere suspect it covers at least some of the same ground as the one I am working on. The thing that every explorer fears is to round a corner in the jungle and stumble over the debris of a previous expedition, quietly rotting in the sun. Richard recognises the symptoms of my malaise immediately and will have none of it.

'I get this with my students; they work for months and then suddenly get depressed because they discover Picasso did something similar fifty years ago. We all live in the world. We all participate in the culture. Because you're in the culture, you have shared the privilege of experiencing an idea. You're in the swimming pool swimming, and it doesn't mean you're not going to proceed – you'll just proceed at another angle. If we find that someone else has worked in the same area, made the same references, it shows we are on the right track. We will bring our own approach and our own perspective to bear, and it will be honest work. We can't act as if our area of interest is a country, and we are not going to let anybody else in.'

He warms to his theme, gesturing expansively with one hand as he drives. 'I like the feeling that others are making the same journey as we are. Sometimes I can be sitting waiting at traffic lights at Baker Street in London and see someone get on the coach for Oxford, then see them get off just as I arrive in the city. Perhaps that night I will be sitting at a table in a restaurant and notice them at another table. If I could hear their conversation, I might find that there were all kinds of shared reasons that we have made the same journey.' He grimaces. 'I don't *actually want to know what they are talking about*. I don't want to be God . . .'

He pauses to change gear as we ascend the hill, past High Wycombe and up onto the Chilterns.

'It is like when you are doing that kind of drawing that is a continuous, spiralling, elliptical mark, and the whole thing is moving like smoke across the paper. But when you look at what is happening, any individual mark is travelling backwards as well as forwards, and what it is doing is crossing the previous act, but it happens so quickly you don't notice it. It is exactly the process I feel we are living in. Half the time we are retracing our steps – I know I left it here somewhere – and then picking it up and moving forwards again. I'm sure there's a great physics model for it. I am supposed to be having dinner with a scientist this week; I will try and find out.'

I have gained, I realise, another metaphor for my journey; a trajectory with an onward momentum as inexorable as drifting smoke that is in fact made up of innumerable movements forward and backward, the retracing of steps and the crossing of tracks.

We emerge through the cutting in the Chilterns and begin our descent; the sun breaks through the clouds, illuminating the sweep of the plain below. Fields glowing the luminous green of an English spring are punctuated with small hills, studded with darker trees. In the distance, the cooling towers at Didcot each appear to balance a solid-looking cloud on its end, a power generator's circus trick. Apart from this modernist detail, we could be looking at the landscape in the background of a Renaissance painting.

'My god,' Richard comments, 'it looks like Tuscany with a power station.'

'And then in summer,' I reply rather glibly, 'Tuscany becomes Oxfordshire without a power station.' But it's true: in July and August, the middle classes migrate south like swallows to France and Italy, returning just before the swallows themselves begin the same journey, without the aid of four-wheel drive.

The atmosphere of Richard's photographs is hard to capture in words. They document small-scale human responses to the sheer cussedness of life, the tricky negotiations we make with the stuff that surrounds us. A wooden clothes hanger is jammed into position in a sash-window in Staten Island, holding it shut. A shopping bag serves as a dressing for a dog's foot. The hammer of an old-fashioned door-bell is muffled by being imbedded in a bar of toffee. These actions, however apparently insignificant, have consequences. A discarded polystyrene cup stuffed behind an electricity conduit on the Caledonian Road attracts another, and another, until the wall is festooned up and down with fungal growths. A broken tile pushed under a manhole cover prevents a street flooding in Valencia. These are not the actions of master craftsmen or trained engineers, but a demonstration of the ingenuity and adaptability by which the human animal masters its habitat. As a species we are, it seems, a collection of artful bodgers. And litter-bugs. None of the photographs are staged, except in the Shakespearean sense (All the world's a . . . , etc.). Together they provide a unique body of portraits of unassuming objects and limited aspirations that is both poignant and hilarious.

As we arrive in Oxford, Richard leans forward,

peering through the windscreen, eager to explain. 'Here is something that I see every time that I drive this route and that in theory I might photograph,' he comments. 'I won't; I'm not that acquisitive.' He points to a bicycle with a crumpled wheel, leant against a fence at the top of Headington Hill, as if awaiting collection.

'It's been involved in some sort of traumatic accident. It lay on the pavement for a while, and now it has found a home there. For how long? It's just like the hats or gloves people pick up and place on railings' (something else he has photographed). 'I'm not really interested in a glove on a railing, but in what it means. What an extraordinary thing it is that you pick up this glove and put it on a railing, giving it an almost medieval prominence, as if it was Cromwell's head on a pole or something. In doing so, you move it from the very place where the person lost it so there is a good chance they won't see it, which is why they stay there for months sometimes, becoming quite emblematic.'

He warms to his theme as we descend the hill.

'Here's another – somewhere around here – yes, there! The old railing has been removed, but when Charlie and George came along to do the job, they found that one section was entwined with ivy. They didn't have a saw, so they just left it standing there, one section on its own, a palimpsest of some previous thing. It's as if the ivy was hanging on for dear life. I'm ignoring those' – he waves dismissively at the spiked railings along the edge of South

Park; several of the spikes have polystyrene cups impaled upon them, a favourite Wentworth motif. 'There are more of them every time I come past. I'm beginning to feel that somebody is leaving me a message.'

I ask him if he sees the world differently when he is carrying a camera.

'Not really. Having a camera in your hand is undoubtedly a force field. I usually just have a camera in my pocket, and you know it is asking something, but I am very suspicious of those kinds of photographs. I never go out looking for a photograph. It is too much like going out hunting, and I don't like being a hunter. I would rather have an encounter, be an encountrist. Sometimes I think I am a bit magnetic.' He laughs, undermining any possible hint of pretension in the admission.

It is this relaxed alertness that interests me and that I wish to cultivate in my own research. 'We don't control our experiences really,' I have heard him say on another occasion, 'although we like to think we do. Human beings are just advanced fly-paper. It's all in the editing process. That's what I try to teach my students – editing.'

We park in a street off Cowley Road and make our way to a restaurant where we are meeting a friend for dinner. The Mirch Masala, a long-time favourite among the Indian restaurants in the area, has recently undergone a transformation. The proprietor is a serene-looking, welcoming woman with a seemingly unflappable attitude to the activities of her customers. We used to visit regularly accompanied by our children; she was quite happy to allow them behind the counter to help themselves to soft drinks from the fridge. In return, they honoured their side of this social contract by spending most of the time sitting at the table, munching on naan bread, and observing the comings and goings as their parents ate. They recognised the place as not-quite-home, but nevertheless a friendly space where their needs were recognised and their presence accepted. Different patterns of work and the arrival of another baby have meant that a couple of years have slipped by since I last ate here, but I have kept an eye on the renovation that has been going on, secretly hoping that the restaurant's relaxed ambience has survived the improvements.

'Hello,' the proprietor greets me, unsurprised at my arrival, as if only a week had passed since my last visit. 'How are you? How are the children?'

The interior has been opened out into one large space, with stripped pine furnishings. I am pleased to recognise the fridge, standing to attention against a wall, marooned in its newly plush surroundings. I mention the renovation.

'Yes, there have been a lot of changes here; I am not sure they have all been for the better. People find it a little bit less intimate, more intimidating,' she says reflectively.

We discuss the advantages and disadvantages of open-plan dining as opposed to booths; the latter are less space-efficient, we agree, but possibly more atmospheric. Such self-criticism is rare in the owner of a business but typical of her approach, which is to treat customers as friends rather than business clients. At the end of the day, it is as much the personality of its owner as the layout of the furniture that makes a restaurant a success or a failure.

Our waitress for the evening is a young, dark-haired European woman with an accent that is hard to place. Richard asks her where she comes from. 'Georgia,' she replies.

'I thought so,' he says.

'Excuse me, how do you know people from Georgia?' she asks, apparently astonished. 'Some people think I am Italian. Or Turkish. No one here thinks I am from Georgia.'

Richard mentions a Georgian he has known who worked in a London-based arts organisation and has now returned to Georgia to sit in its parliament. The waitress recognises the name immediately and nods energetically. In her country the existence of a parliamentary system is not taken for granted.

'But have you heard what has happened in Georgia this evening?' Richard asks.

'No, what?'

'I was listening to the car radio while I was waiting to pick up my friend here. Aslan Abashidze has left Adzharia; he has been overthrown.'

The gangster Abashidze, supported by a coterie of Mercedes-driving minions, had held Adzharia in an iron fist, running it as his own separate fiefdom for the last year. When pro-democracy demonstrations were violently broken up by the police, thousands had come out on the streets and chased Abashidze and his gang of thugs out of town. The president, Mikhail Saakashvili, appeared on television. 'Georgians! Aslan has fled,' he announced. 'Adzharia is free!'

The waitress's face lights up. 'What? That is wonderful! I spoke to my mother this afternoon and she said something was going on, but I did not know how it would end. Thank you so much for telling me!' She beams at us, illuminating our table in a spotlight of gratitude and benevolence that does not fade for the rest of the evening. She is still thanking us as we leave.

Rulers fall and the impact of their collapse is felt thousands of miles away. In Los Angeles and London, Georgians will be dancing. On Cowley Road the news, brought by word of mouth as it always used to be, imperfect and devoid of detail, is enough to spark joy in the heart of a waitress; a joy that, once her shift has ended, will connect with the joy of others and crackle across the city like electricity.

EGYPTIAN VAGABONDS

AFTERNOON MEN, AND THE *MALUS GENIUS* OF OUR NATION

Oxford has always attracted travellers of the less well-to-do sort, as well as displaced kings, dissolute aristocrats, and the offspring of dictators and presidents. Tramps, beggars, Irish tinkers, gypsies, and others who rely on their own feet for transport have been regular visitors. Their presence particularly offended Robert Burton, who saw them as a stain on the glory of the kingdom. At the opening of the *Anatomy*, before beginning his epic dissection of human consciousness, Burton undertakes a brief examination of the state of the nation. Every internal malady has an outward expression, he maintains, and the physical decrepitude of the state can mirror internal ills. After listing the blessings enjoyed by English citizens, he notes that 'amongst many roses, some thistles grow, some bad weeds and enormities, which much disturb the peace of this body politic, eclipse the honour and glory of it . . .' (Quoting from Burton is a perilous business;

the sheer length of many of his beautifully constructed sentences forces one to deploy ellipses as literary secateurs, to prevent one's own text being strangled by the ever-creeping tendrils of his argument.)

The first weed he identifies as fit to be rooted out is idleness, 'by reason of which we have many swarms of rogues and beggars, thieves, drunkards, and discontented persons (whom Lycurgus in Plutarch calls *morbos reipublicae*, the boils of the common wealth), many poor people in all our towns . . . Idleness is the *malus genius* of our nation.' As for the nation, so for the individual; idleness is one of the prime causes of melancholy cited in the *Anatomy*. A connection between melancholy and idleness had long been popularly accepted. Influenced by translations of Arabic texts that in turn had drawn on Roman and Eastern traditions, medieval astrologers had established a link between the black bile that caused the melancholy humour and the influence of the planet Saturn. Melancholics were 'Saturn's children'; and the term gradually came to mean social outcasts in general, tramps, derelicts, and the like. So the rogues, Egyptian vagabonds, layabouts, and 'Afternoon Men' so disparaged by Burton were under the influence of the same planet as he was himself. Yet far from acknowledging his kinship with them, he saw them as visible symptoms of a disease affecting the body politic; a sickness that needed to be purged before the advent of a truly glorious nation could come about.

Aware that this vision was unlikely to be realised, Burton resorted to constructing an imaginary Utopia at the beginning of his *Anatomy*, a perfect kingdom in which no man would be permitted to be idle yet at the same time all in genuine need would be supported by the state. The local authorities in Oxford felt they had no such luxury; a solution had to be found to the influx of travellers to the city, a problem that became more acute in the late eighteenth century. In 1790 they were paying constables one shilling for every vagrant they apprehended, yet even this incentive was not enough to curb the flow. Beggars noticeably increased in number during term-time; sensitive to the shifting patterns of temporary employment, tramps added the fleecing of students to lifting potatoes and picking hops in their seasonal calendars. In 1814 the Anti-Mendacity Society was formed with support from the university. Deserving travellers on their way to and from the harvest fields were supported, and leaflets discouraging the public from giving money to beggars were distributed throughout the city. In 1832 the society opened a small hostel, and by the following year as many as fifty Irish tramps a day were paying it a visit on their way to the fields, 'vagrancy being their trade and their delight,' as one writer puts it. The workhouse in the city centre resisted pressure to cater to the tramps; as they represented only eleven of the city's parishes, they felt the responsibility lay with the city council. When famine struck in Ireland, the numbers of vagrants arriving in the city exploded. During 1847 and 1848, 8,500 tramps were given relief at the hostel. Sometimes the building was overrun, and there was nothing for it but to close the doors and call out the police. In 1862–63 the numbers increased further, to 10,000. With the move of the workhouse to Cowley Road, many more vagrants of a professional kind besieged the hostel in the city centre, their demands sometimes accompanied with violent threats. It had become, it was decided, a 'hotel for tramps,' known throughout the region, and was closed. The new workhouse opened with only two small rooms catering for male tramps and two for females. Further casual wards had to be added in the 1880s, by which time Cowley Road was receiving officially recorded visits from between four and five thousand tramps a year.

A combination of the ongoing mechanisation of agriculture, the impact of globalisation, and the pattern of farm subsidies has put an end to much of the seasonal work for labourers in our fields. As apple orchards are grubbed out and hop fields disappear, and as supermarket chains prefer to buy their strawberries from Israel or Spain rather than English farms, it is not just the landscape that has changed. Those still prepared to strain their backs picking English fruit are now more likely to come from Poland than Peckham. At a local history event, I am introduced to Margaret, who has known Cowley Road since the 1940s, and whose family connections with the area stretch back into the second half of the nineteenth century. She is a small, active woman in her seventies with a deep interest in the area she grew up in. She is more than willing to share her memories of the 'gentlemen of the road,' who were a common sight during her childhood, often on their way to work on local farms. Her memories of them reflect a tolerance widely felt at the time.

'Oh, yes. It was a life: they were no problem. They were accepted as people who lived on the street. They looked after themselves. They took casual labour on the farms, stole, and so on. They were accepted as people who had decided this was their life.'

'Did you feel safe in the area as a child?' I ask.

'We didn't go out at night very much as children. But we didn't really feel unsafe anywhere around here. You knew all the gypsies, you knew all the beggars, you knew the people who came every year with sprigs of lavender or heather and little bits of hankies to the door. They'd say, "You've got a lucky face," and that sort of thing. In those days there were ice-cream men who had a box on the front of their bikes and pedalled along. Of course, they were out in the streets all day and had nowhere to go, and so they used to go up Barracks Lane to have a pee. When we kids were going along, we might see the ice-cream man having a pee in the lane and that used to frighten me. They were big, burly men. There were places along there with hollow trees where the tramps used to shelter;

they were frightening. But we used to go out in gangs, you see, over the allotments and up by the stream.'

Despite the relentless gentrification of East Oxford, it still boasts an above-average quota of eccentrics and vagrants; the kind of people termed 'tatterdemallions' in Samuel Johnson's *Dictionary*. For local residents, their passage is akin to that of seasonal birds in more rural communities. Every now and then, a new arrival takes up residency for a few months, enlivening the road with their particular brand of oddness, until they disappear again, bound who knows where. There is the young black man who walks fast, always doubled up, staggering with hysterical laughter. And the woman who wears large, furry headphones and mutters aggressively at passers-by as she strides, occasionally raising her skirts as if to frighten off potential attackers with the sight of her private parts. Some shout things so strange that they are like messages from another world. Like the woman who stood in a backstreet off Cowley Road at midnight a few days ago and yelled, whether humorously or not it was impossible to tell: *'It's going to be a great fucking Christmas now I found out Jesus is dead!'*

Burton himself, like so many of that institution's employees that have followed him, found the university a place where his own eccentricities were tolerated. Cowley Road is also a tolerant place; it has to be, with the high proportion of Saturn's children it attracts. Through one of the historical coincidences (or slippages) that

characterises the area, on the site of the old workhouse
there is now a mental health charity called Restore,
dedicated to rehabilitating its clients through work; they
learn computer skills, carpentry, design, and market
gardening, selling the produce from their greenhouse in
the shop. Unlike the inhabitants of the workhouse, they
are free to leave at the end of the day, their independence
and dignity intact. There is no knowing what Burton
would have made of such an institution, but one suspects
the Utopia he sketched out in the *Anatomy* may have
found a place for it.

LOSING THE KEY

The body lies at the heart of society in the developed world. Adorning, adapting, decorating, pampering, fetishising, and, above all, displaying the body is a core activity in our culture. This puts us at odds with a large percentage of the world's population, for whom such an attitude to the human form is anathema. While a parade of barely clad female (and, to an increasing extent, male) bodies covers the sides of buildings in the West, in many Islamic countries women are required to embody their society's value systems in their dress and deportment. A man's honour in such places is largely based on how well he protects 'his' women. It is no coincidence that the war the world is currently being drawn into has largely been played out in the realm of the physical rather than the world of ideas. From the start, the aim of the participants seems not to have been to win an argument, but simply to atomise their opponents. When one's enemy is a barbarian, one does not discuss philosophy or terms of peace. A man leaving a mosque in Gaza is pulverised by a rocket descending from a clear blue sky. A pizzeria in Tel Aviv is redecorated with Israeli blood. An Iraqi child tearfully relates how she stepped outside her door, only to see her friends on the school bus incinerated before her eyes. And in Tavistock Square, the top deck of a bus is ripped off and tossed across the street, along with human body parts and mobile phones, as another valiant warrior steps over into Paradise. The bereaved of Madrid, London, and Fallujah howl with equal anguish, yet combatants refuse to acknowledge the humanity of their opponents. Why are your citizens innocent victims while ours are just dust, asks the terrorist leader, in a rare moment of prescience. That is the question. The instant, public reduction of human beings to dust is at the heart of the war. It is the body, that totem of Western capitalism and most potent weapon of the disinherited, that is the object du jour. The cosmetic surgeons of the media decide for us how much we can take; scattered limbs at the site of the latest atrocity are painted out, and the publication of images of American bodies returning from Iraq is forbidden.

The daily journey to work in London becomes a game of cat and mouse, with mouseholes the least safe place to be. To be young, male, non-white, and carrying a bag is enough to have to endure mutterings and suspicious glances. To respond incorrectly to a police challenge is to risk death. Suddenly the Underground becomes not the name of a transport system but the entrance to a

Dantesque nether world, which at any moment might spout fire, pouring the dazed and wounded survivors of hidden conflagrations out onto the street. On the pages of the newspapers, the question of how this could have come about is endlessly debated. Many commentators blame the multicultural model of society for allowing radical Islamist ideas to take root in Britain. At Oxford Railway Station, where during the 'crisis' following the London bombings we are greeted in the morning by policemen dressed in black and bearing sub-machine-guns, I fall into conversation with a well-known right-wing newspaper columnist, who I regularly pass the time of day with while locking or unlocking my bike at the bike racks. The terrorists who are attacking us believe in something, he admits with grudging admiration – believe in it enough to die for it. We don't know what we believe in – we have been a post-faith society for over a hundred years. I can hear the regret in his voice, the nostalgia for a society based on clear-cut ideals. He confesses that he worries there won't be a 'country' left if immigration keeps up at the pace it is.

People who perceive themselves as under siege often come to an understanding of what they value and of what they are prepared to defend. If I take an inventory of my own moral universe, what I believe in is the unique historical experiment that is taking place in our great cities, where people from many different cultural backgrounds are able to live together in mutual respect and toleration. One of the four bombs that exploded in London on 7 July 2005 went off in a carriage on the Piccadilly line. Two weeks later, with forensic work complete, the identities of those who died that day were published in the newspapers. Those unbearably moving columns of names told a story. Twelve of those listed as having died on the Piccadilly line train that day were said to have been of British nationality; three were Polish, one was French, one a New Zealander, one Turkish, one Iranian, one Afghani, one Romanian, one Vietnamese, and one Mauritanian. For me, that carriage and its occupants represent the country I am proud to belong to. Despite the appalling failures of our system – still marred as it is by inequality, racism, and violent crime – urban Britain represents one of the best examples in history of a tolerant, pluralistic society, albeit one based on the Briton's famed characteristic of reserve, of keeping himself to himself and minding his own business. At certain moments, Cowley Road can seem to represent this untrumpeted success, one that appears under attack from all sides.

Tyndale Street – named after the pioneering translator of the Bible who ended up being strangled and then burnt as a reward for his scholarship – is a quiet, residential street leading to the Christadelphian Hall. On Fridays at noon, where it intersects with Cowley Road, a few hundred yards from the Jewish Chabad House in one direction and a Methodist church in the other,

Bangladeshi Muslims prostrate themselves at prayer. Passers-by, many of whom would profess no religious belief at all, hardly glance at the devout, their bodies facing down the road in the direction of Mecca, aligned with the journey that each must make at least once in his lifetime as a dutiful Muslim. The ground feels as layered in history and different traditions as a street in Jerusalem. A friend of mine who lives in a street further along Cowley Road, her back garden overshadowed by the new, larger mosque, works for a Palestinian charity. She tells me that her predecessor in the job came from a Muslim family from Jerusalem who for generations have been the key-holders of one of the principal destinations for Christian pilgrims, the Shrine of the Holy Sepulchre. The question of who should look after the Christian community's holiest site had provoked such squabbles between different Christian sects and denominations that they agreed to appoint a Muslim as its caretaker. The massive key, along with responsibility for opening up and closing the shrine every day, has remained with the family ever since. A few days after hearing and being affected by this story, in one of those strange examples of synchronicity that seem typical of our mediated age, I see the key-holder himself, the massive, ancient key in his lap, interviewed in a documentary on television. While holding no brief for the Christian version of Jesus' family tree – how can the one God have a son, he asks in gentle amazement – he appears untroubled by any doubts as to whether the visitors to the church he looks after should be allowed to believe whatever they want. I am left with the feeling that in the West we, too, seem to have held the key to something precious, without knowing what it was. I can't help thinking that we should cherish this moment and not relinquish it too easily to the soldiers, the politicians, and the terrorists. History teaches that once the key is lost, it is almost impossible to recover.

BED-SITS AND *BIRĀRDARI*

For the first time in November 2003, illuminations were strung across the section of the road between Manzil Way and the churchyard of St Mary and St John, to mark the end of Ramadan. A picture of city councillor Mohammed Abassi switching on the illuminations – beaming broadly and with arms outstretched, surrounded by members of the Muslim community – appeared in the local paper. *'Happy Eid!'* the lights declared; crescent moons, each cradling four stars, decorated the street lights as far as the churchyard. The lights reinforced the message that this is the commercial centre of the Asian community. The southern side of the road is dominated by Bangladeshi and Pakistani shops and restaurants; Bangla Café, Bangla Bazaar, Naz Oriental Grocers, the Aziz and Ashok restaurants, halal butchers, and stores. On the other side of the road, the mosque provides an extraordinary but increasingly common British aesthetic frisson to those descending Divinity Road from Headington, its Oriental profile rising above the roofs of the red-brick Edwardian terraces, as visually incongruous as if cut and pasted onto the landscape by a mischievous architecture student.

Pakistani immigration into Oxford began in the late 1950s and was initially the result of recession in the north of England. Local employers including British Rail, hospitals, and building firms were losing workers to Morris Motors at Cowley, where there were better wages on offer on the assembly line. This created opportunities for Pakistanis who were experiencing a recession in cities like Bradford, Manchester, Rotherham, and Sheffield. Most of the immigrants came from villages in the same areas in Pakistan: Jhelum, Attock, or Faisalabad in the Punjab; Mirpur in what is known by Pakistanis as Azad (free) Kashmir. These communities have had long experience in sending their menfolk out to find employment; in the nineteenth century they had travelled to work on the great irrigation projects set up under the British Raj. Money sent home allowed their extended families to buy land, the only true sign of wealth in rural Pakistan. After the Second World War, with opportunities at home diminishing, family groups pooled their resources to send a representative to England, where a fortune could be earned by those prepared to work hard and able to tolerate the chilliness of both the climate and some of their new neighbours. He in turn would send money back to sponsor the passage of another member of the family. Men lived together, sometimes fifteen to a house, working all the hours Allah gave them. What was needed were not specialist skills, but workers prepared to do anything that was required, outside the rigid demarcations of the British workforce. 'I can't read or write,' a neighbour tells me proudly, 'but I can do electrician, plumbing, plastering – woodwork I can't do. I didn't train to do these things, I just learnt it. I worked in Didcot Power Station, Garsington substation. I worked in a bomb factory. They didn't trust any other foreigner to go in there, but they trusted me.'

Eventually the women followed, some say to keep an eye on their menfolk and make sure that they were not led astray by the temptations that surrounded them. New outposts of Punjabi, Pathan, and Kashmiri villages were planted in British cities, from Glasgow to London. Once in Britain, family members remained in touch, telling each other of employment opportunities that arose in their area. Loyalty to the *birādari*, or extended family group, was thus transferred from rural Pakistan to the Pakistani community in Britain, helping to build a closely knit and mutually supportive community.

The first arrivals experienced considerable prejudice. A hairdresser on Cowley Road called Annette's notoriously refused to accept non-white customers. The premises were picketed by local people, including the minister of the Methodist Church on Cowley Road, the Reverend Sidney Hinks, and an Afro-Caribbean graduate student named Rawlston Williams. They, along with their companions, were arrested, but the incident created such a public uproar that their point was made. Meanwhile, the local bus company operated a quota system limiting the number of Pakistani and West Indian workers they would employ. When the first West Indian started work at British Leyland in 1964, white employees refused to work alongside him. The introduction of the Race Relations Act in 1965 ended employment discrimination on the grounds of race or colour, and British Leyland became a magnet drawing Pakistanis to East Oxford. In the 1960s, a house in the area cost three or four thousand pounds. Pakistanis pooled their money to get onto the property ladder, sharing their living space with their wider family, a style of life that replicated traditional patterns at home.

I meet up with Jamal, a second-generation Pakistani entrepreneur and part owner of a local accommodation agency. Accommodation rental is only one of his areas of interest; he has been involved in enterprises ranging from catering to baggage handling. Like all true businessmen, the actual commodity seems unimportant to him; what matters are the figures it generates, and he is able to seamlessly switch his focus to whichever aspect of his empire requires his attention. Understandably, he is a busy man. In view of the relationship that has arisen between our families through having children at the same school, he has kindly, if a little hesitantly, agreed to answer my questions about the Pakistani community in East Oxford. While he is very far from running a traditional Asian family business, he still sets great store by the values that he learnt as a child and by the hard work that built the prosperity the community enjoys today. I get the impression that, like many self-made men, he does not suffer fools gladly, and I am anxious not to waste too much of his time. I begin by asking how important he feels the family and the *birādari* system have been to the achievements of Pakistanis in Oxford.

'Totally important. It's the main difference between the home-based community and the immigrant community. When my parents first came over and when I was growing up, everyone was a brother or a sister. It took me quite a while before I realised that we weren't all related. It was a close-knit thing because there was such interdependence; everybody reached out for everybody else. There was a glow wrapped around the Asian community because we all looked after each other. It was very hard times and needs dictated. The mainstay has been to get into business with the whole family involved. When the kids came back from school, they'd rack up something. Or when family came to stay, you'd say, "Look, I need help to get these packed up," and they'd do it and every little bit helps. If you sit down and analyse it and look at the number of people involved in the immediate family who are unpaid and get no real thanks for it – without them it would be a loss-making situation. That is why I personally didn't go down that road.

'Now, things are changing. The Asian population is assimilating; all the old values are being challenged. You hear old people, English people, talking about how times have changed; well, you hear the same thing in the Asian community. "Look, when we first came over, or when your grandfather came over, we did this and that . . ." and the kids say, "Oh, give it a rest, Pop; that was then and this is now." Now with a lot of Asian families that would have tended towards starting a business, the kids are saying, "What are you doing? I can go and earn five pounds an hour doing menial tasks, and the hours you work, it is the equivalent of one or two pounds an hour – can't you see that, Dad?" And he says, "No, son, this is all for you . . . It is our property and it remains our property."'

'So do you think that loyalty to the extended family is being undermined?' I ask.

'It's a good system, but you can only take it so far. When the community gets to a certain size, it breaks up into subgroups. We're at the stage where the immediate family is what is left. If you've got no dependence on someone, it's just about "I like you or I don't like you." It's inevitable. It's human nature.

'Now the East European immigrants are the equivalent of what happened with the Asian community twenty or thirty years ago. These guys are coming out of poverty, they're wandering around, and they're saying, "Look, I'll do anything for next to nothing . . ."'

'That's an offer not many people would refuse.'

'Not even the government! It's feeding the economy underground and helping push everything up, and the government can see that. Someone has to do these jobs, and the Asian kids are sitting there and saying, "Thank you very much, but I'm not doing that . . ." Back in the sixties, their parents were criticising the English people for not wanting to do certain jobs, saying, "Work is work, what does it matter." Now the same things are coming around. I can guarantee that the current influx of migrants, in twenty years they'll be saying the same thing – it's a universal rule. Now migrants from previous generations are criticising new migrants for doing things they used to do, expressing the same prejudices and preconceived ideas that used to be said about us – "Look at these people coming here and taking our jobs" – and you say, "What? Excuse me? Where the hell did you come from, and what did your parents have to do to survive?" But I think people have learnt from the first and second waves of immigration; it's not all forgotten – it's built in and there is something there as a reference point.'

Many Pakistanis have entered the property market in Oxford, where there is an insatiable demand for rented accommodation provided by each year's influx of students. Local magnates have been joined by investors from all over the world, several of them landlords on Jamal's books. 'Lots of people have invested in property here,' he explains. 'Business people from Hong Kong or wherever have done the sums and looked at the figures, their percentages and returns, and said, "Let's hit Oxford."'

Property prices in the area have increased fifty or a hundred times since the arrival of the first Pakistani immigrants, forced up exponentially by the last decade of high employment and low inflation. It is hard to see how young people born in the area will be able to get on the property ladder by buying their first home. Yet the neighbourhood retains a large number of houses, bed-sits, and hostels for rent. Professionals buying houses and students from wealthy backgrounds live alongside those arriving in very different circumstances. Certain less scrupulous landlords, perhaps themselves involved in people-trafficking, have been prepared to pack their properties with those unable to complain of the conditions in which they are forced to live. Illegal immigrants have been found crammed into garages and other spaces normally considered unfit for human habitation. These travellers have little in common with those arriving at the universities to begin a new term. In the nineteenth-century novel *Sybil; or, The Two Nations*, Benjamin Disraeli writes of Manchester: 'Within one city, two nations, between whom there is no intercourse and no sympathy; who are as ignorant of each other's habits, thoughts and feelings as if they were dwelling in different zones, or inhabitants of different planets.' In Disraeli's day, the structure of society was fairly easily understood; the 'other nation' was the poor. It is probably specious to apply a quote intended to describe a large city shaped by the Industrial Revolution to one that acquired its industrial base only in the twentieth century, yet the words have an uncomfortable resonance. Despite its historic status as a place of learning, this is still a city full of division, ignorance, and mutual incomprehension, in which many nations live side by side.

'What do you think of the lights?' I ask the newsagent as I buy my paper.

He smiles wryly. 'Well, they are not bad. But I am Hindu, not Muslim. I would like it if they would also put up decorations for Diwali. But these lights will stay up till Christmas, now. So we are missed out altogether.'

WHAT THEY THINK YOU CAN BEAR

Football, Religion, and Nightmares on the Cowley Road

I meet Nick for a drink in an Irish pub in an East Oxford backstreet off the Cowley Road. It is a relief to find ourselves in an establishment honestly dedicated to drinking, without a sofa or the hint of a 'theme' in sight. The middle-aged barmaid has the quiet authority of a woman used to keeping the almost exclusively male clientele in order. The drinkers play cards at tables beneath portraits of racehorses or sit at the bar smoking and watching the television. On the night we visit, there is a big match on; Celtic are playing Rangers, and feelings are running high. A green-and-white-striped Celtic shirt hangs on the wall of the pub, leaving no room for doubt that sympathies lie with the Catholic team. They score and a cheer goes up, fists punch the air; a shaven-headed Glaswegian slaps the palm of a Cork man, the veins at his temples bulging with the intensity of the moment, his grin almost a grimace. Moments later Rangers equalise, and groans of disgust fill the room. By walking through the door tonight, we

191

have struck a seam of complex tribalism that unites two great British traditions – religious sectarianism and football. The men at the bar are the children of just one of the many conflicts that have washed up on Cowley Road.

Nick is a counsellor working with refugees in a therapeutic context; we have known each other for a while, but I have never heard him talk about his work, and I have asked if we can meet up so that he can tell me a little about it. He is also a writer, and we kick ideas about writing around for a while; he tells me that he finds writing a way of resolving conflicts, a subject he knows something about. A local himself, he is justifiably curious, perhaps a little sceptical, about my project. Whether or not he is convinced – I feel he is, but it may just be the Guinness – he starts to talk about the stories he comes across every day. As he does, his voice gradually takes on an intensity at odds with his usual laconic delivery.

'Nearly all of the clients I work with are on antidepressants. Many of the women have been raped; all the men have been tortured or been through something else – perhaps they have been forced to do things at gunpoint, like kill or rape. There are a lot of boy soldiers in the world – they are given drugs, psychedelic drugs, and then sent out into the jungle to kill people. It is not always clear what has happened to them – they only tell you what they think you can bear.'

'What they think *you* can bear?' I ask.

'Yes. Then they escape from one trauma to find

themselves in another, secondary trauma when they get here. Of racism, of being completely disenfranchised, not believed by the Home Office, not valued. There is total confusion in this country, perpetuated by the media, between economic migrants and asylum seekers. People can't tell the difference; they think, "Oh, they are coming here to steal our jobs." These are not economic migrants; in fact, many of them are middle-class people; this is how they paid the agents to get them here. They might have been professionals, doctors, or lawyers in their own country. Here they are not allowed to work; they have to vegetate while their case goes through its first and second appeal or until they get their deportation notice. They can only work for cash, and it isn't easy to find those jobs. In law, once they get their deportation order, they are stripped of all their rights and benefits; they are not even allowed treatment on the NHS; but they can wait for up to a year to be deported. I had a Sudanese man on the floor of my office weeping and gnashing his teeth because he was going to be sent back; a year later he is still here.'

'These people are all around us – they make up an important element in the local population,' I say.

'They do. They all have nightmares, you know. Along Cowley Road there are people in bed-sits, tossing and turning, screaming in the night, not knowing if their family is alive or if they are going to be able to stay in the country.'

193

'How do they arrive in Oxford?'

'Some of them come in lorries and are just dropped off at the Wheatley roundabout on the M40 and left to make their own way into the city. Others arrive at Heathrow, and the agent gives them a bus ticket to Oxford. Sometimes they think they are arriving in France, and suddenly discover that everybody is speaking English. Organisations in Oxford give them some clothes, a bit of money, some short-term accommodation, and put them in touch with the authorities.'

These are stories I want to hear first-hand; these voices should be represented in the pages of my book. Nick is understandably cautious about brokering any introduction. Apparently, researchers who want to demonstrate that they have 'consulted' with asylum seekers are constantly approaching his clients; they suffer from 'consultation fatigue.' 'They want to cooperate, but at the same time they could be excused for asking, "What's in it for me? Will it help me to get a place to live? Or help me avoid getting sent back to whatever hell I have escaped?"' He is worried about tokenism and about issues around the abuse of trust. He can't do anything that would jeopardise his professional relationships.

'I understand completely,' I tell him. 'Everything you say is true. To make this book, I can't avoid intruding on people's lives, poking my nose into their happiness or pain. I am as uncomfortable with it as you are. But I can't stop now.' He nods, and we stand up.

'I'll think about it,' he says. He takes me by the elbow. 'Ring me in a week. That's the plan. Ring me in a week and I will have made up my mind.'

It sounds like a good plan to me. We walk together up the Cowley Road, enjoying the neighbourhood we share and the mildness of the winter's evening, until we come to the parting of the ways. 'In a week,' I tell him.

He nods. 'In a week.'

BETWEEN TWO FIRES

Pulling the Dragon's Teeth

About six o'clock in the afternoon, the Arcade du Saumon became a field of battle. An observer, a dreamer, the author of this book, who had gone to get a near view of the volcano, found himself caught in the arcade between the two fires.

VICTOR HUGO, *Les Misérables*

Predictably, my involvement in local politics, in which I had so far avoided public disgrace, was about to descend into farce, controversy, and paranoia. Along with a small group of local artists and other interested parties, I was invited to take part in the next stage in the public consultation, to be held one evening at a local school. It was called 'Selecting a Palette' and was intended to act as a forum at which proposals for public art projects could be mooted as well as help given in the choosing of building materials for the improvements. A document from the transport policy department of the council reminded us of our main purpose. The redevelopment – or, to give it its full title, 'The Cowley Road Mixed Priority Route Road Safety Demonstration Project' – was intended to allow people to 'move through the space and within it with fewer traumatic collisions than currently occur.' The main logic for any alteration in the appearance of the road was therefore to impact on traffic speed.

After a brief introduction, we listened to a presentation by Liam Curtin, the artist funded by a local arts organisation to lead public art initiatives on Cowley Road. A laconic Liverpudlian with a shock of white hair and a well-travelled face, Curtin, a veteran of regeneration projects across the country, explained the activities of the community artist with a deadpan wit that was immediately engaging. To my intense relief, he started by saying that in his view the vibrancy of the area's activities and culture made the imposition of a monumental, permanent work inappropriate. He also made it clear that he was personally opposed to the idea of gateways at each end of the road, a view to which many voices were raised in assent. Curtin had begun his time in the neighbourhood by filming interviews with local shopkeepers and residents as a way of getting to know the area better. (How *observed* this road now is, I couldn't help thinking. Its inhabitants go about their business shadowed by community artists and local politicians, like Galapagos tortoises lumbering along the beach trailed by Victorian scientists, while a lone author lurks in the shadow of the palm trees.) He had built his first work, a temporary sculpture made out of discarded computer CD-ROMs, with the help of local children in the park at Manzil Way. His proposal for a final piece, the culmination of the project, was that a series of 'ingots,' each commemorating a local personality or event, be set into the new pavements. Those who chose to could then follow the trail they made through the neighbourhood, discovering more about the area as they did so.

This seemed to me a fairly sensitive intervention. Public art located underfoot does not interfere with sight lines or impose an ambience. (At the same time, I couldn't imagine it would slow the traffic, either.) I could see how the collaborative researching and creating of the work might well turn up interesting memories and help bring the community together. The meeting's response to the artist's comments on permanent artworks and gateways was encouraging. I began to relax. Why, I wondered, having spent much of my working life involved at least peripherally with the visual arts, was I so concerned about community art in my own neighbourhood? Successful public art can be among the most vibrant expressions of contemporary culture. I had read enough case studies and seen enough examples, both good and bad, in cities around the world. When I had mentioned my interest in public art to one of the consultants, she had narrowed her eyes and said, 'We don't like experts.' Really, I had felt like replying. So when something goes wrong with your car, you don't take it to the garage? Or when you get ill, you don't visit a doctor? In reality, however, I had none of the certitude of such seasoned professionals; I was still thinking the issues through myself. But at least

I was thinking about them. What the consultant meant by 'we don't like experts' was that *the people* should decide on their community art, rather than have it imposed upon them by outside specialist interest groups, a hard argument to resist. *The people* in this case would mean those who responded to public consultations – already, as I had observed, a select group. The people would then get the public art they deserved, and it would be 'good,' as the only aesthetic judgement of value (and the only one a certain type of community worker felt comfortable with) was that the people themselves had chosen it. This was a magnificent closed system, impenetrable to question, able to dismiss any that challenged 'the will of the people' as elitist. As the same consultant had told me over the phone, in a statement of aesthetic relativism I found even more worrying, 'Good design is all just a matter of taste.' Tell that to the Bauhaus.

The next speaker was a man with considerable influence in the local community, whose views would be carefully considered by those in charge of the consultation. In a very short time, he dispelled all my feelings of reassurance. Public art, he told us, should be *functional* as well as attractive, and it was important to mark this important project with a work of art that was permanent. For the same reason he supported gateways to the Cowley Road. He was keen to put East Oxford on the tourist map and end the city centre's monopoly as a visitor attraction. Animatedly, he outlined his proposal for a public art piece that in his view would meet these criteria. In Arthurian times, he told us (why do alarm bells always ring when somebody uses the phrase 'Arthurian times'?), a dragon was said to have lived beneath the Plain at the beginning of Cowley Road. Therefore he proposed that a series of litter-bins should be commissioned, running along the extent of the road, shaped and coloured to resemble a dragon.

Here I have to confess to a certain difficulty as an author. (Such authorial asides I know are equivalent to a blow-out on the motorway, interrupting the reader's progress and revealing the mechanics behind the stage curtain; occasionally, like other 'traumatic collisions,' they are unavoidable.) In writing of these events, I have to draw certain boundaries establishing where it is legitimate for me to go on the page, even when the argument gets heated. To report what I, and others, at the meeting said in response to this proposal would be unfair, offering no right of reply. Suffice it to say that the speaker had summed up in a few words exactly the kind of thing I most dreaded. A dragon? What next, a statue of Gandalf? I wasn't the first to respond to his proposal. Perhaps when I did speak, the fog of midweek commuter tiredness made my voice more acerbic than I intended. In any case, when I had finished, to the great surprise of all, he got up and left the room. I simply assumed he was going to another important meeting. It was only later that I discovered that I had offended him deeply, and in offending a man so important to the success of the consultation, I had also offended the organisers. They considered his support essential to the successful delivery of the project, and I had jeopardised it. No matter that others at the meeting felt my comments were justified and delivered in a measured way; I now had a black mark against my name. I was left with the uncomfortable sensation of having both unintentionally hurt someone's feelings while simultaneously making it harder for myself to achieve my aims.

After this high drama, there were more mundane matters to attend to. During a coffee break, we went outside into the courtyard to look at examples of building materials, laid out for our inspection by the design consultants. Each of us was handed a thick pamphlet describing the different paving slabs available; they had names like *Chartres*, *Cornish*, *Saxon*, or *Savanna*, intended to be either evocative or reassuring, and were illustrated with colour photographs of high streets and malls. 'The concept of the Chartres modular paving,' we learnt from the pamphlet, 'was inspired by the beautiful medieval city of Chartres in Northern France.' Sadly, the environment in which it appeared in its illustration looked more like downtown Reading. This is the gap between the vision of the town-planner and reality on the ground. When we regrouped, other suggestions for alterations to the aesthetic appearance of the road were taken from the floor. There was a tremendous enthusiasm for the planting of trees, apparently a common feature of public consultations. While I consider myself a great lover of trees, at a previous meeting I had once again found myself adopting a contrary position, pointing out that overplanting would obscure one of the city's most intriguing views of its famous spires, obtained when crossing Cowley Road opposite the main mosque. I was pleased to see that this reservation was registered in the council document. Somebody proposed that a tree should be selected to represent each ethnic community in the area, conjuring up a vision of the road lined with mimosa, baobab, and jacaranda, with a small mangrove swamp where the storm drain regularly overflows. Another that a purple dye be mixed with the tarmac when the road was resurfaced. These suggestions were noted with due solemnity by the consultants, with the proviso that the advice of local tree officers would have be to be taken on the suitability of species eventually selected and the sites of plantings in relation to underground services, an elegant get-out clause that no reasonable person could quibble with.

In debates over redevelopment projects, certain ideas take on a totemic quality to each camp. This was the fate of the gateways that I had so vehemently objected to. I hadn't the time to mount any kind of coherent campaign or raise public awareness among those who had not participated in the public consultation. However, whenever I mentioned the idea, in places where local people gathered together, there was almost universal agreement that they must be resisted. This couldn't just be attributable to the echo-chamber effect of consulting one's own peer group, I believed, and the meeting seemed once again to underline the wide opposition to the concept. I suggested confidently to the convener of the meeting as I left that perhaps we had seen the last of them. To my surprise, she told me that exactly the opposite was true; the idea was far from dead, and we would be hearing more about it very soon. Over the coming weeks, I learned that transport planners on the local council had decided the gateways were absolutely necessary as a traffic-calming measure. They would announce to motorists that they were entering a special area and encourage them to slow down. Once again I found their logic unconvincing. When a driver has seen such a landmark once or twice, it is filed away in the memory and ignored, no more relevant than a bus shelter or a lamp post. In any case, wouldn't introducing new hard objects into the kerb only increase the risk of collision and injury? Why else are the French government cutting down the beautiful avenues of plane and poplar trees that line roads in southern France? For no reason other than that they have discovered that removing them saves lives.

I began to be affected by more sinister suspicions, as lone campaigners often are. What was the real reason for the popularity of the gateways with certain elements within the city? Could it be more than the city official's eternal desire to demarcate and control? Was some people's interest attributable to a desire to have something serve as a permanent reminder of their involvement in the project, for political or career reasons? Were we fighting local Napoleons, intent on erecting monuments to their successful campaign? Surely this was much too cynical a view.

The thing about public consultation, I was told by an old political hand, is that politicians love it, as long as the public tells them what they want to hear. I began to feel the limits of this type of direct democracy. Those in power were unlikely to give ground on something they believed in, just because the sample that took part in the consultation got it wrong. Their job, after all, was to *know* what is best for us. It was easy to feel marginalized; I suspected I was regarded as a single eccentric objector, when in reality everybody I spoke to, *my* unscientific sample of the community – which included bus drivers, builders, artists, carpenters, academics, shopkeepers, teachers, scene-painters, schoolkids, and social workers – agreed that we didn't want our neighbourhood rebranded. It was just that, as is so often the case, they didn't have the time or the inclination to get involved with the local political process.

Fortunately, at this point I discovered a powerful ally. Marian has worked for several years in the publicly funded sector, on community and art projects, and speaks the language fluently; she was even employed in the early stages of the public consultation on the Cowley Road redevelopment scheme, soliciting the views of older members of the community. At the same time, she is a local who feels at least as passionately as I do about the neighbourhood and has lived in it a good deal longer than I have. We began to talk together about how we could make our views heard. Marian had a number of conversations with the consultants to let them know that there was more general opposition to the plans than perhaps they were aware of. We were encouraged to summarise our views in writing and send them to the transport officers in the council to ask for a meeting, which we did, without success. There was now considerable momentum behind the gateways concept: it seemed it was supported not only by the transport department in the council, but also by our elected councillor. In public pronouncements, gateways appeared to have leap-frogged the democratic process and were talked about as though they were a given. Yet another public meeting was called, this time to invite participants to submit ideas to help in the design of the gateways. Marian and I were asked if, as our views were known to be negative, we would mind staying away on that particular evening. With mixed feelings, we agreed. Reports we heard back from others who attended suggested that the pro-gateway lobby had packed the meeting with supporters of their own views. We felt outsmarted, outgunned, suddenly aware of the vastly greater political experience of those we were opposing. At the same time, we became even more determined to make sure they didn't succeed.

MELANCHOLY,
AN AMERICAN PHOTOGRAPHER,
AND THE IRISH WRITER

In the same way that the stirring of the sap and the increased volume of the dawn chorus made Chaucer's pilgrims think of the open road, the turning leaves and crisp evenings of autumn in London or New York signal that the time approaches for publishers to be off on their annual pilgrimage to the Frankfurt Book Fair in Germany. In a bar adjacent to the huge exhibition halls, I meet a famous American photographer. Perched on a bar-stool with his extended belly straining at the fabric of his polo shirt and with his wide mouth, always emitting either laughter or smoke, he looks like a tree frog suspended over a forest pool. Whenever he is introduced to young women, he makes suggestions of astonishing obscenity, all delivered with the same disarming smile. To my surprise, no one takes offence. 'He's the only guy that's got intimate black-and-whites of Sinatra,' a friend says into my ear. The photographer is hawking a new collection of work for publication and going to as many parties as he can, although walking between perches has become difficult with the passing years. There is a photography publisher in our company, but I know he has no money, and he knows that I know, although he is standing drinks for one and all with a bravado bordering on desperation. I think the photographer understands the situation as well, but he is happy to be here shooting the breeze, swimming in the blue light of the bar, guzzling drinks and waving a cigarette between his long, spatulate fingers.

He tells me about photographing Samuel Beckett, on the occasion of the author's eightieth birthday. Despite being one of the most photogenic of all writers, Beckett loathed having his photograph taken, flinching each time the shutter clicked as though he were having his teeth pulled. When the session was over, the photographer told Beckett what an honour it had been to meet him. Beckett's writings had been a tremendous help to him in his youth. 'How so?' asked Beckett, with a flicker of interest. It turned out that when the photographer was a young man, struggling to make his way in his chosen profession as a new arrival in the big city, he had become extremely depressed, suicidal even. Reading Beckett made him feel that at least there was one other person out there who saw the world the way he did. This, somehow, was a comfort and allowed him to carry on. He glanced up at the author's face, with its pale, alert eyes and cheeks and brows so deeply scored with lines that in photographs it took on a timeless, reptilian quality. Suddenly his mumbled thanks seemed impossibly naive, and he flinched from the coming reply.

Beckett leant over and patted him on the back. 'There, there,' he said, 'you're over all that now.'

COWLEY ROAD CALLING

Exploration is not so much a matter of covering the ground as of digging beneath the surface: chance fragments of landscapes, momentary snatches of life, reflections caught on the wing – such are the things that alone make it possible for us to understand and interpret horizons which otherwise would have nothing to offer us

CLAUDE LÉVI-STRAUSS, *Tristes Tropiques*

Patterns of immigration are often referred to in terms of *tides* and *waves*; inflammatory politicians, articulating (or set on creating) a fear in the native population, extend the watery metaphors by employing the word *swamp*. Such movements in nature leave residual signs of their passage behind; as patterns in the sand, a line of driftwood and flotsam on the beach, tide-marks on the harbour wall. The movement of people also leaves markers. Some are semi-permanent and easy to spot: mosques, churches, synagogues, temples, community centres. Others are small scale, non-monumental, part of the ephemera of daily life. Examples of the latter are the advertisements for international phone cards that proliferate in the windows of shops on Cowley Road. To have a telephone installed in one's house is a badge of permanence. Most recent arrivals prefer to use a mobile or a phone in a booth in one of Cowley Road's call centres. The titles of the cards alone paint a picture of the journey some of the neighbourhood's residents have made. *Mama Africa! Pakistan Connect. Hello Arab. Jamaica Direct. Eastern Eurovoice. Taj Mahal.* They provide cheap rates to all the places that a telephone system designed for a British clientele regards as exotic and therefore prices accordingly. The advertisements for the cards are mostly brightly coloured and decorated with an identifying image: a palm-fringed Caribbean beach, an Indian temple, or an African lion. Each lists the countries alphabetically that the card offers rates to, along with the price of calls per minute, providing an A–Z of the market they are seeking to attract. These listings have a certain poetry. The *Asia Card*'s list traverses the continent's alphabet of countries from Bangladesh to Vietnam. *Africa Calling* ranges from Angola to Zimbabwe. *Hello Arab* spans the Arabic world from Algeria to Yemen. The *Eastern Europe Calling Card* straddles Eurasia from Albania to Uzbekistan. Special advertisements appear at holiday times, promoting special prices for the season: 'Cracking Diwali Rates!' promises one. 'Ramadan Mubarak,' salutes another. The world is criss-crossed with low-budget conversations between those who travel to escape persecution or seek their fortune and those who stay behind. The air around us crackles with speech, although we cannot hear it; by studying the handbills in the windows of Cowley Road, we know exactly what it costs per minute.

JUST LESS LUCKY

At precisely the moment when I decide he's forgotten, Nick rings me back with a number. He's found someone willing to talk, a young Albanian from the borders of Kosovo and Serbia, whose appeal to remain in Britain has been rejected and who is awaiting deportation. He's living in Blackbird Leys at the end of Cowley Road; Nick thinks he might have a story to tell. I ring the number; the voice on the end of the phone is soft, deadpan, betraying no surprise at my strange interest. He has been expecting my call, he says. Nick has told him about the book I am writing. He is willing to meet and talk. Over the next few weeks, we have to reschedule a number of times, but eventually we hit on a date that works for us both. I sit and wait for him in a bar in the centre of town on a bitterly cold Saturday evening. Particles of projected light drift across the ceiling. On one wall a large screen shows a film of an aquarium, full of brightly coloured tropical fish, in real time; on the other, logs blaze in a virtual fireplace. Music squirts from overhead speakers, and a group of Dutchmen sit down at the next table, making loud comments about the girls walking past the window. I sit and worry about whether my tape will pick up my interviewee's voice above the background noise in the bar, and about intruding into his life. Why should he talk to me at all? Every time somebody walks in through the door, I look up. To calm my nerves, I start to decode the décor; the brass-look overhead fans and palm trees in pots seem to be attempting to create a 'colonial' feel, but the carpeting, with its pattern of bright shards of stained glass, and the conical shades on the floor lamps are Scandinavian retro-modern, locating us somewhere between Raffles Bar in Singapore and 1960s Helsinki. And then there are the fish . . .

The young man who finally arrives is scarcely out of his teens; dark-haired with a shy smile, his face recently recovered from the ravages of teenage acne, he is smartly dressed in jeans and a white shirt without a coat, despite the plunging temperature outside. He explains he is dressed this way because he is on his way to a party, but he is happy to sit with me and talk for a while. With touching honesty, he apologises for being late: 'I am not very punctual. Nick goes crazy sometimes!' It is clear that he is here out of gratitude to his long-suffering counsellor. I buy him a drink at the bar, and we decide to move upstairs, where we hope we can speak uninterrupted.

He comes from a town with a large Albanian minority that lies just within the borders of Serbia. The conflict that has decimated the region and cast a long shadow across the last years of the old century is encapsulated in his family background. His father was Albanian and his mother a Serb; it is as if the tragedy of the region is written into his DNA. I ask him how common such a mixed marriage would be in the society in which he grew up. He smiles wryly, twisting his mouth down at one corner.

'Not very, because the Albanians and the Serbs don't get on very well. My father came to Serbia to work in a factory, met my mother, and obviously they fell in love and got married. I came here when I was seventeen – I wanted to find my sister. My mum died when I was two years old. My father suddenly disappeared in the 1997 conflict, so I was left alone.'

The ripples of that conflict reached Oxford in unexpected ways. My wife has an allotment off the Cowley Road and often trades seeds and plants with other gardeners. One neighbouring plot-holder in the late 1990s was an elderly Serb woman, nearly bent double but full of vigour, who loved to come and chat, bringing gifts of handfuls of marbled purple-and-white beans from her homeland. When America and its allies finally intervened to restrain Serbia's expansionist ambitions, their plan was to drive back Milosevic's army by unloading thousands of tons of bombs on Serbia. Britain agreed to join in the bombing raids and allowed the US Air Force to use its airfields, including one just outside Oxford. Bridges, power stations, and other non-residential, strategic buildings were targeted, but civilian casualties were high. When my wife greeted the elderly Serb at the allotments one day and asked her how she was, she dissolved into wails of grief. Her family had lost everything in the bombing of Belgrade; their house and all their possessions had been destroyed. Suddenly her old age was devoid of peace, as she worried for them and mourned the dead among her old neighbours. 'Tony Blair is murderer,' she shouted, shaking her fist at the sky, through which American and British planes might at any moment be rumbling towards her homeland. 'Tony Blair is murderer!' Ironically the bombardment unleashed such a savage fury among combatants on the ground that some of the greatest atrocities of the war were a direct result. One of the many thousands of Albanians who disappeared in the slipstream of the retreating Serb army was the father of the young man sitting before me. His son, like so many others, is searching for sanctuary in a nation that has played a dubious part in the history of his people.

'It was a really hard journey to get here. I went to Estonia, and then my cousin organised a trip to Greece. Some people there provided us with Greek passports so I could travel. We went to Germany, then by train to Holland, and then by lorry to the UK. We arrived in Hull. I spoke little English. I went straightaway to the police so that I could claim asylum. The police were quite tough;

there was especially one immigration officer who wasn't very nice – I remember he had these cold, blue eyes. They contacted social services, and the social services people in Hull were really kind. They found my sister, living in Oxford. She couldn't believe her eyes!' He laughs, remembering.

'Did she know you were coming?'

'No. I had never met my sister before I came to England. The thing is that my father was married twice. His first wife was Albanian, and my sister was his first child. My father tried to hide that he was married before, but I found out from my cousin. When I heard, I wanted to know who my sister is – and when you want something . . .'

'How did she react to you when you arrived?'

'She helped me financially and morally. When she knew she had a brother, it made her feel wonderful . . . . She said she realised she always had this love and wished she had a brother or sister, and then this thing happens . . .'

'That's a wonderful thing that has come out of your journey to Britain.'

'Yes, wonderful. I was given exceptional leave to remain until my eighteenth birthday. They sent me to college, where I started learning English – really nice teachers, I had loads of support. My attendance was really good, so they were pleased with me. I did a seven months' English course, and then I took my A-levels. It was very challenging doing them in English; there were loads of essays to write and coursework. I took maths, physics, and chemistry. I got A, B, B. I got offers of places at two universities, to study electronic engineering. But now they say I have to go back. My legal representative has appealed twice, but it has been refused. He thinks my case is exhausted, so he has closed my file and I am waiting to be deported. But my sister has indefinite leave to remain, so maybe I can put in another application on humane grounds . . .'

'Why don't you want to go back to Serbia?'

'The thing is the UK government says that Serbia is a safe country, that it's safe to go back. But I have mixed origin; it won't be easy for me. My mother was Serbian. Where I come from there is a big Albanian majority, within Serbia. I don't know how much you are aware, but at the end of the First World War, there was a big conference in London and they split up Albania. They gave the Montenegro region to Serbia, one of Albania's most beautiful parts. Kosovo was rich in minerals. Greece was given a bit as well. Before the war, Albania was a big country. If they had left it together, I don't think this conflict would have started. The Albanians where I come from live in a very closed society; they don't mix well with non-Albanians. They started to hate me before I left. And the Serbs hate Albanians. I am caught in the middle of two fires; it is not safe for me.'

'What kind of thing might happen?'

'I guess you remember a couple of months back, the Albanians started attacking Serbs . . . Before it started, they marked each Serbian house with a cross; then all the houses marked with a cross were burnt down. The people who live in small towns like mine are not educated. They don't even understand the concept of a nation. The main reason they hate each other is they don't even know each other. There's loads of prejudice – let's beat him because he's Albanian; let's beat him because he's Serb. In the region where I live, it is very traditional. They know their neighbour, and they are afraid of living next to an unknown person. They study your biography, and as soon as they know you are mixed, they can't accept you into their community. I don't believe it's safe to go back like the government says. I think they just want to look tough on immigration because the election is coming. The opposition are using these issues to attack the government. A friend of mine of the same age was deported back to nearly the same area, and he was beaten as soon as he arrived. I don't think they have looked properly at my case. When they turned down my application, it was at a time when they wanted to halve the number of asylum seekers.'

'How does that make you feel? Like a number?'

'Yes, I just felt like a number.'

He lifts his head, straightens his shoulders, looks me in the face with a touch of pride and defiance. 'Actually I could contribute to this country. I could finish university and work here as an engineer. It hurts my feelings. Everyone has a dream. I didn't come here to be an engineer, but I had opportunities because they let me go to college, and I found out what I wanted to do. When people stop you realising this dream, you feel frustrated and angry. I would have been happy if they had refused my application as soon as I came to this country. But I have come too far – I have created a new life, new friends, college, a place at university . . . But now, after all this, they just say you have to go back. Isn't that awful?' He appeals to me, his eyes hurt, baffled by the situation he finds himself in.

'It is awful,' I agree. You don't meet many twenty-year-olds with such a clear idea of what they want to do. I can't help feeling we could use a few more like him. But he is caught in the web of a discourse that portrays all asylum seekers as economic migrants, free-loaders. He is a piece in a political chess game that gets played every time an election looms by politicians not too proud to appeal to an island race's darkest instincts. I wondered how aware he was of the media battle that surrounded cases like his.

'I work in a newsagent – I can't escape it. I read the newspapers every day. I would say that the *Sun* and the *Daily Mail* are the worst, but I don't think they are prestigious newspapers. I have noticed that loads of people who read the *Sun* are not from very educated backgrounds. Students and intellectuals read *The Times* and the *Guardian*, which

I think are prestigious newspapers, and they do not treat asylum issues as the others do. I can admit there are some few asylum seekers who don't behave properly and cause trouble, but there are so many who are hardworking, doing well at school and university, giving so much to this country. Why do the newspapers never show their readers those asylum seekers?'

There are many possible reasons, we decide. Perhaps they tell people what they think they want to hear. Perhaps they have their own political agenda. To be so misrepresented must be a troubling, baffling experience. We talk around it for a while, until he laughs, shrugs his shoulders. His party awaits; it is time for us to go. We finish our drinks, and he leans forward.

'You know,' he says, 'asylum seekers are just like other people. We are just less lucky.'

DREADLOCKS AND RIM-SHOTS

Reggae at the Zodiac

In these days of the triumph of karaoke culture, of manu-factured pop bands, TV soap stars with singing careers, and jet-setting personality DJs, going to watch live music can seem as anachronistic an activity as reading a book. Not on Cowley Road. The Zodiac is situated in what used to be the old Co-operative Society Halls and is one of the jewels of East Oxford. Tonight they are hosting a living legend, a man who has had at least three careers and continues to thrive, the reggae singer Horace Andy. I have left it very late to buy a ticket and am convinced that I've missed my chance, gloomily adding the concert to a mental list of events I have failed to catch at the Zodiac. Support act for the night is a local reggae band; a friend plays keyboards, and in time-honoured fashion, I ring him to see if he can get me on the guest list. Predictably, he has used up his small allocation, but tells me there may be some tickets held back for the door. 'In any case,' I say, 'it's time I came to see you play.'

'I can't promise that we'll be any good,' he replies. 'We're very unpredictable. I'm not even sure who's playing in the band tonight.'

'Hang on,' I tell him, 'you're selling yourself too hard – you'll cause a riot!' His habitually downbeat delivery is exacerbated by the fact that he will be missing Horace Andy; after weeks without a gig, his band has been double-booked and will have to leave immediately after their set to drive twenty miles to another venue.

As it happens, I strike lucky and secure one of the last tickets. I arrive early when the hall is still cold and deserted, smelling of lager and yesterday's cigarettes. For a musician (even an ex-musician), this atmosphere is oxygen, as invigorating as ocean spray. I remember asking a friend why she split up with her drummer boyfriend. 'When you get to thirty,' she told me, 'you feel like you want to go some places where your feet don't stick to the floor.' I walk to the bar, my feet adhering as securely in the patina of spilt beer as if I were a gecko running up a wall. The room is still half-empty when the support band appears; my friend blows on his chilly fingers nervously, his concession to stage gear a woolly hat pulled down to the top of his glasses, as though he'd wandered in out of a snowstorm. Gradually the audience filters in, moving forward towards the stage at the band's insistence. They work hard at warming up the crowd for the great man's appearance. 'Horace Andy has come all the way from JA to be with you tonight,' the singer shouts. 'We have come all the way from the Cowley Road.'The crowd gives an ironic cheer of acknowledgement. I see faces familiar from the road: Celine from the Galeria Brasil, with a group of Brazilian friends; the cameraman from East Oxford Action; Marian and Tony, who have managed to find a babysitter and look as excited as young kids; my friend Chris, the teacher. Something of a carnival atmosphere is building; the temperature and the smell of the air are changing as the crowd thickens.

When the lights dim and Horace Andy's band members stride purposefully onto the stage, Andy isn't with them. It is clear from the first few bars that we are dealing with a bunch of top session musicians; the sound is lean and muscular, stalking the hall like a panther on a leash. They intend to take us back to school and remind us what a great music this is, over three decades after it evolved in the sweat-drenched dance-halls of Kingston. The bass player and the keyboard player are both serious-looking reserved women, dressed in denim with dreadlocks down their backs. The guitarist, cradling an Epiphone semi-acoustic, is a little flashier, his chest exposed and adorned with gold chains. The drummer holds the sound together while taking the lead vocal on a song demanding that politicians deliver world peace – an heroically optimistic aim in the climate of the times.

'Do you want Horace Andy?' he asks as the song ends, teasing the crowd. 'Do you want Horace Andy?' When the cheers reach sufficient volume, they strike up the next song and Andy comes bouncing on, dressed head to toe in camouflage fatigues, ducking and weaving and jogging on the spot. He beams at the crowd, holding both hands out with thumbs up, an endearingly down-to-earth gesture he repeats throughout the evening. His dreadlocks, bobbing behind his head and tied back in a neat ponytail, are beginning to turn white, I notice. Otherwise he looks in good shape for a man who must be nearing sixty years of age. 'Mr Horace "Sleepy" Andy,' announces the drummer, still fulfilling a double role as musician and MC.

'Money, Money, Money,' Andy sings, 'is the root of all evil.' His unmistakable voice floats out across the hall, wrapping us in its embrace. Since his first hits in the early 1970s, it is a sound that has earned him his keep, despite the vagaries of fashion – as a purveyor of sweet lovers' rock melodies; of Rasta-fuelled consciousness raising anthems; and latterly as a foil to the edgy, melancholic urban rumble made by the Bristol-based group Massive Attack. Like so many of Jamaica's greatest stars, including Bob Marley and the Wailers, Delroy Wilson, the Skatalites, and the Heptones, Andy had his first hits working with Clement 'Sir Coxsone' Dodd, the founder of Studio One, Jamaica's equivalent of Motown.* Andy occupies a strange position in this reggae pantheon. Neither blessed with the killer pop sensibility of Marley, the aggressive

---

*A key figure in the evolution of reggae, Dodd died during the writing of this book.

self-confidence of Tosh, or the heavy, mystic aura of Winston Rodney, better known as Burning Spear, at one time he seemed destined to remain in the second rank of reggae performers to cross over to a global audience. His voice was the most mannered of all these singers, a scratchy, fractured falsetto with a built-in trademark echo at the end of every line (hard to explain – you have to hear it done). He could not have predicted being taken up so late in his career by an English musical collective and suddenly being introduced to an entirely new audience. His voice is the perfect counterpoint to Massive's dub electronica, shedding light into their albums' dark corners. By keeping a pace behind the front rank, Andy has avoided both canonisation and hospitalisation – in times past, earning serious amounts of money has been a dangerous business where he comes from – and is well-placed to provide a new generation with a taste of authentic reggae.

Judging by tonight's audience, they are hungry for it. Andy has a huge back catalogue to draw on and the musicians to make his songs relevant to a new century. It is clear he still loves performing. The voice is note perfect; the dancing never stops. *'Do you feel it in your bones? Do you feel it down to your toes? Rock to the music – Skank to the music – Do you love reggae music? Come and tell me,'* he croons. And the crowd is rocking, the heat travelling downward and melting the tackiness so that feet are lifted freely from the floor. He takes us right back to 1970 with his first hit, 'Skylarking,' with its words of fatherly advice addressed to the youth of Kingston *'Begging you a five cent, sir – Begging you a ten cent, sir – Cannot 'elp, no cannot 'elp. So if you all keep on doing what you all are doing, you will end up, up, up in jail.'* In between songs he thanks the crowd, hand on the heart beneath his camouflage T-shirt. 'Mek mi hear it for mi Rasta children,' he cries, ever modest, urging the crowd to acknowledge the efforts of the band. They are having fun with the material, cutting up and rearranging it while never losing the plot. Rim-shots on the snare rattle like hailstones on a window, the drum and bass cut out to leave the vocal harmonies to float, supported only by the chopping guitar, until the bass swoops in once more, as though a great beast sighed and shook itself awake, and the drums are back, locking the rhythm down. Andy urges them each to take a solo; the bass player, who throughout the proceedings has sat on a speaker at the edge of the stage, cannot be persuaded to move to take the central spotlight, and as he entreats her, she turns her head away proudly, a little piece of stage business between them.

Outside the Zodiac the descendants of Abraham are at war, each claiming they are the inheritors of the true revelation, and that their arguments over holy real estate are tied up with the end of time. On stage Andy identifies himself a representative of that other lost tribe of Israel, the Rastafarians. *'Every tongue shall tell, on that Day,'* he warns, *'when the Lord comes again and judge everyone, for*

all the wrongs they have done and all the lies they have told.'
Who could have predicted that at the beginning of the
twenty-first century, these and other millennial texts
would have such a central influence on world events?
Compared to the voices of other Children of the Book
that fill the airwaves, the Rastafarian message suddenly
seems eminently reasonable. Yes, Rastas demand social
justice and warn of impending judgement on the wicked,
but their musical ambassadors generally speak in the
language of non-violence and of enjoyment of the good
things of life. *'Those that sow a good seed shall surely reap,*
plenty of food for your family, eternally . . .' Some might
argue that Rastafarianism, a relatively recent cultural
manifestation, should not be ranked alongside the
major world religions, that is has produced no great body
of literature or coherent philosophy – but look where
coherent philosophies have got us. The news from the
middle of the world, where different imperialist forces,
backed by their holy books, are unpicking the fabric of
civilisation stitch by stitch, seems far away. Cowley Road
is an island, where music melts the bonds that tie us to
the earth, allowing the people, for a little while at least,
to dance.

OF LEPERS, LUNATICS,
AND LAYABOUTS

I

With its mysterious origins, its biblical associations, and
its hideous and catastrophic consequences, leprosy was
the stalking nightmare of the medieval period. Hundreds
of leprosariums or lazar-houses were built throughout
Europe in the twelfth and thirteenth centuries, in which
its victims could be housed at a safe distance from the
local population. The disease was eradicated in Western
Europe around the beginning of the fourteenth century;
however, the French philosopher and historian Michel
Foucault maintained in his book *Madness and Civilisation*
that lepers were replaced in the public mind by other
categories of feared outsiders: the poor, the indigent, and
the insane. The perceived threats from these groups led to
building programmes for different kinds of institutions
of containment: bridewells, work-houses, prisons, and
mental hospitals. Over time, all such buildings tended
to be moved outside the city walls. It was as though

229

the guardians of society, like modern-day frequenters of the roulette table, believed that misfortune could be catching. Life was enough of a gamble without courting ill luck.

Those unfortunate enough to be deemed worthy of exclusion – through disease, poverty, or mental instability – would make the journey east from the city of Oxford across Pettypont, the medieval span across the river Cherwell, that was replaced in 1779 by Magdalen Bridge. Those infected with leprosy were taken to the Leper Hospital at Bartlemas, founded by 'Old King Henry' (Henry I) in the early years of the twelfth century and endowed with £23 5d. from the farm of Oxford. Situated one and a half miles east of the city along the Cowley Road, it was far enough away to prevent contagion yet near enough to be a constant presence, a destination for charitable alms and a reminder both of God's mercy and his power to afflict the sinner. The endowment provided for twelve infirm Brethren and a chaplain, although the number of inmates was later reduced to eight, six infirm and two healthy to work the fifteen acres or so of fields and a small grove that were bequeathed to the hospital along with the buildings. Henry also granted two cartloads a year of hay from the royal meadow near Osney, and firewood from the forests surrounding the city. The Brethren were enjoined to pray for the soul of Henry and his family in the chapel every Monday. These arrangements were confirmed by Henry III in 1267, 'for the salvation of my soul and the soul of my ancestors and heirs.'

Unfortunately, the fate of the lepers and the poor who succeeded them as the inhabitants of the hospital did not remain so close to the royal heart. Where there is a source of income, there is also temptation; and when monies are being received by the lowliest in society, there are those who will see it as common sense to divert them to their own uses. In the early fourteenth century, Bartlemas was a major pilgrimage destination. A miraculous well was sited there, and the chapel possessed some potent sacred relics: Edmund the Confessor's comb; a rib bone of Saint Andrew the Apostle; the bones of Saint Stephen; and even the flayed skin of Saint Bartholomew himself, more often claimed to be preserved at St Bartholomew in the Fields church in Rome. Many miracles were said to have been wrought through these relics, and pilgrims flocked to the site, bringing considerable profits to the Brethren. The Bishop of Lincoln granted forty days' indulgences of sins for those who went 'to St Batholomew's Hospitall without Oxon on the feast of said Saint, or eight days after, and with their prayers, oblations and gifts worship him and alsoe out of charity contribute relief towards the leprus almesfolke thereof.' The income earned by the hospital at this time must have been considerable; in it lay the seed of its own destruction.

In 1312 a certain Adam de Weston became master of the hospital. He immediately set about asset-stripping the establishment with great zeal. Among the possessions of the Brethren he appropriated were four cart-horses with harness, two carts bound with iron, wheat, flour, malt, and a red altar cloth he took against the Brethren's wishes. The income from alms was supposed to be divided equally among them after the Monday service. An enquiry conducted during the reign of Edward II discovered that de Weston took it all himself and applied it to 'bad uses,' including the support 'of a certain Laetitia de Kayso, *concubiniam suam ab antiquio*, and William his son, to the loss and impoverishment of the said hospital and the poor infirm persons there.' In addition, he dismissed the clerk and the servants and labourers who kept up the hospital and farm and sold all the hay and straw it produced so that the animals starved.

The royal enquiry recognised that a new solution had to be found for the management of the hospital. In 1327 it was granted to Oriel College, who were to provide it with a chaplain, as well as paying nine pence a week to each inmate. Sadly, the college treated the hospital residents little better than de Weston had. In the first years of Richard II's reign, they bore away the chapel's relics to their own Church of St Mary the Virgin, 'which caused great complaint from these Hospitalliers.' By the sixteenth century, divine services at Bartlemas were intermittent. Oriel took all the income paid to the hospital, but its buildings fell into disrepair, and the Brethren nominated by the townsfolk to live there found them unfit for habitation. The well was stopped up by the parliamentary troops that besieged the city during the civil war, part of the suppression of papist superstition; they also stripped the chapel roof of lead for bullets and pulled down the hospital buildings, which were rebuilt twenty years later as alms-houses. In the early nineteenth century, these were used as an isolation hospital, when cholera arrived in Oxford on its grand tour of the slums of British cities. By the end of that century, all the furniture had gone from the chapel, and there were no services being held there at all. Only four Brethren were registered as being attached to the hospital; one permanently lived at the workhouse on Cowley Road, another 'was from time to time driven there by want,' while a report prepared for the Oxford City Council in 1896 recorded that the remaining two Brethren 'beg for charity in Oxford, where they drag on a precarious existence.' A member of Oriel College was still receiving a stipend as chaplain but never visited the hospital, and the Brethren didn't know his name. The report found the state of the hospital worse than it had ever been under Adam de Weston.

To the medieval mind, the leper was in some way blessed, as he suffered affliction for his sinful nature in this life, thus bypassing purgatory in the next. The lepers of Bartlemas would have been feared, certainly; but they were also the recipients of special royal favour and intimately connected with a holy site that was a place of miracles. Disease, poverty, and death were intimately bound up with healing, divine grace, and spiritual renewal in an alchemical, transformative process that was at the heart of medieval spirituality. In the parable of Jesus, a leper lies dying of starvation at a rich man's gate, his pitiful condition ignored by those passing in and out. He dies and is borne by angels straight to heaven. The rich man, who has ignored the leper's entreaties, fares less well. In the next world, their roles are reversed; the leper is in paradise, a cherished divine favourite, while the rich man is consigned to the eternal flames. Unsurprisingly, this parable has always been a firm favourite with the disadvantaged.

In other cultures, lepers are also somehow seen as touched by God. Working as a volunteer in a children's clinic in India as a teenager, I arrived one morning to a sweet, slightly cloying odour. One family sat huddled on the floor a little distance from the other patients. Their daughter covered her face with a handful of the miserable rags that constituted her clothing. 'Remember that smell,' I was told; 'that is the smell of active leprosy.' In the local community, those in whom the disease had played its course were a fairly common sight; often they were beggars, rendered unable to work by the loss of digits or limbs. When there was a religious festival at the temple, they came out in force. Those with legs but no fingers pushed the ones with manual dexterity but no legs on homemade trolleys. They owed allegiance to Shiva, warlike God of destruction, as though a blast of his breath had stripped them of their extremities. Long-haired, dishevelled, their eyes red with ganja, they seemed to revel in their startling appearance. In this society, they had a place and a role, at the centre of a community event in the religious calendar, their bellowed chants and the rumble of the wooden wheels of their carts punching a hole in the aural fabric of the day. Very unlike, as far as we can ascertain, the position of the European leper, excluded beyond the city walls in the same way that the Renaissance city gradually excluded animals. Cows, monkeys, and lepers wander the main thoroughfares of cities in India, where 60 per cent of present-day leprosy cases occur. 'At the end of the Middle Ages,' Foucault writes in the first sentence of his extraordinary book, 'leprosy disappeared from the Western world.' Successfully contained and no longer fed by trading contact with the East following the Crusades, it burnt itself out; but a pattern of exclusion had been established that would be the mark of European society from then on.

Turning up a pot-holed lane off a stretch of the Cowley Road dominated by the looming red-brick bulk of the Bingo Hall, one comes across a cluster of buildings that predate their surroundings by several centuries. This is the site of the leper hospital on Bartlemas Lane. The hamlet seems becalmed in this hidden backwater, an urban Shangri-la, untouched by the rapid development that saw the surrounding meadows disappear within the space of half a century. On the site of the original hospital stands the alms-house, built by Oriel College in 1649. St Bartholomew's Chapel is much earlier, dating from the first years of the fourteenth century, a simple building without a spire, built of rubble, a stone quarried locally and known for its durability, set in a grove of apple trees and briars, loud with blackbirds. It stood here when the Brethren of Bartlemas still haunted the lane; men perhaps without fingers or noses, who when chanced upon would have provoked a sign of the cross and a muttered prayer. A farmhouse, part of it dating from the sixteenth century, still stands behind an ivy-clad wall on the site of the original St Bartholomew's Farm. The building has been much added to over the centuries, giving it an irregular, lopsided charm. Its zinc-covered metalwork porch, the walnut tree in the garden, and the wisterias climbing its walls bring a touch of rural France, as well as Elizabethan England, to this hidden aspect of Cowley Road.

II

The evolution of Oxford society, and of the area around Cowley Road as a home for its rejected, marginal elements, continued to conform to the model outlined by Foucault long after the sufferings of the lepers was over. The workhouse on Cowley Road where the abandoned Brethren of Bartlemas found refuge was not opened until the mid-nineteenth century. The poor were a challenge to the local authorities, however, as well as to gloomy philosophers like Robert Burton, from a much earlier date. In 1601 Oxford's city council resolved that Robert Phillis, weaver, be paid twenty pounds a year to employ the poor in spinning wool and linen in the city *'wherein specyall regard must be had that the idle and loytring sort be sett on worcke, and yf they refuse and doe their worcke amysse, that they be punished by whipping.'* By the 1720s city parishes were running their own workhouses, and it was said that 'the fear of confinements' was 'at last promoting the city' and persuading those previously on relief to fend for themselves. The task of housing and feeding paupers was farmed out to private contractors, rather as the care of the elderly is today. Local businessmen employed the poor of several parishes, and in return for their labour and an annual fee, they were charged with providing their charges with lodging, fuel, three meals a day, clothing, and daily prayers. Once a month the inmates were to be taken to church to be viewed by the parish. It was not easy to find entrepreneurs willing to farm paupers, despite the economic potential of their cheap labour. James Piggot, a thread-maker, employed the destitute of seven parishes in the workhouse at Gloucester Green for a period. When he gave up, it was with great difficulty that the services of Solomon Cross, a weaver, were secured. Once again, this was only a temporary solution. In 1771 eleven parishes united in a union, under a board of guardians, determined to provide a General House of Industry that could accommodate and employ all those requiring relief at one location.

The resulting structure – 'a very neat stone building' designed by John Gwynn, the architect of Magdalen Bridge – was completed in 1772 on a central, five-acre site at Rats and Mice Hill (now Wellington Square). It remained there until it was relocated to Cowley Road in the mid-nineteenth century, during the period of the most rapid expansion of East Oxford. On its foundation, workhouse employees, recruited under powers established in an act of 1771, included the master and mistress, an apothecary, a surgeon, a chaplain, a beadle, and a porter. The same act gave the board of guardians the right to compel the poor, the idle, and the dissolute to enter (this was rescinded in 1816). Inmates were allowed meat three times a week – more often, it was said, than they would have eaten it in their own homes. The intention was that they could once more be put to work, their labours not only making the workhouse self-sufficient, but generating a profit. Left in their own homes and requiring 'out relief,' the unemployed were a drain on parish funds. Once confined, they could be used to turn the wheels of industry, so many hamsters in a cage. At the same time, they would be redeemed by their efforts from the stigma of their own social uselessness.

Visiting a mere twenty-three years later, in 1795, Sir Frederick Eden found the workhouse dirty and in disrepair, with the inmates as slovenly as their surroundings and their work unsupervised. Doors and windows hung off their hinges and could not be secured. There was no proper provision for the sick or for children; the sexes were 'strangely intermingled'; and the house was 'in general dirty, unsweet, and in a miserable state of repair, without a single rule or order established for the regulation and government of its numerous family, who were in general idle, riotous and disorderly.' Following Eden's report, great efforts were made at improvements. Incompetent staff were sacked and replaced with those with relevant experience. The sexes were separated, 'as far as their present employment allowed'; the building was repaired and whitewashed; and an attempt was made to 'make the house what a House of Industry ought to be: a comfortable asylum for the aged and infirm, a place of useful employment for those who are able to work, and a House of Correction for the idle and profligate.' Progress was impeded by the rapid turnover in the board of guardians, each of whom seemed intent on undoing the work of their predecessors. In 1833 a report by Mr H. Bishop again found the house verging on a state of anarchy. 'The house stands in the middle of a garden . . . between three and four acres in extent,' he wrote. 'Consequently all men and women, and children, may meet in this space, even after dark. It is hardly necessary to add, that there is, to speak in the most cautious terms, strong suspicion that the bastardy list has been swelled even within the walls.'

On some occasions, the inmates revolted openly against what they saw as the futility of the tasks appointed them. Bishop tells of the arrangement by which 'it was judged proper to employ the inmates of the house in *wheeling* the dirt of the streets out of the city in barrows, instead of carting it away. The men resisted this arrangement and instead of carrying the contents of their barrows to the appointed spot, they one and all emptied them in the centre of the town, where the four main roads meet and cross, at Carfax.' The mayor and city councillors were sufficiently intimidated that they sent for the governor of the workhouse and asked him to abandon the arrangement. He, however, felt that such a surrender would fatally undermine his authority; through a vociferous campaign of blandishment and threats, he brought the men to order. However, his tenure expired at the end of the year; on his departure, the scheme was summarily abandoned.

By 1849 overcrowding was so bad that paupers were sleeping three to a bed. The founders' entrepreneurial intentions had ended in failure; the workhouse only yielded a profit in the very first years of its existence. Sacks and mops were made, and some spinning and weaving took place, but by the 1830s the workhouse looms had been sold off. A contract with the Paving Commission for street sweeping, stone breaking, and road repair was described in 1832 as 'occasional employment for a few old men.' Oakum picking was 'fit only for the idle.' It is unclear exactly how the original vision of the workhouse, as a place where the unemployed could be reintroduced to honest work and rehabilitated through it, was lost. Most likely changes in the labour market outside meant that unskilled workers were no longer at a premium. Whatever the reason, the pattern was replicated across Europe. Workhouses ceased to be houses of work, and became what could only be described as prisons for the poor.

In the Oxford Records Office, situated in a converted church on Cowley Road, I don a pair of white gloves to examine the Baptism Register for the Oxford Workhouse. The register covers the years 1843 to 1866, finishing two years after the workhouse opened for business on its new site on the Cowley Road. P. C. Kidd, the workhouse chaplain, began the volume, recording the name of each child in painstaking copperplate, alongside the date of their birth and baptism, and the name and previous place of residence of one or both of their parents. He also saw to it that the status of each child on entering the world was made clear in uncompromising detail. 'Edward, illegitimate son of Rebecca Martin, late of Highworth, Wiltshire,' reads the first entry. 'Mary Sarah, daughter (illegitimate) of Martha Frankham, lately residing in St Thomas' Oxford,' reads the next. And so the beginnings of these difficult lives are listed, one after another. 'Susannah, illegitimate daughter of Elizabeth Turpin, Shacklewell London. Anna Maria, illegitimate daughter of Mary Anne Pachman, of St Peter's in the East. William, illegitimate son of Elizabeth Barnes.' Sometimes, as if in exasperation, Kidd took to abbreviating the detail of the entry. 'Sarah Anne, Illeg Dau of Sarah Trindler of Stanton Harcourt.' Many of these young mothers, it can be assumed, were women forced into prostitution through poverty; the presence of prostitutes among inmates of the workhouse was a feature of reports by nineteenth-century visitors. Children on the 'bastardy list' did not escape social opprobrium, even here; they were made to dress in yellow, while children born within wedlock wore brown. Only 'decayed' householders, the respectable fallen on hard times, were allowed to wear their own clothes.

In September 1843 a new chaplain, R. D. G. Tidderman, took over the register. He began by copying exactly the form of P. C. Kidd's entries, learning the job initially, as anyone will, by imitating his predecessor. Before long, however, he made changes. The custom of noting illegitimacy in the register was abandoned; whether from humanitarian impulse or a simple pragmatic desire to cut down on the paperwork, it is hard to tell. A child's status could be inferred in any case from the fact that only a mother was present at the baptism. The notes he wrote to himself are still there, on the facing page: *'No baptisms in July and August. Copied and sent in ill. Births.'* It is tempting to read some entries as evidence of his pastoral efforts. Daniel and Sophia Rathbone had two of their older children, one aged two and the other eight, baptised along with their baby, as though yielding to persuasion from an earnest young chaplain. Tidderman gave the best years of his life to the job, continuing in his post for over two decades, during which time he must have witnessed every kind of dissolution and destitution and heard innumerable tales of heartbreak. His flock was mainly made up of locals, their previous habitation given as one of Oxford's parishes: St Aldgate's, St Ebbes's, St Peter's in the East, St Michael's, Holywell, or St Thomas's. Others had wandered from further afield: St James's Dublin, Clonakilty Cork, Deptford, Birmingham, and Yarmouth. Each entry seems loaded with possible narratives. The previous place of residence of Sarah Mapson, the mother of Sarah Anne, is simply given as Oxford Workhouse; perhaps she had followed the same profession, and fallen foul of the same occupational hazard, as her mother. On occasion it fell to the chaplain to name as well as 'dip' an infant. On 29 November 1859, Elizabeth Augusta Church was baptised. Under the column for parents' names, Tidderman has written simply 'unknown – found in St Thomas' Oxford.'

After much deliberation in the middle years of the nineteenth century, a new eleven-acre site for the workhouse was obtained adjoining Cowley Road. The architect William Fisher designed the large brick-and-stone building 'in the Renaissance style,' to house 330 paupers. Three parallel blocks, at the end of a surprisingly long driveway, faced Cowley Road, on a site now occupied by the mosque and the Restore mental health charity. The foundation stone was laid in 1863; an infirmary was added in 1865, and the chapel (the sole surviving building from the workhouse complex) in 1866. A photograph taken during the First World War, when the workhouse was temporarily commandeered as a military hospital, shows the drive sealed by a high white gate, manned by a soldier. The building, its central spire rising above the mature trees that surround it, is forbidding and impressive. The landscaping, the lack of traffic, and the neoclassical architecture recall photographs from the days of the Raj in India – a picture of Bangalore, say, or the New Delhi of Edwin Lutyens. After all, this, too, is the architecture of colonisation. The workhouse was a building laden with symbolism, embodying the power vested in government over the citizens of this outlying colony. East Oxford was another country to the Oxford of Matthew Arnold or John Ruskin. Cumnor Hill, to the west, was the playground of poets, and walks to the north of the city fulfilled Victorian ideas of the picturesque. The east was a place of mission, populated by heathens to convert, the unseen territory to which servants and tradesmen returned at the end of the working day. While Oxford's workhouse was not as forbidding as Manchester's – which Friedrich Engels describes in *The Condition of the Working Class in England* as 'the "Poor-Law Bastille" of Manchester, which, like a citadel, looks threateningly down from behind its high walls and parapets on the hilltop, upon the working-people's quarter below' – it shared some of that building's didactic function. It would be a brave labourer, indeed, who questioned his master's authority, living in its shadow.

The Victorian impulse to create monumental structures for the accommodation of the less desirable elements of society was particularly marked in their treatment of the mentally ill. On three or four occasions, I visited friends confined to the huge mental hospital at Friern Barnet, in North London, now converted into luxury apartments. Situated in extensive grounds, the building itself was planned around a central corridor so long that it was said to contain its own micro-climate, producing mists and eerie lighting conditions. If you weren't mad when you went in, it was said, you soon would be. Most people's reluctance to visit such places is based on the deep-seated fear, to which I myself was not immune, that through some administrative error, they might never be let out again. Indeed, during the brief hours I spent there, I was approached by inmates who begged for small change; ragged, haggard figures who gave every impression of having dwelt for many years in this strange kingdom. Stories abounded of children committed for petty offences such as theft, emerging a lifetime later, thoroughly institutionalised and unable to cope with life outside.

Much thought went into the internal design of the complex of buildings at Cowley Road. Rooms were included for the preparation of oakum, in which old ropes were picked apart for the loose fibres, then used to caulk the gaps between the planks in boats, and the crushing of gypsum, used in the making of plaster. There were special wards designated for use by 'tramps, sick tramps and epileptics,' as well as bedrooms and day-rooms for married couples and a separate day nursery. The infirmary included a surgery, a sick ward, a convalescent ward, and two venereal wards, the latter a reminder of the former occupation of many of the young mothers in the workhouse. The unemployed, the destitute, and the inconveniently pregnant were not the only ones to end up there. The census of 1881 shows a number of inmates, twenty-four in all, whose category is listed as 'imbecile.'

From 1930 the workhouse underwent a change of use and became a geriatric hospital, handed over to the Ministry of Health in 1948. To Foucault's list of the marginalized and excluded today, we should probably add another category, the old. Once we enter our dotage, we can expect to be hidden away to embark on the journey towards death out of sight, where our infirmities and erratic behaviour will not disrupt the smooth running of everyday life. The geriatric hospital continued to function until the early 1980s, when it was finally demolished. The only physical trace that remains of the workhouse, once such a powerful presence on Cowley Road, is its chapel, still in use and now converted into the Asian Cultural Centre.

DANCING SAND AND
ZUM-ZUM WATER

He shoos the women out of the kitchen with flapping hands and starts ferrying pots from the oven to the microwave to heat up the food he has prepared. 'You and me, sir, we will serve,' he instructs me, handing over a plate of lamb kebabs and a plate of bright green, home-made chutney. As an ex-restaurateur, part of his clearly defined role as head of the household is that he is chief cook; indeed, cooking is his main passion and consolation. The smell of the chutney – made from fresh coriander and mint leaves chopped up together with 'a little bit water,' ground coriander seed, fennel seed, and green chillies – fills the kitchen. I take the bowls through to the front room where our families are seated on the sofas and place them on a low table. Soon they are joined by a mountainous drift of pilau rice, the white grains enlivened with green peas and nuts. 'When I put lid on, I put little bit masala,' he explains, with an epicurean glint in his eye, making a sprinkling motion with his hands; 'then when you serve, you get smell of masala – I like it very much.' The daal is creamy and flavoured with lemon and the chicken curry tender. Lastly, a pièce de résistance, there is a bowl of sweet rice, boiled with sugar and flavoured with cardamom, its grains died red and green. Finally he joins us, settling down on a cushion on the floor and helping himself to some food. Whenever he spots something that anyone needs, he shouts in Urdu and one of his teenage daughters, who have maintained a shadowy presence in the background, arrives with it. With their father in the room, they are changed from the streetwise, confident young women of our acquaintance to silent waitresses, a transformation that never ceases to unsettle us. Our sons play together on a video game as we eat; from what I can tell when I glance at the screen, it appears to be based on street-to-street urban warfare. 'Triangle, triangle,' chants his son, as a sniper appears on a virtual rooftop, and he judges that my own son is slow in responding to the threat. 'Press the triangle.'

My daughter asks if she can have a little more food. 'Oh gosh,' he replies, 'make yourself at home. You are like family, *innit*. Anything you see you like in this house, just take it; it's yours.'

'Maybe I'll take your television,' she jokes, slightly embarrassed by the intensity of his generous impulse, but he does not laugh.

To European eyes, the room is bare, the walls without

pictures, except for an ornate Qur'anic text and a view of Mecca. The TV stands in pride of place in a cabinet containing a selection of DVDs and video games, and currently trails long wires across the carpet to where the children are sitting. The ceiling is decorated with an abstract pattern in the plasterwork, a series of swoops and swirls like the flight path of swallows, or writing in a script even more indecipherable to me than the Arabic on the wall. I indicate the picture of Mecca that features the huge, mysterious black rock, the Ka'bbah, that has been a site of worship at Mecca since pre-Islamic times. 'Have you made the hajj?' I ask.

His wife leans forward. 'He has been, not me,' she tells me.

'Yes, yes,' he intervenes, 'I been, fourteen years ago. I take my father. Who else to look after him over there? When you get there, you think you in paradise. So many people. Not like when you go to football, everyone pushing and shoving. No rich and poor there, everybody same, just thinking about God. When you come back, you different.'

We try to imagine what it must be like, this journey that is one of the basic duties of Islam. 'Do sick people go who want to get well?' asks my wife, thinking of Catholic pilgrimage centres like Lourdes.

'No sick people allowed to go,' explains his wife, 'no too-poor people either. But you have to take clothes in case you die there, white clothes.'

'Yes, white clothes,' her husband repeats, 'one you wear, one for washing.'

'If you die there, is good luck, we thinking,' adds his wife. 'My uncle went, he not come back. That's good luck, he die there.'

We sit for a minute or two, thinking about the pilgrims who step outside their lives and, dressed for the grave, focus on the eternal. The previous weekend I had walked along the river to the twelfth-century church at Iffley. It is famous for its late Romanesque carvings, including mysterious beaked birds' heads, a winged serpent devouring its own tail, a merman clutching a sword, and a remarkable king's head, said to be that of Henry II. In the thirteenth century, it was also the home of an anchoress, Annora, the Recluse of Iffley, who lived in a cell built adjoining the church. A well-born widow, she withdrew into her spartan dwelling, staying there until her death in around 1241. A window was constructed in the wall of the church so that she could receive the sacrament and view the altar. Built into the floor of her cell was her own gravestone, a constant reminder of her eventual destination and an aid to contemplation. A thirteenth-century grave slab still lies between the yew tree and the church wall, on the site of the cell.

My neighbour is still transported, remembering his time in Mecca. 'When you there,' he reminisces, 'you forget everything. You forget you left your wife and children. When I went back, I had to go in airport and buy her a ring.' They double up with laughter together at the memory.

'Did you bring anything else back from the journey?' I ask.

'Yes, *zum-zum* water. It tastes so sweet. In the old days, there was no water in that place. When Ismail was a baby, he was playing in the sand, kicking it with his foot – I don't know how to say it – and the water came up. It coming till they had to say *zum-zum* – that means "stop" in Arabic. Most water in that Middle East place taste salty, but this is sweet. I just brought back couple of gallons, not much. Then when people come to visit, you give them *zum-zum* water and dates to eat; that's what you have to do.'

The origins of the spring at Ka'bbah, the waters of which form an important part of the pilgrims' ritual procession around the stone, are linked in Islamic tradition with the founders of the Muslim race. Hagar, the maidservant cast out into the desert by Abraham, was searching the hills of Safa and Marwa for water to give to her son, Ismail. As she ran from place to place with increasing desperation, her child lay on the sand and kicked his heels, and where he did so, water started bubbling out of the sand.

Later on I check references to '*zum-zum* water' on the Internet. The same story has been posted innumerable times, a personal testimony attesting to the purity of the miraculous well, which has refreshed pilgrims to Mecca since the first days of the hajj. The story appears in almost the same words on many different sites; those reading it are urged to forward it to others, to dispel any doubts they may harbour about the water's miraculous nature. In 1971 an Egyptian doctor wrote to the Western press, declaring that the holy water at Mecca was unfit to drink. King Faisal immediately commissioned two engineers from the desalination plant at Jeddah to investigate the well, and it is their personal account that is reproduced on the Internet. They ordered a local man, once he had showered, naturally, to climb into the water of the well, which came up to his shoulders. The engineers then pumped the water out as fast as they could, into storage tanks. Where was the water coming from, they asked the man standing in the well. Could he see any ancient pipes or inlets? At first he was defeated; there appeared to be no explanation for the water's constant replenishment. Then revelation dawned. *'Alhamdollillah!* I have found it!' he is recorded as saying. 'The sand is dancing beneath my feet as the water oozes out of the bed of the well.' Samples were taken to laboratories and tested, and the water found to be perfectly drinkable, free from algae, and high in salts, minerals, and anti-bacterial fluorides, which perhaps account for its refreshing properties.

We finish the meal with cups of tea – a drink that, although secular, has arguably been as revered in our culture as *zum-zum* water has in theirs ('that's English, *innit?*' asks the wife anxiously as she passes round the cups) – and tear our children away from their virtual battle, with its uncomfortable echoes of real-life conflicts in Gaza or Iraq.

JUNIOR JIHAD

A friend is teaching in a primary school just off Cowley Road. His duties include tackling religious studies with a class of eleven-year-olds. As part of the class study of Islam, he asks the Muslim children to bring in their prayer mats and demonstrate to the rest of the class how they pray.

'It's always a good one,' he says. 'It's interesting; the other kids just shut up and watch. I think they're a bit gobsmacked by how seriously the Muslim kids take it. All the Asian kids go to mosque school as well as my class. I get all the kids to write their personal biographies, with landmark events in their lives; they often put in things that happen at mosque, like when they have successfully learnt a passage of the Qur'an. The other day I was doing religious education, talking to them about the Five Pillars of Islam. At the end of the lesson, a girl came up, very self-possessed and confident, and said, "Sir, there are six pillars, you know." "Oh really," I said, "I thought there were only five." "No," she said, "the sixth pillar is jihad: we have to defend our Muslim brothers and sisters anywhere and be prepared to die in defence of Islam." This girl is eleven years old.'

'How did you respond?' I ask him.

He shrugs his shoulders. 'How could I respond? I just thanked her and went on clearing up the books.'

OF BOOKS AND BITUMEN

In fact, it is not entirely foolish to imagine constructing a highway out of words. Each year in the United Kingdom, around 120,000 new books are published, often in print runs of many thousands. Together with those published elsewhere and imported into the country, they represent an unimaginable mountain of printed matter. Readers cannot possibly consume all this information. There are not enough column inches to review all these new titles or miles of booksellers' shelves to accommodate them. Many of them are simply not wanted; their conception was a mistake. Like abandoned orphans or street children, they are condemned at birth to a half-life in shadowy realms beyond the public gaze. They come and go in an unnumbered parade without the committed reading public ever becoming aware of their existence, an existence that has itself become an embarrassment – lingering evidence of a misplaced bet. What to do with them all? Leaving them in warehouses to gently decay

OF BOOKS AND BITUMEN

is not an option; they clog up the book trade's sclerotic arteries that are desperate for new blood. The remainder bookshops cannot shift them; they have a market, it is true, for ghosted biographies of alcoholic footballers or bit-part actresses with unfeasibly large breasts, while the flickering candle of their fame lasts. But what about all these others? The forlorn first novels, the obscure medical textbooks, the forgotten politician's memoirs, the TV tie-ins for programmes nobody watched? Pulping them is expensive, a cost that merely adds to the negative equity they represent.

A solution was required. Someone came up with the idea of mixing surplus books with bitumen and using them in the construction of motorways. Forty-five thousand books are required for every mile, it seems. Many easy jokes can be generated from this situation. An editor who has suffered with a particularly difficult author could get her revenge by driving repeatedly over the section built from the impossible creature's masterpiece. Stretches constructed from romantic novels may be subject to subsidence in warm weather, as they reconstitute as slush. Erotic novels may cause irregularities in the road surface, and so on. Meanwhile, along these highways of the mind – built of daydreams, scholarship, ambition, imagination, and greed – speed the lorries laden with urgent deliveries of next season's new titles. It is a symbiotic system of great elegance and circularity. At last publishers can justly claim to be making a real contribution to the infrastructure of the nation. And none of us need worry that perhaps we are simply publishing too many books.

CARNIVAL

Do you want me to go with you?
If you like, answered Courfeyrac. The road is free, the streets belong to everybody.

VICTOR HUGO, *Les Misérables*

It is Carnival. The smoke from a barbecue outside the Hi-Lo Jamaican Eating House drifts across the heads of the crowds that fill the street, like incense at a Greek Orthodox procession. Trade at the restaurant is brisk, and the Red Stripe is flowing. Skylarkin' Sound System have piled up their speaker cabinets against the front window and are pumping out their patented mix of reggae, ska, and sixties rhythm and blues to an enthusiastic crowd. The man behind the decks is a living legend, the sixty-something, white reggae MC known as DJ Derek. He stands, smiling benignly behind his owlish glasses, an ever-present cigarette dangling from his lip, microphone in one hand, and a bottle of beer in the other. Derek is not some late-arrival revivalist; he has been playing these records since they were pressed, starting out at functions in the black community in Bristol in the 1960s and progressing to clubs and festivals all over the world.

This is why he is regarded with such awe by younger generations of DJs, and why members of the crowd run up to have their photograph taken with him behind the decks, adulation he greets with amused tolerance. The man tending the barbecue lifts its lid, and a cloud of heavily scented smoke obscures the sun. 'I love dat smoke,' Derek rasps, in a gravel-throated Jamaican patois. 'Mi don't smoke ganja, you know, jus' cigarette, and strictly shag . . . not necessarily in dat ordaah!' And he drops another tune, with perfect timing, and the crowd roars its appreciation. A vintage 1960s ska instrumental blasts out, a wild, rasping tenor sax soloing over a beat that rattles the windows.

One of the characters of the Cowley Road has taken a prime position in front of the decks; Bob is a small Jamaican man in his fifties. Usually dressed in a zip-up windcheater with a black baseball cap pulled down over his eyes, he can be found wherever there is music playing in the pubs and clubs of the neighbourhood. Today he is executing a complicated, balletic dance with the can of Red Stripe he is holding as a partner. He looks at the beer at the end of his outstretched arm with the tender gaze of a man regarding an adored sweetheart and circles it, demonstrating his best moves, as if eager for a response from his steely-faced lover. He has the bodily control and range of facial expressions of a silent movie actor, but it is never clear if these performances are for an audience or merely to amuse himself.

A few days earlier, I had been parking my car in the street where I live; as I did so, my daughter and I became aware of a man passing the car window in the street, limping heavily, dragging one leg along the ground. He made a striking figure, wearing a jacket, loose-fitting trousers, and a wide-brimmed straw hat in a Cuban style, his whole body tilting with each step. Suddenly, a few yards ahead of us, he stopped limping and ran a few steps, crossing the road, and striding hurriedly along the pavement. My daughter, who shares my fascination with neighbourhood characters, recognised Bob beneath his Cuban disguise. 'Quick,' she said, 'let's see what he's doing,' and we locked the car and moved to a position where we could observe his progress down the street. Another car was approaching, slowing down to park at the kerb. As Bob drew up to it, he again started his exaggerated gimping, attracting the startled attention of those inside, only to begin walking normally a few yards further on, to the confusion of his onlookers. He didn't look back, to gauge the reaction of his audience, but strode on past the betting shop, a small man made bigger by a large hat and an obscure thespian ambition. Is there a syndrome that compels people to act and dance as others are forced to continually wash their hands or to utter their deepest secrets out loud? Compulsive performance disorder, perhaps?

The Carnival in June is East Oxford's answer to May Day, the university's day of licence, when the choristers of Magdalen pierce the dawn air with their singing and drunken students leap off Magdalen Bridge into the shallow and treacherous river, sustaining terrible injuries and the derision of the national press. While their celebration can appear to be the arcane ritual of an obscure, overprivileged sect, the Carnival engages a wider spectrum of the community. Indeed, the official banners, in slightly worthy tones, encourage us to 'celebrate diversity.' The original impetus for the Carnival came from within the Jamaican community; the Caribbean, after all, along with Brazil and, arguably, West London are the real homes of the Carnival tradition.*According to some, it was then hijacked by what they call 'do-gooders,' middle-class professionals keen to organise the event in accord with *their* vision of utopia. When the Carnival began in 2000, the stalls that were licensed to set up in the park at Manzil Way, instead of catering to the hunger and thirst of the revellers, were all earnestly soliciting donations to various charities. This misunderstanding of the spirit of Carnival was somehow typical of the neighbourhood. The city is the birthplace of some of the most important NGOs in the world, including Oxfam, and a number of other organisations deserving our support. Sometimes those whose profession is fund-raising for worthy causes cannot help seeing the gathering together

---

*I am, I admit, ignoring those European Carnival traditions played out in the chilly mists of Venice or in Munich's wide, leafy boulevards.

of large crowds of people simply as an opportunity to proselytise, instead of a time to forget the world's troubles and live for the moment. What do you need at a Carnival? Red snapper barbecuing on the street. Music in unlikely places accompanied by unlicensed dancing. Alcohol, freely available. A large benevolent crowd that can control anyone who, after a day of drinking and smoking in the sun, becomes confused and aggressive. Above all, the quickest way to increase the sum of human happiness is to ban motor vehicles. Allow people to wander through those spaces usually rendered dangerous and noisy by traffic, and you unleash a feeling of liberation, a glimpse of a better world that when it vanishes leaves a trace in the human heart. (Bicycles, of course, are still permitted. Cyclists are, for the most part, heroes who risk life and limb every day to make the world a better place and should always be made welcome.) Getting the agreement of the city council to close Cowley Road to traffic for the whole of the Carnival was the greatest achievement of the Carnival committee. Once that happened, the Carnival began to outgrow its beginnings and develop organically.

My youngest son is taking part in the Carnival procession with his fellow pupils at preschool. He is wearing a T-shirt that he has printed and a crown cut from red and green rubber that resembles something between a Native American headdress and a floral display. The day starts for us in a hall where hundreds of children from different schools are milling about trying to find their teachers, their parents, or their costumes. The tumult is impressive. My son is finding it daunting and is keeping a firm hold on my hand. I listen to his worries with one ear while the other is glued to my mobile phone. I have just returned from Montreal on a red-eye flight without my suitcase, which has gone on a brief holiday on its own. I am jet-lagged and bereft of almost all my worldly possessions, as well as the notes of meetings at a book fair in New York, and am engaged in a continuous long-distance conversation with airport baggage handlers in an attempt to track down my belongings. In my sleep-deprived state, I am almost moved to tears at the thought of the gifts I had bought for my wife and children lying abandoned in some God-forsaken luggage bay. With an honesty that I would rather have been spared, a man on the end of the line tells me that my case has disappeared from the computer tracking system. It could be in Hong Kong, he muses – the belts at La Guardia for London and Hong Kong are adjacent – or it could be in Toronto. Or perhaps it never left Montreal. Teachers are shouting above the hubbub made by the kids in an attempt to marshal their groups. Tears are being shed, whistles blown, hands tugged. I terminate the conversation, and we follow the crowd out to take up our position at the head of Cowley Road. The procession waits for the signal to begin. We are positioned right behind the local samba band, and their infectious rhythms are putting everyone in a party mood.

A Carnival procession is the embodiment of organised chaos. Unlike a military procession, for instance, each element within it has its own irregular momentum. The samba musicians come to the end of one set of rhythms and halt, acknowledging the cheers of the crowd, bringing the procession behind it to a halt in turn, before their leader gives them a new set of instructions through a combination of sharp beats on her drum and blasts on a whistle, and they set off again, preceded by a group of frenzied dancers. Behind us a woman in a gold bikini supports a massive structure that represents the sun. One of the bamboo poles that anchors it to her waist comes adrift, and the whole thing totters dangerously, threatening to fall on our heads. Helpers rush to her aid, and she moves forward cautiously, now with her own attendants in train, an uncrowned Carnival queen. We do our best to maintain our position behind the banner carried by pupils from my son's school, but it isn't easy. He sits on my shoulders to get a better view. My phone rings. The baggage handlers at Heathrow confess that they are confused. The behaviour of my suitcase confounds their systems. It could be anywhere or nowhere, in the air or on the ground, they can't say. Behind us, supporters of Greenpeace bounce a giant inflatable globe up into the air above our heads. Like my suitcase, it becomes detached from its moorings and begins to spin dangerously out of orbit, before they haul on the ropes and bring it back under control.

The effort of remaining mentally attached to my absent possessions is too much; the ties connecting me to my suitcase are unravelling as the samba rhythms infiltrate deeper into my consciousness. My son is overtaken by a desperate urge to pee, and we have to flee the procession in double-quick time. I put my phone away. The Mirch Masala restaurant is closed, the proprietor out front on the pavement selling ice-cream to passers-by, but she kindly waves us inside to use the facilities. By the time we rejoin the procession, it has lurched forward and we have lost our position. We struggle through a chaotic collage of sounds and impressions: a troupe of bhangra drummers in purple and gold costumes spin like dervishes; African dancers in fake leopard-skin bikinis crouch low, running through the crowd; a Chinese brass band of serious-faced elderly men in black suits blast their long-stemmed trumpets in our faces, while an orange dragon writhes furiously at their feet. As we inch forward, I look up at the people hanging out of windows and the groups sitting on flat roofs, smoking hubble-bubble pipes and lifting drinks aloft in salutation as we pass. All neighbourhoods need to be picked up every now and then and shaken, rearranged; they emerge, once the streets have been hosed down and the debris swept away, rubbing their eyes and their sore heads with a rueful smile, a little looser, a little friendlier. A measure of anarchy is good for any highly controlled society. The forces of law and order demonstrate that they are secure enough in their position to relax the reins for a day, step back, and allow people to break a few rules, enjoy themselves, thereby increasing the chances of public cooperation when normal business resumes. 'WARNING,' reads the printed notice pinned to every stage. 'Noise Levels in excess of 85 dba. Ear damage possible. Earplugs available from the Information Tent.' This seems to me the right balance of official intervention. Go ahead and party, they seem to say, but don't sue us if you go deaf; if you are worried about your ears, we have earplugs. Otherwise it's up to you.

It feels good to retrace my route down Cowley Road accompanied by thousands of revellers; pilgrimages were ever thus, part solitary, part communal celebration. Groups of my son's fans among the onlookers lining the pavement reach out to us, asking, 'Where were you? We waited ages for the school banner to reach us and then we couldn't see you.' My son shrugs nonchalantly, licking his ice-cream, as if to say a man's gotta do what a man's gotta do. Speak to his agent, I feel like saying, I'm just the chauffeur. On the main stage there is a power cut, and the London Community Gospel choir are forced to perform a cappella above the noise from the street; the audience members sit silent, spellbound through 'Amazing Grace.' We meet my son's friend Abdullah, who introduces us to the bhangra musicians who are resting

in the shade of some trees in the park at Manzil Way. My
son sits on a man's knee, holding a drum, while I take a
photo. He is laughing; the man's impressive moustache
tickles the back of his neck. 'This is good boy,' the man
tells me earnestly, pinching his cheek. We shake hands
with the music troupe and retire to sit in the graveyard
under the trees, eating chicken curry and chappati from
a Bangladeshi stall. I lie on my back on the grass, the jet
lag seeping out of my body into the ground, my son's
head on my chest, glad to be home. Sometimes this is
the most precious communication between parent and
child; two human beings inhabiting the same moment of
time without words, the larger used as a piece of furniture
by the smaller. I am reminded that the families of most
mammal species sleep in piles. The phone in my pocket
vibrates. It is a text telling me that my suitcase has been
located and picked up from the airport by couriers; it will
be delivered to my home within the next twelve hours.

RETURNING TO THE SOURCE

I come across the work of artist Jo Thomas by chance, looking through a leaflet issued by the council to promote a festival of events associated with the waterways of Oxford. On 21 June, the longest day of the year, it tells me, Jo would be walking through the city, visiting the places mentioned in ancient records as being the locations of wells or springs. In the evening, she would meet anyone who was interested in discussing the subject at a suitably aquatic location, the bar of the Waterman's Arms on Osney Island. Needless to say, by the time I see the leaflet, the date of her walk, and the evening meeting, has long passed. Nevertheless, I am intrigued enough to make enquiries in order to get in touch with her. Here is an artist working in the same city, whose researches must have overlapped with my own. It doesn't take long to track her down. My initial email remains unanswered for a number of weeks; she is out of the country, in Romania, looking at fountains. However, when we finally make contact and I explain a little bit about what I am up to, she seems as keen as I am to talk further.

We arrange to meet in the Excelsior Cafe, a famous Cowley Road landmark, on a clear, crisp, autumnal Saturday afternoon in September. The Excelsior is what used to be called a working-man's café and, as is usual with such places, is much frequented by the unemployed, as well as workers of both sexes and a sprinkling of the bohemian demimonde. Presided over by two elderly Greek gentlemen, Costas and Andrew, the place inspires fierce loyalty in its clientele. In the Excelsior one can smoke (in fact, merely by choosing to breathe in its interior, one forgoes the non-smoking option),* order milky coffee that comes with an impressive discharge of steam from a 1950s-style Gaggia machine, and while away the time for minimum expenditure. Here, political cadres can plot coups, poets pore over verses, building workers get a hearty cooked meal, impoverished students keep warm, and street people conduct their business (although woe betide anyone that Costas believes is engaged in anything untoward; they will be unceremoniously thrown out, and it may take months before they are readmitted). The Excelsior has several customers who eat there every day. At least one gives it on his card as his office address before ten a.m. Inside,

---

*Recent legislation means that this aspect, at least, of the Excelsior's atmosphere will soon change forever.

the brown walnut-veneer wallpaper absorbs the light, which is further furred by cigarette smoke and the odour of fried food, so that the place is simultaneously so dark and yet so conducive to conversation and speculation as to resemble Plato's cave.

While I am attaching my bicycle to a lamp-post, I think I recognise Jo on the other side of the street. She is of medium height, with long, dark hair, and has the erect, unhurried, yet purposeful stride as she crosses the road of someone whose shoes are used to eating up the miles. Giving directions on the phone, I had asked whether she would be coming by bus or bike. 'Oh, no,' she told me, 'I walk everywhere.' Once we are settled at a table with two cups of milky but deceptively strong Excelsior coffee, I ask her what led her to the subject matter of her recent work.

'I decided it was time for me to go back to college, and I came to Oxford to do an MA at Brookes. I came across Hope's book on *The Wells and Springs of England*. In that, I discovered that there had been seventeen wells in the Oxford area; I decided to walk through the city and find the sites of the wells and what evidence of their presence continued in the life of the town.

'I began with Bartlemas, partly because I liked the name. Bartlemas is beautiful; it's like stepping into another world. I learnt a lot about the spring-line from chatting with the allotment manager' (allotments adjoin the lane that runs up to the chapel). 'The allotments and the old green road behind them are like a wedge of greenness coming into Oxford. He told me they get deer coming right in from the surrounding countryside, to the edges of Cowley Road. A lot of the old roads around here used to end up at the shrine of Bartlemas.'

As she walked the streets around the site of the old pilgrimage site, Jo experienced some strange slippages between past and present. In Highview Road, a few hundred yards from Bartlemas Lane, in what appears to be an abandoned garden, someone has built a wishing-well. Was it just a typical piece of garden vernacular or a gesture towards the past? At Bartlemas itself in the immaculate garden of the alms-house, now a private residence, a concrete-edged ornamental pond reflects the sky in the same place as where the lepers used to go down to bathe in a pool fed by the well, to treat their affliction. (A similar leper's pool existed at Harbledown, in Kent; Edward, the Black Prince, was reputed to have bathed there to treat his leprosy, his royal lineage no guarantee of immunity.)

As part of her project, Jo has made an artist's book. Gingerly I leaf through it on the Formica table, which is treacherously stained and gritty with spilt sugar. One page shows a map of Oxford with the roads removed but the rivers still in place, the sites of the wells marked with small circles. These have then been punched through the pages of the book as a motif, a constellation of miniature absences; each page is dedicated to a particular well and the appropriate hole is circled to locate it, so that it can be matched with its position on the map. A photograph taken at a well site and a few epigrammatic words, as brief as an ancient Greek fragment, appear for each entry. I am anxious not to spill coffee on it and hand it back before I have had a chance to study it properly, but it continues to resonate in my mind over the next few days. The circles are like ellipses in the text, yet they also represent the way that wells pierce the fabric of the city, connecting the strata laid down over the centuries. Perhaps they are also places where the past leaks though into the present? If the city is a text, the wells are punctuation points. And if the city is a body, wells are openings within it that ooze mysteriously, like stigmata, or statues of the Virgin that weep real tears.

'So what is the work,' I ask her, 'is it the books, the walking, or your meeting with people?'

She shifts slightly uncomfortably, as if at the intrusiveness of the question. 'What I've been doing is marking the sites with a disc of copper leaf on the ground – marking them very gently – just making a slowing. I've been using different glues in different environments; they last three to four months. The first glue I used took a setting time of about twenty minutes, which was nice, because it meant you had to wait on that spot as part of the process, and you'd meet people, who'd ask what you were doing. On the other side of town, I met a milkman who only contributed a few words, but he brought his own story to the project. He told me it was a great place for a well because the sheep would pass there, being taken to market. Others believe that their fruit and vegetables are growing better because they are getting spring water rather than piped water. Or that the dampness creates a kind of melancholy.'

At this point I am unable to restrain myself from leading the conversation onto a diversion about *The Anatomy of Melancholy*. The worst interviewers are those who listen back to their recording and find it full of the sound of their own voice. Fortunately for us both, Jo hasn't forgotten the previous question, about the nature of her work.

'I suppose it's what actually happens on the street when someone walks by and sees a disc; seeing if there is any kind of slowing down in that area. I've also done sound recordings of travelling through the town in the places of water. You get the birds in Bartlemas Lane and the sound of the traffic gradually crescendoing. There's a well in the middle of Castle Mound where there's an amazing silence. You go into the metal cage at the top of the mound, and there are steps going down; there's a well, sunk right through the middle – I suppose in times of siege it was a source of water. Being in the centre of the city inside a mound in that silence is very powerful.*

---

*Since the completion of this book, Castle Mound has become a paying visitor attraction and presumably no longer functions so effectively as a reservoir of silence.

Then you come out onto Hythe Bridge Street, and your route takes you gently out towards Port Meadow and the quiet again. Because I don't live in Oxford, I have a real feeling of travelling through the city and finding breathing points that relate to a quality of specialness.

'I started off thinking that it would be good to make people take the walk through the city to all the sites, but I realised it was quite a big expectation of people – walking it took an awfully long time. They can travel imaginatively, using my map – and I am just as happy with that.'

About ten people had turned up to Jo's meeting at the pub, all of them interested in different ways in the points where water rises to the surface in the city. They had included an archeologist, someone writing a thesis on holy wells, casual observers, and those wishing to visit the sites. They decided to share contact information. 'In a sense it is what happens next,' Jo explains. 'I do feel a sense of responsibility. They've given their time and trust.'

We decide to walk up to Bartlemas. We circle the tiny chapel, the lawns surrounding it scattered with windfalls from the apple trees, and speculate over the pool. I've visited the place many times, but nearly always on my own. It is strange to do so now with someone else for whom it has a significance beyond its physical reality, as a leaping-off point into the past. 'Did you know that there's a story that Saracens bribed the lepers to poison the well?' Jo asks, as we walk back down the lane towards the hum of Cowley Road. This strikes me as extraordinary. After eight centuries, the West has once again become embroiled in a war with Islam and is terrified of attack from within. Poisoned wells were key to the arsenal of terror in the Middle Ages, just as devastating to a community as a car bomb on a busy street. We pause to admire the oak that grows at the entrance to the lane, a tree in the prime of life, 150 years old, perhaps. Old enough to have given shade to shepherds driving their flocks across the meadows to market, but not to lepers or pilgrims to the wonder-working well.

The street is busy. Unusually, among the brightly coloured *shalwar kamiz* and neon T-shirts, there are a number of traditionally dressed Jews in black, walking along the road towards the Chabad House. It is the Sabbath following Rosh Hashanah, I realise later, the time of year, according to orthodox Jewish belief, when G-d created Adam and Eve. It is also when creation is called to account, and G-d decides whether it merits another year of existence. The ten days remaining before Yom Kippur are a window of opportunity for men and women to change their fate, which, though inscribed for each individual, is not yet sealed. The methods recommended are repentance and the giving of alms to the poor. There is no sign in the sky on this sunny afternoon that the fate of so many hangs in the scales. As we enjoy the ambience of the street, concentrating on the shifts and changes in atmosphere as different features dominate – here a mosque, there a supermarket or a betting shop – we are unaware of the cosmic deliberations in progress behind the surface of the sky.

We are heading for St Edmund's Well; once again I have been brought back to the starting point of my journey. Jo has pored over old maps, spoken to local experts, and managed to gain access to the grounds of Magdalen College School in her attempts to pin down the exact location of the site. 'It took me ages, because the roads and the rivers were marked in the same way on the map I was using, so which were rivers and which were roads? And, of course, the roads have shifted . . . There's so much water around here. There used to be a shrine to Our Lady on the other side of the river, and the two shrines related to each other. When they were building Christ Church, they talked about moving the dirt down towards the shrines of St Edmund and Our Lady. St Edmund's has become the elusive one, but in a way I like that . . .' We walk away from the Plain, where I had placed the well in my imagination, down the cul-de-sac of Cowley Place. At the end of the street, we stand outside the impressive gates of St Hilda's College, looking across the immaculately kept lawns towards the river. At our back are the equally verdant and inaccessible grounds of Magdalen College School. Movement everywhere in the centre of the city is circumscribed by these barriers, of water and private property, making pedestrian routes almost as liable to full stops and retreats as in a city of waterways, like Venice. As Jo puts it, the waterways are like a 'pelvis for the city: the whole town is constricted by these two rivers.' She had been keen to have some kind of authorisation for making her marks upon the street, however temporary. 'In a way, they are an act of graffiti. So I thought, let's go to the council and see how absurd they think this is, and I found that the pavements are owned by three different authorities: the university, the city, and the council – and so how do you know which pavement belongs to who? The whole place has so many barriers that are designed to keep one sort of people in here and one sort of people out there . . .'

In her quest to find the location of St Edmund's Well, she ended up making a judgement and placing the disc on a pavement in Cowley Place, outside the entrance to a sports and recreation hall; (are such places a twenty-first-century equivalent of wells, as places of restoration and refreshment?) We search for it, pushing with our feet at the wallflowers that have crept under the railings and are lying prostrate, like exhausted travellers, in the dust, but without success. Other aspects of Jo's project have disappeared as completely as the disc in Cowley Place. She had built a wooden travelling case in which she carried her artist's books, divining rods, and a series of Polaroids taken at the sites of the wells from place to place. On the way back to Reading, she fell asleep and, waking up disorientated and in a hurry to get off the train, left the case behind. She laughs, ruefully. 'I can tell you, I know a lot about lost property departments!'

'The first thing you learn is that you never get anything back,' I say sympathetically. 'In the old days, before they broke up the railway system into its component parts, so that different companies are responsible for the tracks, the trains, the stations, and the lost property offices, I hear that things were sometimes returned. As a regular rail traveller, I have lost many things, some of which I was quite attached to. Useful things, beautiful things, stolen, dropped, forgotten. Sometimes I feel like saying, "I know, I know, I shouldn't become too attached to possessions. I *hear* you. I don't need to be reminded of this again." '

She smiles, bravely. 'There was something lovely about it. I was taking it out of Oxford; it would have become a relic. And it's just vanished. It's nice to know it's out there somewhere. I've learnt a lot of good lessons from it.'

'I have learnt those lessons as well, but they are very painful.'

'Yes,' she agrees, 'it was painful. But it makes a good story, too.' And I have to agree that this is one of the consolations that life offers; that its most difficult episodes can be resolved into anecdotes shared with a friend or collected on the pages of a book.

THIRD PARTITION

A JOURNEY IN THE HINTERLAND

It is dusk when we hear something moving slowly and deliberately through the undergrowth. We are standing surrounded by the debris of generations of badger excavations, the fortified city of an embattled tribe, and the badger is returning after an early evening foray. He becomes aware of the presence of intruders in his kingdom at roughly the same moment as we notice his. Gradually, almost imperceptibly, his mask materialises in the gloom, between the dark, lower leaves of a naturalised rhododendron. The black-and-white stripes on his head, so distinct in daylight, are remarkably effective camouflage in the twilight. We peer at each other short-sightedly. Suddenly, and silently, he is gone.

Dudley has brought me to the woods on a humid weekday evening, straight from the train station. He walks most evenings in summer, leaving behind the stress of his job and the pounds that publishing lunches threaten to add to his waistline, emerging from the woods, like Thoreau, a leaner and wiser man. As we stride briskly through the sweltering gloom, our shirts sticking to our backs with sweat, we talk, startling muntjac deer that catapult across our track, their young scarcely bigger than hares. At a turning in the path, a fallow deer stands poised for a moment, regarding us over its shoulder with an affronted expression, as though we were gate-crashers at a private party. Its departure is literally *flight*, a series of graceful parabolas involving minimum contact with the ground.

At first sight, the woods resemble deep nature; on closer inspection, they are carefully and scientifically coppiced, the undergrowth between the trunks thinned out, with here and there a fallen trunk left to decompose, to encourage those insect and vegetable life forms that feed upon and engineer decay. This protected natural world, five minutes from the busy ring road around the city, is artificially maintained, the site of academic studies and wildlife documentaries. Every inhabitant of these intensively settled islands learns to accept that the managed landscape can be as beautiful as any wilderness. This one is farmed not for financial profit but scientific knowledge, a crop that requires less rather than more intervention, a helping hand rather than a war of conquest and chemical attrition. There are no scientists about tonight, unless we count ourselves *natural scientists*, bent on triggering beneficial chemical reactions within ourselves through this most ancient of pursuits, tramping the woods, hoping to shed something that has adhered to us in the city, like grass-snakes intent on sloughing their skins.

We are discussing our working lives. We both find ourselves inhabiting a position on the outer edges of large organisations. For him, as the publisher of a small but significant imprint that has been swallowed by a huge multinational publishing group, it is the first time he has experienced being an outsider in his own workplace, expected to plead for the life of his books at board meetings that have begun to feel more like hanging assizes than a gathering of creative minds. His own position, he knows, could be signed away at the stroke of a corporate pen, the imprint retaining only a ghostly existence as a 'brand' to be applied to certain projects as his overlords see fit. He finds this position particularly uncomfortable because he is someone used to being at the centre. I, it becomes clear as we talk, have operated on the fringe my entire career; even though I currently work at a major national institution, it is still in a position at its edge, with a remit rather different to that of many of my colleagues. It is always an option to complain about the difficulties of such an existence. It is more interesting perhaps to recognise the element of unconscious choice that has shaped its trajectory. It could be that it derives from the same impulse that has led us both to settle in the area in which we live, a place outside yet adjoining the main city, from which one can observe and comment, while retaining a sense of independence. This is not, after all, such a bad place to find oneself, we decide, either geographically or professionally, our breath getting shorter as we climb a steep slope. We are not yet ready to trade our souls for corporate advancement. Yet we need to work; therefore we must succeed at this precarious and sometimes uncomfortable high-wire act. We emerge from beneath the trees to look out across a valley, raucous with wheeling rooks, to the car factory in the distance at the end of Cowley Road, glinting in the evening sun. The science is working; our hearts are lighter. I am usefully reminded that sometimes, when there is no train or plane fast enough to transport you beyond the reach of your troubles, a long walk may be your only way out.

INTO THE FURNACE

I

The extreme heat warps people, just as the road surface warps and shimmers in the relentless glare of the sun. In parts of southern England, we hear that cars have become bogged down as tarmac turns to black treacle. The tracks on the railway expand, and the lives of those foolish enough to be travelling into work descend into chaos. As temperatures climb towards 40 degrees, or the mystical figure of 100 Fahrenheit, depending on your age, tourists are too stunned to remember that in this country people drive on the wrong side of the road. They step off the pavement without looking, making cycling hazardous. The crazies are more visible – shouting, snarling, waving their cans of Special Brew. Cowley Road is strangely empty, scoured by a hot, dry wind. It is the cooks from Nile Vallie Fast Food who sit on chairs on the pavement outside, still dressed in their aprons, tall, fine-looking African men searching the horizon for customers. 'BAGUETTE COUSCOUS CHICKEN RICE KEBAB,' they have chalked on their blackboard, hopefully.

The drunks from the churchyard of St Mary and St John have become increasingly voluble in the warm weather. Every evening they hold a drinking party; young and old are invited, the halt and the lame and the plain staring mad: the kind of crowd Jesus used to pull, from what we hear. Some of the women have children, toddlers who seem quite happy to play on the grass while their mothers drink and banter with their friends. Their dogs lollop among the gravestones. The drinkers either gather in a hollow under an ancient yew tree at one side of the graveyard or around the steps of a cross, erected in 1917 in memory of the Reverend Richard Meux Benson. Some, overcome with the beauty of the evening, lie on their backs with their heads on a grave. Occasionally they sit on the wall, as though surveying Cowley Road from their front porch. Benson was the force behind the construction of the Church of St Mary and St John, a process that began in 1875 but was painfully slow due to lack of funds. For nearly twenty years, the congregation met in a temporary structure on Stockmore Street, known as the Iron Church. Such buildings were constructed from kits supplied for overseas missions. 'The whole structure was about as primitive as it is possible to imagine,' wrote the photographer and local historian Henry Taunt, in a handwritten note preserved in Oxford Library, 'even to the plain deal benches with which the interior of both nave and aisle were filled. But how the church filled, plain as it was, there were seldom seats to be found vacant, and the hearty sermons, so different in those times from the great majority of churches, were enjoyed by many, but spoken against by a few who did not understand them.' Despite its evident popularity, the congregants complained that the structure leaked and that local youths delighted in throwing pebbles onto its roof during services so that they clattered down with a tremendous din, distracting the worshippers. The permanent church that replaced it is a series of compromises; the west tower replaces the tower and spire originally proposed by the architect. Benson had intended the interior to be richly carved and ornamented so that 'the whole building may speak of God's work in nature and in grace'; however, only a few details were completed.

Although it has a loyal congregation, it is no longer a question of standing room only in the imposing structure, its scale and monumentality speaking of the beliefs and certainties of a different age. I cycle through the graveyard every night on my way home from the station, and the drinkers allow me free passage. (One evening one of them lurches towards me and, in a joke with uncanny historical overtones, says, 'Don't you know this is a toll-gate, mate?') When two policemen cycle in on their new mountain bikes to remonstrate with them over the noise they are making, they explode into righteous indignation; I see the fear on the young constables' faces. One evening I notice that all except one of the drinkers are out in the sunshine. As I approach, I realise that the solitary figure remaining beneath the tree is not alone; a woman is bending over his lap, her hair obscuring her face, addressing his personal needs. He has removed his shirt, and his ivory back is incandescent with spots. I glide past, as discreetly as I can. This may be the closest his personal life comes to a private, intimate moment.

The following evening the graveyard is closed off with police tape. My wife tells me that she had driven down Divinity Road from a dental appointment earlier in the day, joining Cowley Road opposite the church, when a man had staggered out in front of the car with blood spurting out of his neck – 'like a fountain,' she said. A passer-by was trying to help him, but he was struggling, still intent on pursuing the man who had stabbed him, the drink rendering him insensible to the horrific flow of blood. Meanwhile, his companions emerged from the graveyard, shouting encouragement to the fighters as if they were at some chemically altered football match – a scene out of Bosch or a Romero film – the zombies from *Night of the Living Dead*, with the volume turned up.

II

Do certain spots have an aura that attracts drama or violence as others are reputed to allow access to a more spiritual plane? Six months after the stabbing at the junction of Divinity and Cowley roads, a twenty-year-old female student from Oxford Brookes is knocked down and killed by a police car that is answering an emergency call. A police notice appeals for witnesses to what it terms a 'serious incident.' Someone has scrawled on the notice 'THE POLICE DID IT.' Bouquets of flowers are tied to a lamp post outside the Londis supermarket. There is a feeling of outrage and sadness in the community. How could a car strike and kill someone at the junction of a residential side street and a main road, at the bottom of a fairly steep hill, if it was being driven responsibly? Gradually, the story changes. The girl was drunk and stepped out in front of the police car. How terrible for the driver, who was just doing his job. A nineteen-year-old woman of my acquaintance, who is known to be a bit of a 'party animal,' vows to give up drinking. 'It could have been me,' she says.

In London, on my way to work, I buy a copy of the *Big Issue* from my usual seller. I chose him as my vendor of choice because he hears voices. Often they say things to him about his customers as they approach, causing him to giggle or grimace at the moment he needs to make a sale, which makes life difficult for him. 'Oh all right, mate, you're a diamond,' he says as I come into focus; one of his regulars. He wants to find work as a film extra, he tells me. Perhaps he dreams of discovery and stardom, of a different kind of performance than the one he puts on outside the Tube station every morning. Today the magazine carries a story about pedestrians knocked down by police vehicles in London. A young black woman was killed in South London the year before, and initially the papers had run with the story, demanding an enquiry. Then it began to trickle out that the woman was a drug dealer who apparently walked among the traffic to sell her wares. Suddenly the story disappeared. Is this a pattern? When a pedestrian is killed by a police car, are their characters subsequently blackened in an effort to diminish the crime? Suddenly I feel ashamed at the way my attitude shifted when I heard that the student had been drinking. What would student life be without the occasional bout of excess? And since when did police cars become instruments of judgement, sparing upright citizens but weeding out the dissolute and degenerate from among us?

BLESSINGS AND TRIBULATION

I rejoiced with those who said to me, 'Let us go to the house of the Lord.' Our feet are standing in your gates, O Jerusalem.

PSALM 122:1–2

It is a baking, airless Sunday morning in August when I decide, for the first time in several years, to go to church. The assembly I am visiting meet in a prefabricated office building in a yard set back from the Cowley Road, opposite a petrol station. The congregation are arriving, in minibuses, cars, and on foot, as I make my way to its door. Many are attired in beautifully starched traditional African dress. A man in a maroon shirt edged with white embroidery around the neck and matching loose trousers is pushing his baby to church in a buggy. He walks without haste, impossibly elegant in the grimy urban surroundings, and when he notices me, he halts and indicates with a silent, open-palmed gesture that I should precede him with my bicycle. It is ten minutes before the starting time advertised on the sandwich board propped up on the pavement, but the courtyard is busy and the interior that I glimpse through the window already appears crammed with people. I prop my bicycle against a wall and hover uncertainly. A young West Indian man dressed in a smart blue shirt and tie, with his hair arranged in neat cornrows, approaches me and takes my hand in both of his. 'God bless you. Do you mind coming this way?' I am guided to the back door, which stands open. I had been hoping to enter unobserved and watch the proceedings from somewhere near the back, but it is not to be. Another tall, shy young man, his eyes modestly downcast, takes my hand. 'Welcome,' he says, softly. He is dressed in a buttoned-up, three-piece grey suit despite the sweltering heat, and guides me gently but firmly to a seat halfway along a row and near the front. When he has successfully deposited me, he turns towards the stage at the front of the hall, draws a clean white handkerchief from his pocket, and dabs the sweat from his brow. The ceiling is low, tiled in grey polystyrene; all the windows are open to try and catch whatever breeze may limp along the road and into the back yard that I glimpse across the rows of heads, where derelict garages with buckled, gaping doors stand empty in a savannah of scorched yellow grass. My eyes return to this landscape during the service. For some reason, it draws me; I want to be out there, hearing the leaves of the grass crackle underfoot and looking up at the cloudless sky.

The band is tuning up. Two bulky men in dark glasses wearing matching green African shirts are playing guitar and bass, respectively; they stand, shifting slightly from foot to foot, their instruments already slung around their necks, occasionally bending to fiddle with the levels on their amplifiers. The drummer adjusts the height of his stool, and a boy of around twelve years old takes up a position behind a set of congas. Ripples of sound float from the speakers as the guitarist allows his fingers to wander over the fret board. The boy responds with flurries of conga beats. More and more people are coming in, greeting friends and settling into their seats. The women of the choir file onto the stage, dressed in matching West African outfits, statuesque in their tall head-dresses. One of them detaches herself from her comrades and comes forward to the microphone to lead the worship.

The words of the first song speak of God being like a goldsmith, refining the human heart like gold, a biblical motif beloved of Job and the prophets Malachi and Zechariah. The worship in this predominantly African congregation is very different from the Afro-Caribbean Pentecostal church services with which I was once familiar. There, ancient standards like 'Amazing Grace' and 'The Old Rugged Cross' are continually renewed by astonishing feats of virtuosity from soloists; the mass choirs are a balancing act between tight control and spontaneity; and a contemporary edge is added by the younger members of the congregation who listen to the latest gospel CDs from America and eagerly import the best new songs into the church. Here there are no old eighteenth century London hymns, transported across the Atlantic and refashioned on the plantations; no gospel standards written in the storefront churches of Chicago in the 1930s. The songs are newly minted, mainly by British and American evangelistic movements of the last two decades. The singing is deep, rich, and heartfelt, but the emphasis is all on participation rather than performance.

Again and again, the simple chorus is repeated with hypnotic intensity. A man standing a few rows in front of me acts out the words, demonstrating his desire to surrender his being to a higher power with expressive gestures, his head tilted back as though engaged in a private dialogue with his creator. Then the woman who has been directing the proceedings halts the song with a raised hand. She leans on the Perspex pulpit, staring at the floor, as though listening. 'I feel that God is telling us that he wants all of our hearts,' she says. *Amen*, calls out a voice behind me. 'He doesn't want us to hold back. It is very easy for us to grow complacent as Christian people' – *yes* – 'and to see it as a Sunday thing. But our Christianity should be a way of life. Jesus is a way of life!' There is enthusiastic assent and the music resumes, with interludes of extempore prayer in which the whole congregation joins simultaneously and out loud, in the African manner. It is interrupted once again when a slight, middle-aged West Indian man dressed in a pale blue suit and with an engaging smile gets up on the stage. He is obviously one of the leaders of the church.

'That song we were singing when the sister was leading us in worship, about God being like a goldsmith – didn't the choir look good today, by the way? – I wonder if you know anything about makin' gold.' He smiles and looks around the room, appearing as relaxed as if he were at a small gathering of family friends. I get the feeling that he is speaking with the confidence of someone who has seen the inside of a manufacturing works. 'The goldsmith has to make the gold really 'ot, and then he take it off and skim off the impurities. If he look in' – he mimes bending over and looking into a vat taken from a furnace – 'and he still see impurities, he 'as to put it back on the fire. And that's not going to be very comfortable, is it?' *No.* 'That's not going to be very nice, is it? But that's the way you make gold pure. So don't complain when things get a little tough. Do you like being persecuted?' The congregation laugh. *No*, they answer. 'No, but you will be persecuted. You will get sick. You will have misfortune. God allows it to refine your heart. Amen?' *Amen.*

This is the message at the heart of this strand of Christianity, one that speaks powerfully to the disadvantaged. When life is going well, God is blessing you. When chaos breaks out and troubles threaten to overwhelm you, God is allowing the devil to afflict you to bring you closer to him. The Lord disciplines the one he loves, the Good Book tells us, as a father the son he delights in, while the devil prowls around like a roaring lion seeking whom to devour. This message is also present in Islam; after all, followers of the Prophet are also Children of the Book. Life is a succession of challenges, preparing Muslims for the life to come. 'We shall certainly test you with fear and hunger and the loss of goods or lives or the fruits of your toil,' instructs the Qur'an. 'But give encouragement to those who patiently persevere, and when calamity befalls them, say: "We Belong to Allah, and to Allah we will return . . ."' Fatima, a neighbour, had visited our house the previous week to explain her family troubles. She has a noble face of the kind made more so through the trials she has experienced, framed by a purple scarf wrapped loosely around her head and shoulders. 'I do not understand what is happening,' she says, 'but' – and she raised one arm, the hand bent back in a dancer's gesture, palm upwards – '*he* knows. God says we *must* hope. *Must* hope. He commands it. Whatever happens, he commands it.'

'But it must be difficult to hang on to this belief when things are so difficult,' I say.

'Yes,' she says, shaking her head sadly, her hands once more clasped in her lap, 'is difficult. Very difficult. But we must carry on, *innit*.'

Depending on your point of view, this is fatalism, faith, or a mechanism that prevents the human psyche crumbling under intense pressure. Probably all of these. In any case, it seems that her words, uttered softly in a back room in Oxford, lift the curtain that divides two great world cultures. That which separates us makes us the same.

Back in the church, they have shifted focus to financial blessing. Every week an entrepreneur among the congregation is invited to come up and tell their brothers and sisters about their business. In this way, it is hoped that other church members will be inspired to set up their own enterprises, supporting each other in any way they can. A young Ghanaian in a well-cut suit, with a quiet but confident manner, is given a rousing introduction. He explains that he has bought the rights to a telecommunications 'gateway' that will route calls from calling cards to West African countries. 'It has taken a long time and a lot of investment,' he tells us. 'There's a lot of politics involved. Sometimes in those countries, it's difficult to get things done.' He smiles and there is knowing laughter from some of the congregation. 'Every time you make a call to an African nation using one of those cards, your call is routed via many different countries. People complain about the quality. Now you will get 100 per cent clear calls, and we will get £5,000 a week from the traffic.' *Amen*, someone calls out. 'Now the big telecommunications companies want to route their calls through our gateway. The business could grow very big.' He returns to his seat amid applause, smiling modestly. The pastor bounds back onto the stage.

'It's good to have entrepreneurs in the church, isn't

it? They are as important as the leaders. It's good to hear when their businesses are going well. And when they are faithful men and women of God, they will tithe 10 per cent of their earnings, and that is good for the church!'

There are moments in any religious service, however welcoming, that separate the observer from the committed participant. When an announcement is made that the collection is about to be taken up, I realise uncomfortably that my pockets are empty. I had come on impulse, and it hadn't crossed my mind to bring money with me; I have to hand on the basket that is passed down the row without placing anything in it. To do him justice, the man taking up the collection does not register my want of generosity by a single flicker in his expression. While the baskets are travelling from hand to hand around the room, the choir perform a Kenyan song; a Kenyan from the congregation replaces the boy on the congas, and some of the ushers carrying the money to the front break into a dance. In West Africa I have seen the whole congregation in a tin-shanty church dance forward and throw their money into the basket, in the full expectation that tithing at least 10 per cent of their meagre income, however painful at the time, will result eventually in God's blessing. The same thinking is at work here, even if its expression is more muted, in tune with the reserved culture in which the church is planted.

The second awkward moment occurs when it becomes

clear that the congregation members are going to take Communion. They clearly have no problem with visitors joining them in this, the time within any Christian service that is most intensely loaded with meaning. Wars have been fought, friendships broken, and families divided over the interpretation of Jesus' command to 'do this in remembrance of me.' My forehead breaks out in a sweat of anxiety. On the one hand, I do not wish to offend by refusing the offered bread and wine. On the other, I have too much respect for the sincerity of their beliefs to partake just for the show of it. Perhaps if I had lived a life untouched by religion, I would find such dissembling easier. Like many of my nation, I was inoculated against Christianity at an early age by its lukewarm expression in the established church, and by hearing its precepts in the mouths of unsympathetic teachers and dubious politicians. However, if the ability to have a religious experience is carried within the genes, as some suppose, a Darwinian version of the doctrine of predestination, I had a predisposition to it. Just one example of this tendency was a Norwegian ancestor who traveled to North America in the nineteenth century to preach the gospel to the Native American population. The New World claimed the life of his wife, who died shortly after the birth of their first child, a little girl. On the long journey back across the Atlantic with his baby daughter, the ship encountered a storm. Emerging unobserved from his cabin, the pastor heard the crew attributing the storm to the 'bad luck' of having a baby on board, a situation they were planning to remedy by throwing her over the side. I owe my existence to the fact that he persuaded them otherwise.

I emerged from childhood a staunch atheist but found it harder to shake my background than I expected. For six months or so, I had a job washing dishes in a hospital kitchen. I worked with three women: one was a Muslim from Morocco, another a Greek Orthodox from Cyprus, and the third a Catholic from Northern Ireland. I was the only unbeliever in the place, and they were united in their horror at my shameful state; we used to have long, friendly arguments, our straight speaking somehow acceptable in the steamy half-light, while my hands peeled inside my rubber gloves from the scalding water. 'No God, Jim?' the Moroccan used to ask me, looking searchingly, mournfully in my face (her own was decorated by the fine blue lines of a traditional tattoo). 'No, none at all,' I would reply with certainty, tipping another load of metal containers into the sink with a crash.

It is strange the paths down which life can lead you. Like the elderly photographer on the bar stool in Frankfurt, I, too, experienced a time of existential despair in my twenties, caused by a combination of factors too tiresome to relate. The thing that kept me going, that literally got me up in the morning, was not Beckett, but black music. Anyone with more than a passing interest in the output of the great American soul labels of the 1960s and 1970s soon realises that all the best singers come out of the black church. What these voices have in common is an almost transcendental sense of yearning, a spiritual quality almost entirely missing from white popular music, even when they are singing about love of an entirely physical kind. Years later I came to recognise this as akin to what Roland Barthes, writing about Russian choirs, called 'the grain of the voice,' the combination of the singer, the language in which they sing, and their physical body. 'Listen to a Russian bass,' he writes. 'Something is there, manifest and stubborn (one hears only that), beyond (or before) the meaning of words, their form (the litany), the melisma and even the style of execution; something which is directly the cantor's body, brought to your ears in one and the same movement from deep down in the cavities, the muscles, the membranes, the cartilages and deep down in the Slavonic language, as though a single stain lined the inner flesh of the performer and the music he sings.' The language of the music I was listening to was not Russian, but a remarkable collision between African-American speech rhythms and the cadences of the King James Bible. Inevitably my interest had led me to the source of most African-American pop, to gospel music. I got to know the work of the great quartets with their magical names: the Swan Silvertones, the Soul Stirrers, the Mighty Clouds of Joy, the Pilgrim Travellers, the Spirit of Memphis Quartet, and the Dixie Hummingbirds; and the searing majesty of the female vocalists: Aretha

Franklin, Clara Ward, Shirley Caesar, Mahalia Jackson, Mavis Staples, Rosetta Tharpe.

For a time the joy, sorrow, ecstasy, and anguish embodied in these voices, and the faith they drew upon, seemed to offer some sort of answer to the problem of finding oneself alive on the planet, towards the end of humanity's tenancy upon it. I began playing guitar for a black gospel singer, often finding myself the only white musician in the venue; it was an entrance into a parallel culture, where groups can appear in packed halls in the heart of the city, yet not receive a mention in the mainstream media. It brought its own challenges. We would rehearse, but once on stage the singer might shout, to whoops from the audience, 'Let's have church,' and launch into any one of hundreds of songs the other musicians had at their fingertips after a lifetime spent in various Pentecostal denominations. I had to follow as best I could.

Predictably enough, encountering the reality of the human institutions that embody religious faith in our world led to disillusionment. At the same time, to listen to that music even today is to be reminded of a dimension to human experience seldom encapsulated in art or literature, that shapes the lives of countless millions around the world. Perhaps in the end it is as instructive to lose a religion as to find one; to do so is to realise that none of the things we think of as fundamental to our being are incapable of alteration. It is more likely to be the small things that endure: tastes, unconscious mannerisms, characteristic vocal inflexions that allow friends to say, after being out of touch for years, that we really haven't changed at all. 'Why do we not remember how many contradictions we find even in our own opinions,' writes Montaigne in the *Essays*, 'how many things we regarded yesterday as articles of faith that seem to us only fables today?' At odd times, perhaps in the middle of the night, we do remember, replaying the opinions and beliefs we held with such conviction in the past, and the sensation is not always a comfortable one. The sweat on the brow of the man apologetically edging his way through the crowd to stumble out onto the Cowley Road may not have been merely a symptom of social embarrassment, but of relief at escaping once again from such blazing certainty, into the half-lit world of doubt and difficulty that remains the habitat of that minority in our world who somehow survive without a God. Believers, I salute you; but the path of this pilgrimage cannot run backwards. My destination is elsewhere.

A GRAVEYARD REBORN

And smale foweles maken melodye,
That slepen al the nyght with open ye, –
So priketh hem Nature in hir coráges, –
Thanne longen folk to goon on pilgrimages

CHAUCER, 'Prologue,' *The Canterbury Tales*

Built as it is on the clay of Cowley Marsh, the soil of the graveyard at St Mary and St John shifts with changes in the levels of groundwater, so that its gravestones move over time, in places jutting out of the ground at crazy angles like gapped teeth. This – along with the trees that for many years were allowed to grow untended, the abundance of brambles, and the trailing ivy – gives it an air of antiquity far exceeding its real age. In certain weather conditions in winter, the ground emits a mist that hangs in ribbons between the gravestones, taking on a sulphuric tint under the street lights and causing children to divert from their accustomed route back from school.

The graveyard is home to a variety of wildlife. Chaucer's 'Prologue' speaks of the 'Smale foweles maken melodye

... that slepen al the nyght with open [e]ye.' The birds here do not wait for April to rouse pilgrim's hearts with their nocturnal song. I have heard them even in the depths of winter and after dark, as late as midnight, rehearsing their spring serenades sotto voce in their urban roosts. Male robins in particular, those most territorial of birds, are apparently tricked by the glow of artificial lights into treating the night hours as a perpetual semi-dawn. Grey squirrels thrive here, rats flicker among the gravestones, and pipistrelle bats fly in and out of the church tower in the summer months.

However, there is no denying that the graveyard has also been a sanctuary for less appealing activities, situated as it is conveniently near to the health centre, the pharmacy, and the off-licence. Over the years it has been much frequented by hard drug users, who went to ground like foxes in the brambles, creating leafy shooting galleries in the cover they provided. My daily trip between the graveyard gates has made me a witness to a transformation brought about by collaboration between various agencies and local volunteers. Initially soldiers were detailed to hack down the undergrowth, clearing the ground of thousands of used syringes. The wall along Leopold Street was lowered, to increase visibility. New paths were laid and lighting introduced to encourage the graveyard's use as a pedestrian route. Then conservation volunteers and members of the church congregation began the task of pruning healthy trees and felling dangerous ones, clearing ivy from the gravestones, and planting spring bulbs. By late April the path onto Magdalen Road is lined with bluebells. New signs announce that the graveyard is an alcohol-free zone; cans of beer are depicted struck through with red crosses, and a £500 fine is threatened for infringement.

There is one witness to all these changes, a familiar spirit of the graveyard who makes an appearance virtually every day. Roberta is a stocky woman of indeterminate years, her curly hair still dark; she comes every day with two bulging carrier bags to feed the birds and the squirrels, and to meditate on the passing of the afternoon. The graveyard is her garden, a place to sit and relax and observe nature. When I first noticed her, she was usually on her own or surrounded by the feral cats that left their lairs in the shrubbery to swirl around her ankles, their battered faces turned imploringly upwards in homage to their patron saint and only champion. For some reason, the cats disappeared; either they found another haunt with richer pickings, or they fell victim to a vermin extermination programme. Roberta did not remain alone for long. During the summer months, when the graveyard attracts alcoholics, it becomes apparent that Roberta is drawn to their society also. To start with, she is often on the fringes of their group, sitting quietly, head resting on her hand, and looking into the distance as they entertain each other with riotous drinkers' tales, their laughter ringing between the gravestones. Gradually her role seems to become more central, and it is often her voice I hear as I cycle past. Her presence is clearly not only tolerated but also welcomed.

One Saturday afternoon I am cycling my normal route and pause to read a new notice board that has been erected at the back of the church, announcing the times of work parties in the graveyard. A spry woman in her sixties approaches me, dressed in work boots, a woolly hat, and an anorak against the drizzle, her face lit up with a welcoming smile. 'Ah, there you are! Well, we're all ready to start. Thanks for coming along.' She doesn't seem at all put out to hear that I am not the person she is expecting but merely a passing stranger, and readily answers my questions about the progress of work in the graveyard.

She is particularly pleased that a wider section of the public is returning. 'We've recorded all the names on the graves and put them on a CD,' she explains. 'You can see it online. People are coming back to visit family graves and tend them; they were too frightened before.'

'Really?'

'Yes, they were too nervous to come and spend time here, because of the drinkers and so on.'

I explain that I have watched the changes in the grave-yard over the past five years or so, and compliment her on the work that has taken place. 'What,' I wonder, 'does Roberta think of all this?'

'Ah yes, Roberta. It's interesting. She has a kind of

maternal attitude to the alcoholics, and they claim that they come to the graveyard to look after her . . .'

'So it's a kind of symbiotic relationship?'

'Exactly.' Ruth looks distracted for a moment. 'She *will* feed the squirrels – I've told her that they aren't good for the bird life here, but it doesn't make any difference.'

'Where will the alcoholics go now that this is an alcohol-free zone?' I ask. 'After all, they are part of the community too . . .'

She furrows her brow. There's nothing judgemental in the tone of her reply, merely frustration at a problem unresolved. 'Of course. The problem is that all the shelters round here are dry shelters, so they can't get a place for the night. What's needed are some wet shelters so they can get off the street without stopping drinking . . .'

It is time to return to work. She tells me the dates of the next days when they are seeking volunteers, and I agree to return. I watch her stride off in search of the person she thought I was, my doppelganger perhaps, in the shadow of the dripping trees.

A few weeks later, I take her up on her invitation and report for duty on a work party, accompanied by my four-year-old son. Ruth isn't around, but the others seem pleased of our offer of help, although they are clearly a little nervous at having such a young child about the place. Syringes still lurk in the undergrowth, and we are given a pair of long-handled grips to pick up any we find and a yellow plastic sharps bag* from the city incinerator to place them in. We are assigned to stripping the ivy from the stump of a yew tree that has been cut back; the hope is that it will regenerate once it is liberated from the creeper's anaconda-like embrace. Equipped with secateurs, a hand-saw, and a wheelbarrow, we soon settle into a rhythm of work. I slice and saw my way through the tendrils, some of which are as thick as a man's arm, and my son, who stays on the path, uses the grips to pick up the clippings and put them in the barrow, a suitably absorbing task. After an hour or so, our job is done and we relax on a bench. A drinker, who has been sitting on the steps of the monument to Reverend Benson, stands up, drains his can, and tosses it onto the grass, before walking off unsteadily past the rubbish bin towards the gate, listing to the right like a man on board ship. The rest of the work party are in another corner of the ground, hidden by trees. I look up at the leaves of a silver birch that dance above us against the brilliant blue of the sky. For a moment this Cowley graveyard is Cofa's Glade once more.

---

*Sharps bag: garbage bag designated for disposal of dangerous needles.

FINDING A CLUE

On a summer's day on my journey into the city, I pick up a copy of a newspaper that someone has left on the train. I no longer buy a paper every morning; I rely on my wind-up radio to bring me news of the outside world, and I use my travelling time for reading, writing, or conversation. Or perhaps I'm just one of those people who goes through swing doors without pushing. In any case, I have a theory that the discarded newspaper often contains more interesting news than the one purchased in the normal way. I scan it, bearing in mind Louis Pasteur's dictum that 'Chance favours the prepared mind.' Or Jonathan Ames's even better observation, from his description, published in *Artforum*, of stumbling across a particular, very rare edition of Cervantes he was seeking in Strand Books in New York: 'Chance is sort of like a dog-whistle: it's only perceptible to those with special senses.' I have my own Strand Books story. At the end of May 2001, I walked down Broadway, on my way to Greene Street. I was researching the life of an American artist who had lived and worked in SoHo in the 1970s; my head was full of images of his work and the playful, punning language of the interviews he had left behind that I had read over and over again. I made a diversion into Strand, enticed by its tempting slogan: '*18 Miles of Books.*' I descended to the basement and walked straight to a rack containing some battered old exhibition catalogues and a couple of magazines. I picked one of the magazines up; it was an issue of *Artforum* from the early 1980s on the artist I was researching that included an article I had seen cited many times but had never managed to find. I had been in the store for five minutes. In a state of shock, I took it to the till, where I bought it for two dollars from a guy with dyed black hair falling over one eye who looked like he'd rather be rehearsing with his band.

'Do you have any more old art magazines like this?' I asked.

'We don't sell magazines; we're a bookstore,' he told me, and turned away.

Sure enough, the newspaper I pick up on the train contains three stories related to pilgrimage. The first is written by a correspondent who is covering Kumbh Mela, the vast Hindu religious festival that on this date is rendered especially auspicious by a particular conjunction of the planets. Nashik, in the state of Maharashtra, is one of the places where the nectar of immortality fell to earth, spilt from an overturned pitcher during a squabble between the gods and demons. Blowing conch shells and waving saffron flags, thousands of ash-smeared holy men, many of them naked, plunge into the Godavari River in Nashik as the religious festival recalling the story nears its peak. Such immersions during Kumbh Mela are said to wash away the sins accumulated over the previous eighty-eight lifetimes. Predictably, the offer of such benefits has been known to provoke stampedes among the vast crowds that gather along the riverbanks. Thirty-nine people died in a narrow alley in Nashik on 28 August 2003; six hundred were trampled and crushed to death at Hardvar in the 1980s; eight hundred were killed in Allahabad in 1954.

The second story concerns the trial of a 'people trafficker,' an Albanian gangster convicted of smuggling as many as twelve thousand illegal immigrants into Britain from Belgium over a two-year period. The scale of the operation is staggering; the man's human cargo has been the equivalent of the population of a small English town such as Selby in North Yorkshire or Sudbury in Suffolk. People 'looking for a better life' have been transported by speed-boat from Albania to Italy and then on by lorry or train to safe houses in Belgium, where they were concealed with or without the driver's consent in the back of trucks bound for Britain. The judge in his summing up told the court that the thirty-five-year-old 'businessman' had 'exploited the dreams of illegal immigrants to live in a land that to them was paved with gold.'

The third piece is little more than a caption

accompanying a photograph of Deandra Harris, a twenty-three-year-old black American soldier, kissing the ground at Hunter air base after returning from Iraq. Ironically, spreadeagled face-down on the tarmac, with her pack on her back and her helmet on, she looks as though she hasn't made it; just another American corpse in a car park somewhere, in a country invaded for reasons that still evade credible explanation. Riding the Tube train in London later that day, my eye is caught by an advertisement on the carriage wall. 'Live and Work in America! 55,000 visas to be given away by the American State Department,' it trumpets. Apparently the American Visa Lottery is 'open to people from most countries in the world . . . Ending soon. Enter Now!' The advertisement confirms a fundamental truth that governs the lives of today's global poor: membership of the most powerful country on earth depends on nothing more or less than a winning ticket. A phone number and website address follow. A few – those able to hear the dog-whistle of chance, perhaps – are summoned, their lives changed forever. I can't help but remember the judge's words when he spoke about those prepared to exploit the dreams of immigrants.

OF BATS AND MUTTON CURRY

Man is born to trouble, as the sparks fly upward.

JOB 5:7

A neighbour is explaining the labyrinthine troubles into which his family has sunk. His round face with its grey moustache, always ready with a greeting, wears an air of sorrow; the eyes behind his glasses are divided by a deep furrow and focused on a point in the far distance, as if awaiting deliverance. Casting around for something helpful to say, I make the mistake of suggesting that he approach a prominent figure in the Pakistani community for help. His face creases with pain, and he flicks away my words with his fingers. 'Oh please, please don't tell me that. I am knowing this man for more than thirty years,' he says dismissively. 'When I came to this country in the 1960s, he was telephone lineman. He was clearing nine pound a week – nobody asks how he is making so much money. Then he left this country and act as agent, bringing people in here. Then he came back and now he is big shot.'

'But isn't he from a high caste?' I ask, persisting in my folly. (I have recently read a book on the social structures of the Pakistani community, including a chapter on caste. As the saying goes, a little knowledge is a dangerous thing – to one's dignity.)

He doubles up with laughter. 'How many top people you see in this country, working like donkey? His name might be good. But it is inside, the heart that is important. Unless foundation is strong, you can't build, isn't it. Do you see any of his children lawyers or doctors? No. But they are driving expensive cars. How they get all that money? You telling me.'

It is a recurrent theme with him: the straight man can't get ahead. There are so many temptations around, with ready money available for helping those he endearingly terms 'asylum secrets' (he means asylum seekers) to enter and remain in the country, drugs to be traded and property deals to get involved with. Keeping one's children safe and on the straight and narrow is a full-time job. Several young women, or 'virgins' as he unambiguously calls them, have disappeared in recent months in the local Muslim community. As I understand it, some have undoubtedly run away of their own accord, to avoid arranged marriages or escape the restrictions of a family life that contrasts so strongly with that of their non-Asian school friends. Others may have fallen victim to more sinister forces, enticed away or kidnapped to be sold as brides, either in Britain or Pakistan. My neighbour suggests that the problem is larger than the authorities realise because many families are too ashamed to report their daughters missing. The moral code inherent to Islam combines with the deeply embedded traditions of rural societies from Pakistan and Kashmir to make it difficult for young women wanting a different way of life to find acceptance in their community. Once they have made the break, it is almost impossible for them to come back; they no longer have a place in the strictly demarcated social hierarchy. Despite all the trappings of modernity, some say that Pakistani society in certain British cities is more traditional than it is back home, frozen in time by its transportation across the world half a century ago. On the other hand, it is easy to forget the huge, comparatively recent, and arguably uncompleted revolution that has taken place in our own society with regard to the rights of women. Some of the attitudes expressed in the Muslim community that seem alien to the British way of life today – on morality, religious belief, and the conduct and deportment of daughters, for instance – would not have raised so many eyebrows in the working-class community in East Oxford in the 1950s.

I sit in the small back garden of my neighbour's house at a wooden table, eating mutton curry and rice, with a salad of chopped cucumber and onion. As always it is inordinately good. Often, when he has made a meal, the door-bell will ring and I will find him there with a plate of food. We reciprocate with figs from the tree in our garden, onions from our allotment, watermelon, or a box of mangoes from Cowley Road – it is disrespectful to hand back an empty plate. Food is both the thing that separates us and binds us together. Islamic regulations regarding halal make them suspicious of accepting cooked food from our kitchen. On the other hand, they are proud of their own traditions and pleased to share their food with us. On one occasion, we all crowd into the kitchen as our neighbour's wife teaches us the correct way to cook chappati. The secret lies in the way the dough is tossed in cupped hands before rolling; once the chappati has cooked in an iron skillet, it is thrown onto the open flame of the gas ring and turned quickly to char its edges, a skilled and potentially painful business. In return, their girls want to learn how to make pancakes. 'Stand back,' my wife says theatrically, making the most of the opportunity, before tossing her pancake almost to the ceiling and catching it neatly in the pan. The girls scream with excitement, and their father strikes his forehead with his hand, for once rendered speechless. 'I love to cooking!' he tells me, his face beaming. 'I like make big shopping, buy Coke for the kids, and cook. I not interested eating, just see my family eating. I swear to God, most times I cook, I haven't even tasted!' His face darkens.

'Not much I ask, is it, just to make cooking, have little good times with my family. I don't want big house, lot of money. But whenever I get something, it is snatch away.' We return to our discussion of his problems, in which my function is mainly to listen; like one of Job's friends, there is little I can practically do to help. 'What you think,' he often asks me. 'You a man been to some countries, you got children, you educated, not like me!' He laughs. 'What your opinion?' I struggle to find some comfort in the words of officials in British institutions, the workings of which are still a mystery to him after so many years' residence in the country. Not only can he not read; it emerges that he does not know his real age. 'I am sixty-four years old,' he said on one occasion, with a certain amount of self-importance.

'You can't be,' my wife told him with conviction. 'You look much younger.'

'It says so on my papers,' he insisted, but his own wife, giggling softly, explained that when he was asked his birth date, he had made one up, as it seemed to be required. Now it has entered the official record. It is refreshing to know someone who has added to their age, rather than trying to take years off it, as is more customary in Western culture.

The sounds of splashing water and excited voices drift across the garden as his children take a bath in the extension behind the kitchen. I like the fact that this time of day is called *evening*; as if light and darkness were sand in two ends of an hourglass, moving towards a brief equilibrium, an evening out, at twilight. The summer sky darkens over the cucumber patch, neglected since the onset of the difficulties that beleaguer the family, and the wheeling, screaming swifts are replaced by bats that flutter silently above our heads, the intricate calligraphy of their flight paths indecipherable as daylight fades and night pours into the gardens of East Oxford.

MARGARET'S STORY

Margaret has agreed that I, accompanied by my tape recorder, should visit her at home to ask some more questions. She lives in an Edwardian house next door to the one in which she was raised, a few feet from the road in which she played as a child during the Second World War. Apart from a few years spent in London as an art student, and a few more teaching in the north of England and South Africa, she has been here all her life. The room we sit in is dominated by paintings and books; at the back of the house is the small studio where she works on her drawings and the designs of the stained glass that is her favourite medium. Her voice on my tape is that of an educated woman, but it still has some of the inflexions and cadences of the neighbourhood she grew up in. It is an afternoon in early November. As we speak, the room grows darker and she does not rise to turn on the light. As the memories begin to flow, it is as if the present is fading and the distant scenes she summons up are becoming as real as anything happening outside the window.

'My father's family moved here from Jericho in North Oxford, in 1860 or thereabouts. My grandmother must have lived here a long time.' She walks over to peer at an embroidered sampler hanging on the wall. 'This is her "Our Father," that she did when she was twelve, in 1867. My mother was born on Cowley Road. I've got two different addresses. I've been going up to the record office up at St Luke's, going through things there. In 1891 my mother's family were living at 118 Cowley Road.

'My mother was born in 1892. Grandfather built a house with a friend in Bartlemas Lane around that time – I think she was born there. Number one wasn't built when he bought plots three and five. He made an orchard on plot three and built a house on five with his friend. Now plot three has been built on. My grandfather was a carpenter; he made a fretwork fence round the property. He died in the 1930s, but that fence was still standing until fairly recently, with a little wicket gate that let you down the side of the house and into the kitchen. Yes, he was a good craftsman. He made oak tables – that one in the bay there is one of his. He came here from Gloucestershire to work for a firm in Oxford.

'I don't know how long my grandmother's family lived here – I am still trying to find that out. They lived in Longwall. They didn't live on the front, which was the posh houses; they lived in little cottages round the back, which Teddy [St Edmund] Hall owned and later took down. The husband of a friend of mine was the architect of the improvement at Teddy Hall, and he found the kitchen where my mum used to sit – in the inglenook, with lovely old Dutch tiles – and he saved a Dutch tile and brought it to her and she remembered it.'

She hands me a local history book that has a cover featuring a sepia photograph of four young women on bicycles with the face of a man just visible over their shoulders. 'These are my mother's cousins that lived on Cowley Road. Their name was Streaks. Malcolm Graham put it on the cover of his book *Oxfordshire at Play*. John Streaks – his wife was my grandmother's sister, so she was a Williamson as well. They had four girls and then a boy.'

'Is the boy the one coming up behind?'

'No! No, the one behind is Harry Beckley; he married one of the sisters, you see.'

'So he was in pursuit!'

'He certainly was, and you can see his little face behind the four women in front. He was a chemist all my childhood on Cowley Road, I remember. He was a small man. I said to Malcolm Graham, this wasn't what you said in the book; it was my mother's cousins.'

When we begin talking, Margaret is hesitant, the flow interrupted by phrases like 'wait a minute,' 'hang on,' 'I should remember this . . .' As she gets into her stride, the stories roll out fluently, in an unbroken thread of recollections reaching right back to her early childhood.

'My father was born on Sydney Street. I'm not sure

which one, because they changed the numbers as they built more houses. The area round the far end of Magdalen Road was called Robin Hood in those days, because it was really rough, where my dad's family lived. He wasn't a ruffian, my dad, he wasn't that sort, but his brothers might have been . . .'

'The road must have changed tremendously since your family arrived.'

'Oh yes. All these buildings opposite here were built in the 1930s. These were fields along here, from the Regal Cinema, that's now the Bingo Hall, all the way along. Howard Street finished at Cricket Road. Before that, opposite the old bus garage – you can see it in one of Henry Taunt's photographs – there were sheep in the field there. This was a really rutted, muddy road down to Cowley. Earlier, I don't think this bit of the road was much. My son did some research for his architecture degree, and he thinks the Cowley Road came down as far as the shops and then at Southfield Road it launched off into this road – but the old road was Barracks Lane that runs along the back here, out towards Garsington.'

This is a bombshell: the road has been pulled from beneath my feet like a carpet. According to this theory, the original extent of Cowley Road would reach only as far as Bartlemas; this last section would be a recent addition, while the old road turns into a footpath and cycle track alongside the allotments. A mighty river transformed into a trickle in a ditch. Margaret is unaware of the impact of her revelation.

'The houses were built for workers coming to jobs in the car factory; the Regal Cinema was built to cater to them too. There was always a Saturday matinee for the kids.'

'Did you go along to those?'

'Oh no, we weren't allowed to. Looking back, we had quite a sheltered life. We did things together. We used to play out in the street when my mother was making tea or something like that. There were always buses on the road. We used to play games like jumping the shadows of the buses, because the lights were in the middle of the road then. You made games up to amuse yourself. On the way home, we used to play marbles all along the gutters. There were no cars. If you owned one, you were extraordinary. Even doctors didn't all own cars.'

To twenty-first-century ears, battered by the perpetual roar of traffic, this sounds idyllic. Life was not without its drama in the East Oxford of Margaret's childhood, however. Poverty and violence were never very far away.

'I can tell you all the houses where there were ghastly murders, just murders, and I didn't go out at night to see all the brawling. Fifty years ago there was a murder along here in a house that always seems to be up for sale. And there was a murder in Leopold Street. In most cases, the people ran out of the house and just dropped to the ground dead, and the police drew around the shapes of

the bodies on the pavement, so you could see them after-
wards; each day you walked down, there was the outline
of the body.'

'You are making East Oxford sound like Chicago in
the 1930s.'

'Yes! Then there was, years ago, my mother used to
tell me about this, there was a family where the wife
killed the husband and her children and then I think she
committed suicide. They were all buried together in the
corner of St. Mary and St. John churchyard. My mother
told me that they had the funeral – she was a small girl;
it was the 1890s – and her mother and grandmother and
everybody went. It was like a Jamaican funeral today,
where everybody turns up; she said that there were
hundreds of people there. It was a terrible tragedy. I
expect she had serious depression.'

These dark tales are swiftly forgotten as she walks
through the neighbourhood in her mind's eye as it was
sixty years ago, its inhabitants now mostly vanished.
She summons up the backstreets when they were full of
shops and small businesses, instead of vehicles parked
on the pavements; when they were places of work instead
of dormitories for exhausted commuters.

'One of my school friends lived in Howard Street with
her aunts and uncles, and the back garden was full of
rabbit hutches and chickens; some people had pigs. One
of my dad's cousins lived along there as well, and when
we went for our walks, he'd be leaning on his garden

gate, and Dad would have to stop and have a chat with him. If you went down Howard Street in those days, on the corner of Cricket Road was a shop, run by an elderly couple called Archer; the husband had a taxi, and the wife ran the shop. The next road on the right going through to the school, there was a general store run by a Mrs Mason . . . I can see her now; I can see 'em all. On the corner of Golden Road, on this side, was a fish-and-chip shop. The old man did all the work, and the old woman stood there and swore and served you. She used to push an old pram around with stuff in it, not kids – I don't know if it was stuff from her allotment or what.'

She pauses for a moment, leaning forward, as if looking into a bowl full to the brim of memories.

'Where that garage is now, next door was a little shop where they made dental repairs – you could go and get your teeth fixed. Further up was just the old slipper baths . . .' (In the days before bathrooms were added to the back of the terraced houses in the neighbourhood, locals used to walk to the bath house to wash, often in their slippers, carrying a towel and soap.) 'On the corner of Magdalen Road was a boot-mender's, Mr Giles, where I used to take all our boots and shoes to be repaired. There was a huge grocer's where the Goldfish Bowl is now. Then there was the Paramount Sewing Machine Shop, that only closed a few years back – I love haberdashery shops; they sold all the buttons and everything, wonderful. We did most of our shopping in those shops on the Cowley Road between Leopold Street and Randolph Street. The first shop was bread and cakes; the next was knitting, a wool shop, needlework, needles and pins, all those things. They also had sanitary towels there – I used to have to go and get my sanitary towels there, which embarrassed me no end. There was a confectioner's shop, newspapers, and a lending library . . . The lending library was in the middle of those shops, opposite the hospital. What else can I tell you? Oh yes, when I was a child, local people used to go with a jug with a cloth over it and get their beer from the pub. And you used to be able to get your Sunday roast or your big cake cooked at the baker's.'

Mention of the baker sets off another train of associations and family connections.

'Next door to the baker there was a side way down to an orchard, with a horse in it, a horse and cart. It was a funny little horse, more like a pony really, and the bloke that owned it was called Mr Bricknell; he was a farrier. On the other side was a cousin of my dad's, Harry Smith. They were right next door to the baker's, and their back yard was a builder's yard. There were two of them, Harry and Alf, Alfred – he was a one . . . He lived in Henley Street. The first house down is a funny house; it's long, double-fronted, but only one room deep. Their son went to be a chef at University College, and his specialty was cakes and icing and things like that. I know we were taken round one day to see his latest creation. It was put in the window of the front room, so you could see it from the street. He drank too much, and he died of cirrhosis or something; he must have had access to all that lovely food at the college.'

The city Margaret evokes can seem strikingly different from the one we inhabit today. It is a place in which a garden was not just somewhere to have a barbecue but a place to fatten a pig. In which backyards contained horses, and the public could be entertained by the sight of a cake in a window. Yet the depth of view she is able to apply allows her to see beyond the obvious changes that have taken place and notice those things that remain constant; the continuities that are part of the essential character of the area.

'People talk about the immigrants coming in, and I say that the only thing that's different is the colour of their skin – they are still doing the same things, trading, shopkeeping, working-class stuff that my relations did in Victorian times. When the Jamaicans first came over, they were all bus drivers and hospital helpers; we couldn't have done without them ... .'

Margaret's son comes home, and I decide it is time for me to leave. To remain ignorant of what happened before you were born is to remain always a child, Cicero maintained. (These scraps of ancient wisdom I have gleaned from the shelves of second-hand bookshops and market stalls, fragments of a broken, larger mirror I hold up to the present. My wanderings in books, like my wanderings down Cowley Road, have been intermittent

and undertaken without a compass, so that, like Robert
Burton, but with greater justification, I can confess
that 'I have read many books, but to little purpose, for
want of good method; I have confusedly tumbled over
diverse authors . . . with small profit for want of art, order,
memory, judgement.') If Cicero was right, is this then
adulthood at last; to walk home along Cowley Road,
with the present overlaid with the past, the pavements
populated by ghosts, and the traffic quietened by distant
echoes of children's games and horses' hooves?

A HIDDEN POOL

A stone's throw from the Eau-de-Vie Flotation Centre, another very different place of immersion exists, hidden from public view. I am alerted to its existence by an interview with Rabbi Eli Brackman and his wife, Frieda, published in the local paper. The article celebrates the building of the first Jewish *Mikvah*, or ritual bathing pool, in Oxford since the Middle Ages, paid for by subscription from the local Jewish community, at the Jewish Chabad House on Cowley Road. Orthodox Jewish women mark the end of the period of separation from their husbands dictated by their monthly cycle by bathing in a *Mikvah*, completely immersing themselves over their heads in water. A rain-water tank on the roof of the building is linked to a tank next to the pool to fulfil the necessary legal specifications. 'Some *Mikvahs* use spring-water, as it should be as natural as possible,' Mrs. Brackman explains to her interviewer. 'There will be a very small opening, so the tap water can touch the rain-water. The natural water then turns the tap water into a natural source of water.'

It seems I have stumbled on another miraculous, restorative bathing-place on the Cowley Road, its waters charged with properties that defy natural laws. Such things seem characteristic of the area. The Chabad House is situated in an ordinary-looking Edwardian building, its hand-painted sign, in English and Hebrew, faded and without a phone number or email address. I decide to write to Rabbi Brackman, explaining my interest and asking him to get in touch. As always, I worry that my curiosity will seem like an intrusion. I hand-write my letter and post it through the front door; in this electronic age, the gesture seems archaic, yet at the same time respectful. I think of it as planting a seed from which, if I am lucky, a story will grow.

It is some weeks before he calls. Meanwhile, I do some research into the Chabad, an offshoot of the Hasidic movement founded by Rabbi Yisrael Baal Shem Tov in the Ukraine in the eighteenth century. The youngest of Baal Shem Tov's disciples, Rabbi Shneur Zalman was the author of a key text that explained how the mind could be used in study and contemplation to arouse spiritual dedication in the heart. His emphasis on the importance of the intellect led to his followers being labelled Chabad, a Hebrew acronym of the first syllables of the words *Chochmah, Binah, Da'at* – wisdom, understanding, and knowledge. Understandably, the Chabad movement historically has had strong links with centres of education; present in Oxford since the 1960s, it ministers to

Jewish students at the university, as well as providing a centre to those in the local community who hold Orthodox beliefs.

Summer is turning to autumn the evening my son comes into the room and says, 'There's a rabbi on the phone for you, Dad.' Brackman's voice is friendly, curious, with a slight American inflexion. He is happy to answer my questions, and within a few days I find myself sitting across from him at a Formica-topped table in the Chabad House, sipping a pale pink soft drink. The room's décor is dominated by a framed photograph of the movement's most revered twentieth-century leader, Rabbi Menachem Mendel Schneerson, affectionately known as the Lubavitcher Rebbe, who died in 1994. A smallish, alert looking man, he gazes down at us from behind his impressive white beard, his eyes seeming to twinkle with amusement at a private joke. (His resemblance to the German-Jewish artist Gustav Metzger – inventor in the 1960s of auto-destructive art, who painted with sulphuric acid on nylon with spectacular results – has probably not often been remarked upon in Hasidic circles, but the likeness springs up unbidden from the visual database life has consigned to me, and there is nothing I can do about it.)

Over the next couple of hours, we have a wide-ranging discussion about the history of Hasidism, the historic relationship between Judaism, Christianity, and Islam, and the differing visions the world religions portray of the end-times. It is clear that Brackman is comfortable with debate and used to hard questions. Still a young man, perhaps in his early thirties, his international accent is the result of extensive travel in America and Eastern Europe. He sits in his shirtsleeves, occasionally twisting his beard between his fingers as he contemplates an answer, or leaning back and raising both hands to push them under his skull-cap so that it appears to levitate above the top of his head.

As befits the times we live in, and the location in which we find ourselves speaking, I begin by asking him for his reaction to the current debate about multiculturalism. The fact that we inhabit a moment in history when a small group of people born and raised in this country are so determined to destroy it that they are willing to take their own lives, along with those who happen to surround them at their moment of self-immolation, has led to much questioning in the media of the meaning and purpose of a multicultural society. The vision of a nation in which people of different origins are allowed to maintain their individual cultures and beliefs without interference from the state while living alongside people of radically different outlooks, and the belief that this plurality is something to celebrate, is under threat. It is proposed that everyone, whatever their origins or beliefs, should subscribe to an idea of Britishness, although it is hard to find anyone with a clear notion of what this should be.

'The key word now is to be tolerant,' Brackman suggests, 'but actually what people mean by the word is "I don't identify with you and I despise you, but I will tolerate you." Really, society needs to go a step further and look at people as equal, different but equal. It doesn't mean embracing somebody else's beliefs; I think maybe postmodernism goes too far in believing that everybody is correct, and that you are not allowed to believe that you have the truth – one can totally lose one's identity by believing that. Why shouldn't a person believe that they have the true belief? I think it is very helpful and makes them confident in who they are. At the same time, they should show understanding and interest and embrace other people – there is nothing wrong with considering oneself special.'

'Your own faith is not a proselytising faith, is it?'

'Certainly not and this makes Judaism very different from other major religions. Christianity and Islam historically have believed that unless you embrace their faith, you are not going to be redeemed and are going to go to hell, and they actively went out to proselytise, whereas Judaism believed you can be who you are, if you are upright and decent and a just person and believing in God, without necessarily becoming Jewish. On the contrary, we discourage people from becoming Jewish – although there are a lot of people interested in Judaism, from students to academics and local people, not necessarily wanting to embrace Judaism in their lives but just intrigued and fascinated by its teachings. It is such an ancient religion and its teachings are so rich – it is the source to Christianity and Islam. Many people are very interested, despite what is going on in the Middle East – or maybe because of it . . .'

'Isn't it true that Jews were largely tolerated under Islamic rule for many centuries, and perhaps treated better than by Christian rulers?'

'That is very interesting and 100 per cent true. When the Muslims came to Spain in 711, they permitted Jews to observe their faith, unlike the Visigothic Christians who preceded them. For centuries there was what is called the "Golden Age" of Jewry in Islamic Spain. However, in the twelfth century, the fanatical Almohad sect arose, which insisted on conversion to Islam and which brought Jewish life in Muslim Spain to an end. By contrast, in Christian Spain there was altogether a more pervasive attempt to force the Jews to convert to Christianity, culminating in the time of the Spanish Inquisition. Many Jews, especially those high up in government, had to conceal their identity and went into hiding; they would have secret cellars underground where they could practice Passover – the persecution was much more extreme.

'Generally Muslims were good to the Jews during the Ottoman Empire – although people now paint it as more rosy than it was. Islam says nothing about not being allowed to engage with other faiths – on the contrary, Jews and Muslims always got along. I like to be optimistic, but I think religion has gone through quite a crisis over the last few years and people are discovering true religion again. Sometimes religion has to go through a crisis to get back to its true roots: that faith is about believing in G-d and in good values and is mainly internalised within oneself. And Judaism is the only religion that has been consistent in that way. We do not try to proselytise; we do not look down on other faiths – on the contrary, they can have the same destiny of what we call paradise, if they live their life in a moral and just way and believe in G-d.'

I ask him to explain a little about the origins and definition of Hasidism.

'Because the teachings of the Torah are divine wisdom, because we are talking about something that is intrinsically divine, there is a lot that is not necessarily appreciated on the mundane level but needs to be understood on a deeper level; these are the esoteric teachings that are called Kabbala. The understanding of these teachings on a mystical level has always been available but only to a select few, going right back to Moses. What the Hasidic movement did was to tap into that spirituality and bring it to the surface, making it more available to the Jewish masses. It is not replacing any other law or tradition, but it is infusing Judaism with spirituality.'

'What made the Chabad different from other branches of Hasidic belief?'

'In a nutshell, the difference is in how to actualise the

vision of the founder of Hasidism, Baal Shem Tov. Some saw this as a developing vision which had to continue to evolve even after the passing away of his son, Dov Ber, and others saw it as static, something that should not be developed further. The question was, to what degree should the mystical teachings be made available to the Jewish masses? The Chabad position was to take the ethos of the founder of the movement very literally. He said that the Messianic era could only come about if these teachings, that he called the wellsprings, were brought forth to the outside world – only then could the world be brought to a state of absolute peace.'

He leans back, unable to resist an academic analogy.

'There is a similar debate in theoretical physics: you have some physicists who want to teach scientific theories in school to children or through popular science books, and you have other scientists who are just not happy with that – they don't like seeing science becoming a popular presentation on television or being watered down for the masses; they think it should be studied in the labs in a proper setting. This is a similar debate to the one that took place between these great rabbis. It is a legitimate debate. Should these profound spiritual teachings, that for many years were held under great secrecy, be taught to the masses, or should they be restricted to a perhaps growing circle and only allowed to enter society when understanding reaches a certain level? Chabad took the view, basing itself on the teachings of the founder of the

Hasidic movement, that times had changed and that these teachings should be taught to infuse world Jewry with a new sense of spirituality and enthusiasm.'

I ask him to tell me a little more about the *Mikvah*.

'It is performed in one of two ways – either in spring water or in rainwater. In Israel and certain other countries, there are springs where a woman can find a private area where she can be immersed. We are talking about complete immersion – water represents spirituality. In today's times a *Mikvah* speaks of luxury – there is no more going out to the river and finding a secluded area to immerse in not very clean water in the cold, as it used to be in Russia and those sort of places. The rainwater must be collected in a certain way, by the most natural method as it lands – it is then channelled down a pipe, and the pipe must be without any curves. Basically there are two tanks, the rainwater tank which cannot be refilled regularly because it depends on it raining enough to fill it, and next to it a pool of sparkling clean water with chemicals and so on. When the waters touch, the rainwater validates the pool water.'

I am intrigued by this 'validation' of one type of water by another, the chlorinated swimming pool water with the rainwater that has travelled down a pipe without any curves. Just as I ask him to explain, however, the telephone rings; Brackman just has time to tell me 'it is a legal requirement,' before he goes off to answer the call. He has already explained that Judaism is primarily a religion of practice rather than faith, based not on just ten, but 613 commandments, although some cannot be followed until such time as the temple is restored. I wonder at leading a life so proscribed in a century so obsessed with choice. It would, whatever else, give an extraordinary sense of continuity, of connection with generations past who have led the same life in different lands across the globe. When he returns, we speak of Jewish history, of persecution, of the changing attitude of the church to Jews, and of the rise of Islamic fundamentalism. 'I don't think Judaism has really changed over the centuries,' he tells me, 'unlike Christianity, which has changed so much from medieval times and the Crusades, the Spanish Inquisition through to modern times, it is almost non-recognisable, would you agree?' The Jewish community in Oxford has been a part of the city as long as the university itself. 'There was a Jewish presence here in medieval times; they had a synagogue and cemeteries, and with all the rivers around Oxford, they would have definitely had a *Mikvah*,' he tells me. 'So the building of a *Mikvah* in Oxford is the completing of a circle, the modern community mirroring the medieval community.'

We touch on the situation in Palestine and Israel. His faith does not allow him to evade the issue of possession of the land that both Jews and Palestinians believe is theirs by birthright. The original temple in Jerusalem will be rebuilt, he believes, notwithstanding the fact that a mosque is now situated on its site, and the whole of the law, as given in the Torah, reinstated. Despite the fact that, as he puts it, Israel needs friends, he is suspicious of the support of fundamentalist Christians of the type that are so vocal in North America, as he knows their support is based on the belief that a restored Israel will lead to the coming of a Christian Messiah. From the Jewish perspective, the Messiah must, by definition, uphold Jewish laws and tradition, and so cannot be a Christian.

'We don't believe that the Messiah is going to come to punish the wicked,' he explains. 'The Messiah will come to let people see the truth and be inspired to lead the good life. The Messiah is for the world, not just for the Jews – the coming of the Messiah would mean the world evolving into a peaceful world, with governments coming to the realisation that war is not the path to peace. If the world was at peace, poverty would disappear because countries would not spend billions of pounds on armaments. [The Jewish sage] Maimonides said that in the time of the Messiah there would be no jealousy. If people are not jealous, they will be content – if they are content, they will live in peace – if they live in peace, then people can focus on spirituality and living a good life. That is basically the vision of the Jewish Messianic era.'

The phone rings and our conversation is interrupted once more. I ponder Eli's description of this utopian future. I cannot help thinking of the barber I now visit on Cowley Road, whose home is in East Jerusalem. He doesn't take many holidays; he is always the one to cover for his colleagues. I suspect that going home gives rise to very mixed emotions for him; joy at seeing his family, coupled with a sense of hopelessness at the political situation and the condition of his people. When we talk politics, he speaks calmly, quietly, but the pain in his face is plain to see. I cannot help asking myself how a paradise can be built in a land surrounded by a concrete wall that separates farmers from their vineyards, their flocks from water, their countrymen from their ancestral homes. 'I think people of the faith should return to their faith and get out of politics,' Eli had told me earlier. He is a spiritual man, trying to remain true to the precepts of his religion and making as few judgements as he can on those who follow other beliefs. Unfortunately, the equating of physical territory with spiritual goals and ideas of nationhood is hardwired into the hearts of the three Abrahamic religions, as it is in their holy books. An essay I find on the main Chabad website (not, it goes without saying, the responsibility of Rabbi Brackman) equates the current wave of suicide bombers in Israel with the ancient enemies of the Children of Israel, the Amalek, described in Deuteronomy 25:17–19. 'Remember what Amalek did to you on the road, on your way out of Egypt. That he encountered you on the way and cut off those lagging in the rear, when you were tired and exhausted; he did not fear G-d. Therefore you must obliterate the memory of Amalek from under the heavens. Do not forget.' Torah commentaries point out that the numerical value of the Hebrew word Amalek is the same as that of *safek*, doubt. The attack can be both physical and intellectual, the writer of the article explains. Jews are enjoined by the Torah to wage war against Amalek, who comes in a different guise in every generation, to do everything in their power to destroy every last vestige of him from the face of the earth, and to keep alive the memory of what he has done to the Israelites. The appalling suffering endured by the Jewish people over the centuries has made this a resonant passage for many succeeding generations. However, if the writer is implying that in this generation Amalek has returned not only in the guise of the blood-soaked terrorist but also in the shape of all those who would question the current dispensation in Palestine, there seems little hope of a peaceful resolution. This is not returning to the faith and getting out of politics; it is returning politics to the heart of the faith. Thus the poetry and insight of the ancient texts are subverted to serve current political needs and ancient enmities are kept alive.

Perhaps dialogue is more possible far from the front line, where walls have not yet been built that prevent people from meeting on a daily basis. The Chabad House attracts visitors of many nationalities to Cowley Road. 'We have services on the weekend, and we have a packed house for dinner every Friday night,' Eli says. 'When the students aren't here, we have tourists who find their way to us; we have visiting academics, summer school students

– our main work is with the students – you could look around the room and find people from all over the world here, which actually reflects the Cowley Road quite well, which is interesting.' While Brackman confesses that his heart lies with the students at the university rather than in East Oxford, it is clear he has a certain affection for the area. 'I ride a bike; there's no point driving anywhere in the city. I do my shopping on Cowley Road. We put out an annual Jewish art calendar, and businesses on the Cowley Road promote it, including Muslim businesses. My car mechanic is a Sikh; we are very good friends, and he also sells my calendar – in fact, the calendar is probably the tool that brings the community together, which I really enjoy actually.'

A cycling rabbi shopping on the Cowley Road whose Muslim and Sikh neighbours advertise his calendar is some sort of symbol of hope in a world where hope is in short supply. His remarks remind me that it is these small interactions of trade and exchange that allow relationships to develop across cultural divides. The activities taking place along the road are largely old-fashioned ones that were common in the time preceding the electronic age we inhabit. Working in a shop or a small business not only provides a living; it also gives a person a visibility and status in the community, a way of relating to others based not on difference but on the things one has in common. My own experience of such employment comes from managing a map and guide shop in what was then an insalubrious district of London, where the immediate neighbours were a Greek tailor, a Spanish café, and a Hindu newsagent. Unlocking the padlock on the door in the morning as Giorgiou pulled up the shutters on his tailor's shop, crossing the road to get a cup of coffee and a paper, all the people I had contact with treated me as part of an extended family that was made up of the tradespeople of the locality. Cultural differences were rendered irrelevant through the rituals of our shared routine. This is the dynamic of the complex, pre-modern city street that is so abhorred by city planners. Of course, it is easy to sentimentalise. Small businesses of the traditional kind are disappearing everywhere as a result not only of higher rents and pressure from the property market but also because people now demand more financial return for the work they do. If I missed the sense of community that job gave me when I moved on, I didn't miss the wages. Yet as the city street changes, we should not be unaware of the further isolation and alienation that is the result.

THE LIQUID KINGDOM

Many and sundry are the means that philosophers and physicians have prescribed to exhilarate a sorrowful heart and to quiet those fixed and intent cares and meditations which in this malady so much offend; but in my judgement none so present, none so powerful, none so apposite as a cup of strong drink, mirth, music and merry company.

ROBERT BURTON, *The Anatomy of Melancholy*

Streets in a city have a different character at different times of day. Cowley Road changes as darkness falls from a shopping street into a place of entertainment. Most of the Asian grocers shut up shop for the night. Bouncers appear at the doorways of pubs. A queue appears, contained by metal barriers, outside the Zodiac. In a city that boasts two universities and a local population many of whom are as intent on the pursuit of pleasure as the students, there are an enormous number of people walking the street whose primary aim is to get as drunk as possible. It is as if the water-table, perilously high at all times in the area once known as Cowley Marsh, has risen, seeping through the ground; a road that during the day exists for the transaction of solid goods becomes one where units of liquid are the chief commodity.

Young girls in short skirts with straightened hair and bare legs crowd the pavements, leaning on each other for support, screaming with laughter, their exposed midriffs bulging over their waistbands like uncooked dough. They may be from an exclusive college or from the estates of Barton or Blackbird Leys; only their accents tell them apart as they call across the road to their friends. They exist here in a democracy of feverish expectation, camaraderie, competitiveness, scuffles at the bar, sticky-sweet alcoholic drinks, unpredictable, disappointing men, and vomit. It is safe to presume that if they have fairy wings attached to their shoulders or if their male companions are wearing Roman togas or a crude approximation of female dress, they are students. At certain dates in the calendar known only to themselves, they mark themselves out like this, dressing up in outlandish costumes and embarking on a voyage through the city fuelled by alcohol, seemingly oblivious of anything outside the magic circle of attention they lavish on each other, as they shout, stagger, kiss, and stumble their way down Cowley Road. Normally these bedraggled processions are just part of the micro-climate of the street, tolerated and ignored for the most part by those locals whose livelihoods do not depend on providing the catering for the mobile fiesta. To be dropped into this panorama of the paralytic unexpectedly, however, is to arrive on the surface of another planet.

One evening we come out of the Ultimate Picture Palace, where we have spent the past two hours, along with an audience of eight others, watching a film set in eighteenth-century Korea. (I know how many people were in the audience because I always count; it is part of an underlying anxiety I have about the survival of my favourite cinema, a place where films are played without any trailers, there is no popcorn on sale, and where the ancient seats smell of memories. It is also the only cinema I know where if you are standing in the street outside at the right moment, you will see the projectionist, a small man dressed in a dinner jacket, climb up a ladder on the outside of the building, push open a hatch, and take up position in his eyrie.) The film we had watched that evening was created from a series of extraordinary visual set pieces featuring elaborate costumes and endless ceremonial, with lust and cruelty ever-present beneath a surface like a highly polished mirror. In the closing scene, the tragic heroine commits suicide by walking in measured steps out across a frozen lake until the ice cracks beneath her and she slips silently beneath the black water. We are in a reverie as we mount our bikes to cycle home, but as we turn onto Cowley Road, we notice something is wrong. It is as if the earth has shifted on its axis while we were sitting in the darkness of the cinema, and we have emerged to find it tilting; the pedestrians on the pavements seem unable to move forward, but instead stagger sideways, laughing and cursing, like passengers on a pleasure boat caught in rough weather. Just to be amongst them is destabilising; disorientation can be catching. How many times, sitting in a stationary carriage, have I glanced through the window to see a train move away from the platform and imagined that I myself was moving? It is like that, riding a bicycle in a place where no one else is sober enough to walk straight – to regain your sense of equilibrium, you must keep your eyes fixed on the road ahead or you, too, will lose your sense of balance and round off the evening with a tarmac kiss. Welcome to the liquid kingdom.

THE GATEWAYS CLOSE

'Dad, are buildings made by people?' my son asks me one day.

'Of course they are,' I tell him. 'Who else do you think makes them?'

'Abdullah told me that God put them there,' he replies. Abdullah is his best friend, a couple of years older than he is, someone he looks up to, an authority on cars, computer games, and religious matters. On this occasion, he has sensed that his friend's opinion is questionable but has decided to check with me. For a short time, we discuss how a building is put together – he is a keen student of construction cranes and cement mixers, for instance, so on reflection he knows that buildings do not just appear by divine appointment – before he leaves to go about his business, satisfied. His question remains with me. Pre-industrial societies saw the natural landscape as symbolic of a creator's awesome power, inhabited by demigods and spirits, alternately inspiring and threatening. For Abdullah, who never leaves the city, the artificial urban environment is the only one he knows. He experiences it viscerally rather than conceptually, negotiating its pavements on his BMX bike, scaling walls, balancing on kerb-stones on his way to the corner shop, chaperoning his sisters to the park. For him, office blocks and houses replace the mountains and gorges beloved by Romantic painters; alleyways and streets, the song lines of the Australian Aboriginal or the pathways of the pilgrim.

In fact, most of us live our lives as if we agreed with this childlike view of the city. The urban environment constantly changes – often in ways we don't like – but we (and I include myself) act as though these changes were caused by some abstract force of nature, as beyond our control as the weather, rather than being the result of a series of decisions by people who often hold elected positions, decisions that can be questioned or opposed. Merely by not going away, by making a few calls and writing a couple of emails that become part of the public record, it appears that Marian and I are becoming a fully fledged thorn in the side of those running the consultation. At the same time, we are finding it hard to set up an opportunity for a dialogue with those in positions of real power. Finally we have a breakthrough. A councillor who has spoken enthusiastically to the local press of his vision to lure the tourist buses that patrol the centre of the city into East Oxford so that they can disgorge their cargo of cash-rich passengers for the benefit of local businesses has agreed to meet us in a pub on Cowley Road. We have encountered each other before, for he is the same man that proposed the dragon-shaped litter-bins at the ill-starred public meeting I had attended a few weeks previously. As we have arranged this rendezvous through a succession of emails, I am not entirely sure he is aware of my identity as his public opponent on that occasion, an uncertainty that serves to increase my nervous anticipation. He has given up one of his few free evenings to be with us, and therefore his partner, another local politician, will be joining us at the meeting; they are sticking to their plan of spending the evening together and eating out in one of the local restaurants.

If he is surprised to see me when he enters the pub, he hides it well. We begin, as is so often the case in such meetings, from a point at which we are divided by language. In the interview he had given to the local paper, he had used with enthusiasm the vocabulary that makes so many local residents uncomfortable, speaking of 'rebranding' the area to attract visitors. He, despite coming from the left of politics on many issues, has adopted the terminology of the advertising world when talking of urban planning. This is not surprising; such thinking has pervaded politics at every level. It is now enough to change the appearance of things – or even merely the way in which they are described – to win public approval and stimulate the gastric juices of consumers; real change begins when the public start spending money. In my efforts to explain my misgivings, I am acutely aware that I have no such pre-packaged set of terms or overriding belief system to help me explain my case. My argument is based in equal measure on urban theory and gut instinct, assembled piece-meal from the language of architects, artists, planners, novelists, anthropologists, topographers, and other students of the city. Fortunately Marian has a good grasp of the parlance of local politics and is the perfect foil for my somewhat obscure polemic, intervening each time our visitor's bafflement threatens to become total. Our manner is both serious and friendly. We are, we begin to realise as we find our rhythm, a fairly devastating double act, one that takes no prisoners. Furthermore, sitting together around a table in a neutral location rather than in the adversarial context of a public meeting, it gradually becomes apparent that our little group is not as irredeemably divided as we might have supposed. None of us want to see the area slip further into recession. Marian and I are not, like Victorian romantics, merely drawn to the picturesque; neither are we tourists – we have no interest in living among ruins.

Our new friend has listened to the local traders' tales of woe; he knows that once a big new shopping centre in the heart of the city opens in a couple of years' time, trade on Cowley Road is forecast to decrease even further and more business closures are predicted. He is committed to trying to find ways of combating this trend; our disagreements are merely over how this can be achieved. For his part, he seems to hear for the first time the force of our arguments against the gateways. It had not been his intention to package the road in any crass, commercial way, he assures us, merely to make it more attractive, to brighten it up a little. His desire is not to make it more like everywhere else but to enhance its individuality. One of his constituents has suggested putting carved and painted totem poles at either end of the road; would we object to that idea? Yes, to his surprise, we would. He listens politely to our reasons and seems to accept them. When we part, we have his assurance that we have won the argument with regard to the gateways as far as he is concerned; he will withdraw his support for the idea at whatever power-broking forum it is that he attends. After months of frustration, it takes a minute or two for the impact of his words to sink in. We part with warm handshakes all round.

As Marian and I gather our possessions and make our way to the door, our faces frozen in polite smiles, we remain silent, as though fearful that any more words might shatter this fragile moment of accord into a thousand pieces. Once outside we walk a few yards and then slap palms, whoop for joy. I can see us now in my mind's eye, floating down the road in a bubble of hilarity and relief, a flickering mental image like a home movie of life from some lost era, when the shape of the future could be decided over a glass of beer in a pub on the Cowley Road.

OF ROBOTS, WILD RHUBARB, AND
THE NEW OXFORD WAY

We affirm that the world's magnificence has been enriched by a new beauty: the beauty of speed. A racing car whose hood is adorned with great pipes, like serpents of explosive breath – a roaring car that seems to ride on grapeshot is more beautiful than the *Victory of Samothrace*.

F. T. MARINETTI, 'The Futurist Manifesto,' in *Le Figaro*, 20 February 1909

I arrive at the car factory, the final destination on my pilgrimage, on a chill, misty Friday evening at the end of March. Looking back down the Cowley Road towards my starting point, I see that the sun is sinking, swollen to twice its size in a glowing ball of vapours, like a planet in an alien solar system. Has my journey been one from the medievalism of the old city, lost this evening in a golden haze, to modernity? From the life of the mind to the brash new world of intoxicating speed and foreshortened perspectives that so excited the Futurists, a century ago? Arguably nothing has done more to shape the modern world than the automobile. This site, where cars have been built for close to a hundred years, has drawn workers to the area from across the globe, creating a second city alongside the first, giving rise to the witticism during the car industry's heyday that Oxford was merely a settlement on Cowley's left bank.

William Richard Morris, later Lord Nuffield, the founder of the car industry in Oxford, was himself a working-class Oxford boy who came to live as a teenager in a terraced house a few streets from my home. The story of how he left Cowley School aged fourteen to be apprenticed to a bicycle maker and how within a year he was making his own bicycles behind his parents' terraced house is well known, as is his progression to manufacturing motorbikes and eventually assembling cars. What is perhaps less often commented on is that at one time his grandfather Richard Pether, along with his great-uncle, held the tenancy of Bartlemas Farm, the land that hundreds of years before had been worked by inmates of the leper hospital. This piece of information, stumbled upon by chance in the parish records, resonates in my mind. The more I think about it, the more it seems to pull a taut thread through the historical scope of our narrative, drawing the centuries tightly together so that past and present overlap, each adding its patina to the other.

The famous Bullnose Morris, that was to overtake the Model T Ford as Britain's most popular car in the early years of the twentieth century, began production at Cowley in 1912, laying the foundations of Morris's fabulous fortune. His masterstroke was to decide early on that, unlike Henry Ford, he was not interested in manufacturing cars, but only in assembling them. Other factories, including the Oxford-based Osberton Radiators and Pressed Steel, provided the parts that were put together at his factory in Cowley using the revolutionary new conveyor-belt system of production. Although he swiftly earned a reputation as England's most munificent philanthropist, Morris's workforce did not always benefit from his generosity. He was passionately anti-union, a paternalist and a 'divide and rule' man to his bones. Over the years he endowed the university and local hospitals with huge donations, changing the face of the city forever, even building a substantial church on Cowley Road where his workers could give thanks for their good fortune. He was not above making political donations; in 1931 he gave £50,000 to Oswald Mosley's New Party, the forerunner of the British Union of Fascists.

Within the factory gates, twelve- or fourteen-hour shifts were common; at the same time, when orders were scarce, workers could be laid off, sometimes for an entire summer, without pay. Wages were based on 'piecework,' set at different rates for different employees, fostering greed and division. This arrangement, common to the Oxford factories supplying Morris Motors and the foundation of the wages structure in the wider British car industry, meant that if a machine broke down, employees ceased earning until it was repaired. Before the development of health and safety legislation, men often tried to fix a jammed machine themselves to avoid waiting for the repair crews to arrive, leading to horrific injuries. While both safety conditions and wages undoubtedly improved as time passed, relations between management and the workforce did not necessarily follow the same pattern; the legacy created in the early years seems to have been passed down to the businesses that succeeded Morris Motors at Cowley; BMC (British Motor Corporation), British Leyland, and Rover. By the 1960s, the works had a reputation as the most militant factory within the industry.

Shortly after coming to live in Oxford, I passed the factory as the shifts changed. The gates swung open, and in an instant the road was filled with hundreds of men on bicycles dressed in identical overalls, riding a dozen abreast at their own pace and serenely blocking the traffic, a scene more reminiscent of Communist China than a university town in southern England. This sight, so long a feature of this part of the city, has disappeared as suddenly and silently as the factories, pitheads, and shipyards that fell into disuse across the country in the recessions of the eighties and nineties; another example of modernity erasing itself.

Bicycles were the flash-point of one of the many disputes that characterised the Cowley Works from its beginnings. In one typically petty gesture, the factory management refused to provide sheds for the thousands of workers' bicycles that lay in rusting piles outside, triggering one of countless stand-offs. It is hardly surprising that on occasion the workforce took it into their own hands to gain compensation. A friend who was employed as a builder on site at the works in the 1970s doubles up with laughter as he recounts the story of a shift worker who was constructing a car at home piece by piece from parts he was stealing from the factory, an ambition as seemingly impossible as those wagers where a man sets out to eat an automobile. He was doggedly determined, however, and left work at the end of each shift with another part taped to his body beneath his clothes. When the authorities got wind of his project, they stopped him one evening as he rode out of the gates on his bicycle. On that particular day, he was so heavy that when he came to a halt, he simply toppled sideways and had to be helped back to his feet.

I hear another story that conveys something of the atmosphere of the factory in the old days while visiting a well-known artist in his studio in the East End of London to discuss a publishing project. He asks me where I live. When I mention East Oxford, he asks, 'Cowley? I like Cowley.' In the 1960s as a student, he tells me, he spent one summer working at the car factory. On his first shift, his foreman explained to him that he had to 'make himself scarce' for two hours in the middle of each day.

He asked where he was meant to go. 'Go to the toilet,' he was told. So he would pass the summer afternoons in the factory toilet, with the window open, reading. His studiousness didn't go unnoticed. One day he was called over by the foreman again. 'What the fuck have you been doing?' he was asked. 'Well, you told me to go to the toilet for two hours in the middle of the day,' the budding artist replied. 'Yes, but I didn't tell you to read a fucking book,' said the foreman with disgust.

Industrial relations under the current regime are very different. I am here to take the tour offered by the site's new owners, the German car manufacturer BMW. It took an overseas buyer to see the potential in the site, dogged for so long by disputes and falling productivity, and to recognise that there was a future in one of the most recognisably British designs the Oxford car industry ever produced. In the public mind, the Mini was inextricably linked with the Swinging Sixties and with the classic British heist movie *The Italian Job*, with sharp-suited gangsters with cockney accents, leggy models in mini-skirts, and mop-topped youths in psychedelic jackets. By the 1990s its appeal had worn thin. The strategists at BMW, however, recognised that the market for small cars in the congested cities of the future could only expand – the Mini's brand needed refreshing, that was all. A Hollywood remake of *The Italian Job* was the perfect product placement opportunity, backed up by quirky, individual advertising, designed to create an instant, artificial 'cult status' for the product. The works at Cowley were deconstructed from the inside out, fitted with the latest technology and ergonomic, worker-friendly assembly lines. A completely new basis for employment called NOW (the New Oxford Way) was agreed with the unions to avoid any possibility of a recurrence of the 'British disease,' the factor that most often scared off inward investment from overseas.

I arrive a little late, parking my low-status, nondescript vehicle in the large car-park at Gate 7, as instructed. I have to admit that I have never been too interested in cars, at least since I was too old to play with them on the kitchen floor, and have always spent the least I could get away with on four-wheeled transport. I would have arrived tonight on a bicycle if I hadn't been running behind schedule. My lack of auto credentials marks me out from the dozen or so others who are taking the tour, enthusiasts all. One man is a life-long Mini owner, who finds his current model, a diesel, 'too sluggish around town' and is on the five-month waiting list for a lemon-yellow cabriolet. A couple from Doncaster have driven down for the weekend and haven't even found a hotel yet but have rushed straight to the factory to join the tour. Two elderly Australians are contemplating purchasing a Mini back home and are looking around this evening rather in the manner of diners at a fish restaurant selecting their meal from a tank.

Jack, who is to be our guide, first came to work at

Cowley as a fifteen-year-old in 1962, becoming one of six hundred tool makers in the tool room. At that time the works employed 28,000 people and extended for 250 acres. Although he can be persuaded to reminisce about his days at the factory in times past, I never hear a note of nostalgia in his voice. Under his instructions, we all don orange and black protective jackets and take a pair of goggles and a headset with a receiving device so that we can hear his commentary above the din of the factory floor. After watching a DVD about the paint shop, a place the size of twelve full-scale football pitches and too toxic for us to visit, we board a bus to begin the tour. Jack points out the crèche for employees' children aged between six months and five years old as we drive past – 'at five they're old enough to start spraying Minis,' he jokes – and a new quality-control centre, part of the £100 million further investment BMW is making in the site. Within a few minutes we arrive at the body shop, a building covering an area a quarter of a mile square, still known by its old name of Body and White after the white colour of the steel formerly used in car manufacture. Here Jack tells us to each take a pink earplug from a dispenser to muffle the ear not already protected by our headset ('Too late for me, unfortunately,' he says nonchalantly), before we enter the factory proper.

We pass through a couple of doors and climb up to an observation platform manned by a single quality inspector with a large computer screen who nods to us indifferently. Workers – or, as they are called in the language of the New Oxford Way, *Associates* – are vastly outnumbered by machines in this building. Below us, the orange KUKA robots are at work. A pair of robot arms operate now independently, as one picks up a panel and the other measures its thickness to the nearest micro-millimetre, and now together, as they shoot an electric charge between their claw-like fingers, sending a plume of sparks far into the air. The delicacy of the operations they perform and the balletic elegance with which they accomplish them makes it almost impossible not to see them as sentient beings. The language used to describe their constituent parts compounds this illusion: Jack points out wrists, arms, elephant trunk cables. Surely, I think, as I watch their unceasing activity, whoever programmed their movements has allowed a little of their aesthetic sensibility to creep in, adding an Italian waiter's flourish here or a pause in a movement there, to increase the dramatic effect of a gesture.

But, of course, this response from the human brain confronted by a creation complex beyond its imagining is probably involuntary, the same one that in other contexts leads to theories of 'intelligent design.' There is no denying that watching the machines at work amid the noise, the puffs of smoke, and the columns of shooting sparks that fall and scatter at our feet gives rise to feelings of awe, probably as intense as those felt by visitors to a nineteenth-century steel foundry. I feel a surge of enthusiasm for the sheer ingenuity of humankind, a marvelling at the technical accomplishment I see all around me, despite the fact that it is dedicated to the production of an object that is doing so much to destroy our world. I can only echo the 'Futurist Manifesto'; the noise, scale, and visual drama of this spectacle make it at least as enthralling as most exhibitions of contemporary art. This *is* the future that modernism promised; one in which mankind is set free from manual labour by machines to pursue a life of leisure – although its prophets were probably thinking of something a little different from a life on the dole on the estates of Blackbird Leys. There is a voyeuristic quality to observing the machines at work from our vantage point above the factory floor. I am reminded of an old black-and-white movie in which a group of travellers come to the edge of a cliff and look down on a hidden valley to see it browsed by dinosaurs long presumed extinct. Except here the dinosaurs are at the centre of our civilisation rather than in some remote Shangri-la, and they have taken over.

'How long do you think it takes to make a Mini?' Jack asks the group, his voice remote and tinny through our headsets. 'Twenty-four hours, that's right. And how long did it used to take, in the old factory? Twenty-four hours as well. But there used to be two thousand people on a shift in the old body shop; there's only two hundred Associates in this building today.' He tells us that work at the plant is organised in two eleven-hour shifts, with the remaining two hours out of twenty-four set aside for running repairs to the robots and other machinery. We walk through to another building, where we watch the hemming press add rubber seals to car roofs. The man operating the press gestures to Jack, who goes over to him. 'All right,' he tells us when he returns, 'Giovanni is going to put a sun-roof through the press for you to watch.' We stand, dutifully attentive, as the robot arm and the massive press complete the manoeuvre, clearly one Giovanni feels is of particular technical accomplishment, signalling our appreciation when it is over with gestures before we move on. This is the only time that anyone working on the line acknowledges our presence or noticeably alters their behaviour because of it, although they all seem to know Jack, who greets man after man with a few words or a cheery wave. 'See him?' he asks, pointing to an older man working on the line. 'He was a tinsmith by trade. That one over there was a panel beater. We had a few ex-tradesmen in the old days, but nowadays they are mainly trained on the job. Mind your backs!' He pushes us out the way as a young man on a forklift truck drives up the central aisle. Jack watches him manoeuvre his vehicle through a narrow space appreciatively. 'He was on my team. He left school at sixteen but did all his training, his GNVQs.* He's a very good worker.' Like game

---

*General National Vocational Qualifications.

on a reserve, Associates have learnt to get on with their daily tasks and ignore their gawping observers. It is all part of the transparency of the New Oxford Way, typified by the large windows at the corner of the plant through which the assembly line is visible to onlookers outside. 'Those are the Windows on the World,' Jack tells us as we pass them, 'so that wives can check that their husbands are at work!* We do have problems with the cars driving past on the ring road bunching up to have a look, though, and then not all accelerating again at the same speed,' and he chuckles to himself.

Once in the assembly room, I am again astonished by the degree of coordination that keeps the factory running, turning out six hundred Minis a day, year in, year out. Here the cars advance down an assembly line, each one a different colour with a different combination of fittings, wheels, and electrical gadgetry reflecting the choices made by the individual customer who has ordered it. At one point on the line, each car is matched with the dashboard that has been assembled for it at a factory a hundred miles away in the Midlands. The dash takes less than thirty seconds for three men to fit into place. Jack explains that it isn't paid for until it has been fitted; if the bar code on the dash doesn't match the one

---

*It is not only wives who keep the workers under surveillance. Some of those now employed on short-term contracts or through agencies complain that in this way their rights have been eroded and that they are liable to summary dismissal for minor misdemeanours.

on the car and the line has to be stopped, the supplier is liable to a charge of ten thousand pounds a minute. This is how the new world order works, with risk pushed back onto the supplier. Parts are coming to the factory from sixteen sources in Europe, and the Minis' engines are made in Japan and Brazil. We come to another point on the line where a car's electric cabling is pulled through its body. Again, each wiring loom is different, packaged in individual blue bags in a factory in Romania, delivered in plastic trolleys to the line in the correct order, bar coded to make sure they reach the right car. There are hundreds of different combinations. 'You see that lady there, with a clipboard,' Jack says. We notice a small, dark-haired woman walking among the cars, making notes and checking the progress of the workers. 'She's an auditor from Romania. It's worth their while to have her living here permanently, checking the work, to make sure there's no mistakes. She loves it here.'

She is one of many thousands who have made the journey to this site over the years. Between the two world wars, the population of Oxford virtually doubled; much of this increase was the result of migration to the car factories from the recession-stricken regions of Britain. The South Wales coal fields had been particularly hard-hit by the collapse of foreign markets for Welsh coal in the 1920s and the increased use of fuel oil in the shipping industry. Visitors to the pit villages sent on a fact-finding mission from Oxford brought back shocking reports of communities where starvation and tuberculosis were common. Many of those who left the valleys in search of employment did so on foot or by bicycle. One of those who made the pilgrimage to the car plant at Oxford was Arthur Exell, who told his life story in a history journal, copies of which I found in the city library.* His account makes light of the 125-mile walk he undertook. 'A contingent of the National Hunger March went from Pontypridd [in 1929] and I went with them,' he remembered. 'I was fit, if hungry, and my only worry was my mother, who cried her eyes out when I left. When we got to Oxford they put us up in the Corn Exchange and people brought us soup . . . I was about 18. I didn't know a soul in Oxford and I was lucky enough to get digs with a Mr and Mrs Sawyer up the Cowley Road. It wasn't easy to get digs. In the first place the women found I was Welsh and told me to leave. The Oxford people didn't like the Welsh because [we] were undercutting the English . . . The hatred . . . against the Welsh was terrible.'† This antipathy was increased, as it so often is, by the way the new arrivals clung to friends and relatives from home and to familiar activities that further emphasised the differences between them and

---

*Arthur Exell, *Morris Motors in the 1930s, Parts I & II*, in *History Workshop: A Journal of Socialist Historians*, issue 6 (Autumn 1978) and issue 7 (Spring 1979).

†In recent years a kind of reverse pilgrimage was undertaken by descendants of the Welsh workers who came to the city on foot; a walk retracing their ancestors' steps was staged from Oxford back to Wales.

the native population. They had their own music – they were liable to burst into song after a few pints – and their own religion, as they were all strictly 'chapel,' worshipping at the Congregational Church in Temple Cowley. At the end of the 1920s, a group of Welsh workers who drank, and sang, in the Cape of Good Hope pub at the head of Cowley Road, the same establishment that was later to adopt Munch's *Scream* as its emblem, founded a Welsh voice choir. It started as an octet and was known among its members informally as 'the Party.' After a few months, they were invited to rehearse at the Congregational Church hall; by 1931 they had grown in size and become the Oxford Welsh Prize Glee Singers, although at that time there were no glee songs or Welsh language songs in their repertoire. Soon they were performing at social events all over the country, from social clubs and village halls to the Welsh National Eisteddfod. They are still performing over seventy-five years later.

Certain villages in Wales supplied a disproportionately large part of the incoming population, with migrants relying on each other for help in finding work and accommodation, exactly in the way that the Pakistani *birārdari* system was to operate thirty years later. To men who had been down the mines, work in the car industry seemed light. Arthur found a position at Osberton Radiators, one of the main suppliers of parts to the car factory. He lodged with a friend and then moved with him into a tent, sleeping out the year-round down by the river, the two young men living out a Huck Finn fantasy that must have contrasted strangely with the rest of their working lives. (From the train I still occasionally glimpse campfires flickering in the copses along the river in the evening and shelters made from tarpaulins stretched between the branches of the trees, homes to those who as yet have no permanent place in the city.)

Arthur found Oxford people cold and politically apathetic. Most of the original employees in the industry were ex–farm workers, used to extremely low wages, or college servants, with no experience of activism or trades union membership, schooled in a culture of deference. Arthur became a member of 'the Party' (a communist, rather than a chorister) but managed to avoid losing his job over it, unlike many others. The infusion that took place in the 1930s and 1940s of highly politicised workers and activists from Wales, London, and the industrial heartlands of the Midlands and the north transformed industrial relations in the Oxford industry, gradually winning workers' representation and better conditions.

Before long, Arthur found his eighteen-year-old brother a job at Osberton Radiators, but he watched his progress with mixed feelings. In the press shop in the 1930s, the sheets of metal that had to be lifted in and out of the press were slick with oil and had edges like razor blades, claiming many fingers, even hands and arms.

At Osberton Radiators and perhaps even more so at Pressed Steel, the noise of the presses, the trip hammers, and the clatter of sheet metal being dragged through the workshops on hand trucks was literally deafening. Other health risks the workers faced included being blinded by flying metal splinters, asbestosis, and lead poisoning. An inspection in 1930 discovered that only seventeen of the thirty-six machines at Pressed Steel had the legally required safety guards. 'He hadn't done that sort of work before – he was only eighteen at the time – and I could have cried when I saw him coming home,' Arthur writes in his memoir. 'There were blisters on his hands, all across. The blisters stood right up where he'd [been] picking up this metal and putting it in the press. That's what they had to do, a hundred every hour, nearly two a minute. And that's how you'd go, all day.'

Arthur himself followed the pattern of many immigrants by courting and eventually marrying a local girl. Accommodation for young couples was scarce. The landlord of the rooms they found made them promise there would be no children; in fact, Arthur's bride was already pregnant, and although their landlord was seduced by the baby when she arrived, they knew they needed to find a place of their own. Little provision had been made for the thousands of workers who had moved to Oxford during the inter-war years. In 1933 work began on a new estate of houses adjoining Cowley Road, built on land formerly known as Pether's Farm, further evidence of William Morris's family ties with the land connected to the old leper hospital. Previous applications to develop this site had always been turned down on the grounds that it was too marshy and prone to flooding to be suitable, but the new developer, Fred Moss, sat on Oxford City Council and was able to push through approval for his scheme. He shipped in Welsh workers who were prepared to work for a shilling a day, and building took place at great speed. The estate was named Florence Park; indeed, at the centre of the estate there was an enclosed and entirely new park, presented to the city by the grateful Moss and named in memory of his sister. Promotion for the estate was aimed squarely at clients like Arthur and his wife. A handbill of the period describes the new 650-house development as 'One of the Finest Estates in Southern England. Seven Types to Choose From. Early Application Essential. Book NOW.' The bill certainly made it sound attractive. 'Very Healthy Site Overlooking the City,' it continues. 'Hundreds of Satisfied Tenants. Come and Join Them. Why Stay in Rooms?' Why, indeed, they must have thought in their cramped quarters. The local press was enthusiastic. The *Oxford Monthly* seems to have swallowed Moss's publicity whole, describing Florence Park as 'the only estate in Oxford building houses to let at rentals to suit the working classes as well as the others. It will have a magnificent main avenue 10 feet wide and a 24 foot carriageway with a 30 foot grass verge on the edge of the road leading to Florence Park (Councillor Moss's gift to Oxford) . . .'

Arthur and his wife put their names down for a house at a rent of seventeen shillings and sixpence a week – a not inconsiderable amount and an interesting comparison with the wages of the men who built it. On the day they moved in, there was a torrential downpour and the cart they had hired to transport their belongings became mired in the unpaved road; their furniture had to be carried through the rain to its final destination by hand. The young couple soon found that not everything was as it should be in their new accommodation. The estate flooded regularly, and no one could shut their front doors, as the wood of the door-jambs swelled. 'One day I saw the concrete floor crack and a type of wild rhubarb come up,' Arthur recalls in his memoir. 'Another day when the chain [of the toilet] was pulled, the cistern came off the wall. Most people had that complaint. And then when we had some heavy rain, the water rushed down the back garden straight through the back door, rising to a depth of six inches and out through the front door. It made my wife ill.'

Arthur discovered, along with fellow workers who had rented on the estate, that complaints at the estate office were futile, as the promised improvements never materialised. However, the management of the estate had not reckoned on the tradition of workers' organisation that some of the residents brought with them. Oxford in the 1930s was a hotbed of political activism. The local Communist Party along with the wider Labour movement were fighting for workers' representation in the car industry. During one unbearably hot night in 1934, women employees on the night shift at the Pressed Steel factory joined with the mainly Welsh male workers in staging a walk-out after their wages were docked, beginning one of the most historic strikes in the British Labour movement. With no unions or shop stewards in the factory to bring their grievances to the management, the women played a vital role in both initiating and maintaining the strike. 'The Girls Are Game – Are You?' read a banner held by one of a group of women picketing the factory gates. Their laughing, excited faces are captured in a black and white photograph reproduced on the cover of a pamphlet produced by the TGWU* on the seventy-fifth anniversary of the strike. Four of the sixteen members of the strike committee were women. One of their demands, radical for its day, was that women should receive equal pay for equal work. The local branch of the Communist Party invited a London-based activist, Abe Lazarus, to come to the city and help them shore up the strike. Lazarus was a fiery and charismatic speaker who could stand on a chair and galvanise an audience of hundreds with no need of a microphone. The strike lasted six weeks; by the time

---

*Transport and General Workers Union.

it ended, the American-owned company, in danger of losing lucrative contracts to its competitors, was forced to concede union recognition (although equal pay for women mysteriously disappeared from the settlement). Other employers within the industry had little choice but to follow suit.

After this victory Lazarus stood as a Communist for the Cowley ward on the Oxford City Council, polling a thousand votes, only two hundred less than the Labour candidate, shocking the political establishment to the core. It was against this background that the residents of the Florence Park estate, encouraged by Lazarus, decided to organise themselves into a Residents Association. After a series of rowdy and impassioned meetings and fruitless negotiations with the estate management, they decided the only course of action was to go on a rent strike; their rents were paid into a bank account to be held until such time as they got satisfaction from their landlord. An issue of *The Florence Park Rent Book*, an informal publication issued by the strikers dated 9 June 1935, has a cartoon at its masthead. On the left there is a sketch of a castle with the caption 'BUILT 934 AD AND STILL GOING STRONG.' On the right are a group of Florence Park–style houses, their walls comically skewed, with the caption 'BUILT 1934 AD AND STILL GOING WRONG.' The editorial features the views of the residents of the estate, whose description of it is very different to the picture painted in the handbill or the *Oxford Monthly* article.

'For these houses, *which are scarcely better than condemned slums*,' one wrote, 'we have to pay rent which is in no case less than 13/6 a week as well as rates (including the rates for six months before the houses were built) in addition to doing our own repairs.'

A delegation was sent to the House of Commons to meet with the housing minister and lay out their demands. The minister was sufficiently impressed to commission an architect's report on the estate from a Mr F. Skinner, who noted that although the building had been undertaken on marshy ground, he could find no evidence of land drains having been laid. 'It is surprising to an architect,' he wrote, 'that a city with such fine architectural traditions as Oxford should have left the housing of a section of its working class population to speculative private enterprise, which has resulted in the erection of these jerry-built houses.' Strong words, but not strong enough to challenge the power base of Alderman Moss or the bias of the judiciary of those days towards the property owner; the eviction of those on rent strike was upheld in the courts.

It is hard to believe today, walking the quiet streets of the estate, that such bitter struggles took place on this soil. The ground-springs of Cowley Marsh have been tamed, and the houses in what is now a sought-after suburb bear evidence of their occupiers' individual tastes; a stroll through the estate reveals individual examples personalised with carriage lights, wooden wagon-wheels, satellite dishes, leaded windows, hanging baskets, gravelled forecourts, privet hedges, rustic porches, and Venetian blinds. The park today is full of mature trees, including an avenue of horse-chestnuts beneath the branches of which in summer the light has a cool, subaquatic luminosity. The band-stand, made of the same brick as the houses of the estate, has not seen a band for many years, but the playground is always busy. The ornamental main gates of the park, facing onto what the *Oxford Monthly* termed the 'magnificent main avenue' of the estate, bear plaques that commemorate its presentation to the city by Councillor F. E. Moss. Above the inscription is the coat of arms of the city of Oxford, with its Latin motto: *Fortis est Veritas* – Strong is the Truth. Whether it was truth or strength of another kind that upheld the rent strikers' eviction in the courts, the park survives today as a haven from the din and clamour of the assembly line and the busy streets of the city.

Back in the factory, we have reached the end of the tour. The cars roll off the end of the line, highly polished, gleaming like scarab beetles. We stand and watch as the Associates whose job it is to start them up for the first time and drive them out of the building get behind the driving wheels. 'They don't always start,' Jack tells us. 'It's human error mostly. By the end of an eleven-hour shift, you're so tired you don't know what you're doing. You see those over there' – he points to a pair of wheeled jacks standing by the wall – 'they're so that if we have to move a Mini that doesn't start, we can do it cleanly. The last thing you want is to have three sets of hand prints all over your brand-new car.' Right on cue a car fails to start. Its driver is swiftly joined by two other Associates who, despite Jack's words, push it by hand off the line and round the corner to where it can be attended to. Jack shrugs. 'Ah well,' he says with a wry grin, 'you can take a horse to water . . .'

THINGS FALL APART

An Ending of Sorts

Whenever a thing changes and alters its nature, at that moment comes the death of what it was before.

LUCRETIUS, QUOTED BY MONTAIGNE IN *The Essays*

I always knew my journey would be intermittent, my progress interrupted by the demands of daily life. The account of my wanderings has ended up more akin to time-lapse photography than a chronological documentary. There have been weeks and months when other duties have kept me from pursuing my quest. For long periods I have spent more time either *anticipating* or *remembering* my journey than actually making it. Given these ellipses, it is logical to expect the object of my attention to have changed, even as I observed it. Even so, I am surprised by the rate of mutation all around me as the Cowley Road shrugs off its skin and long-established landmarks disappear. Returning, I feel like a scientist whose eye has wandered from the microscope only to find that the specimen on his slide has changed while his gaze was elsewhere.

Edvard Munch's painting *The Scream*, for some years past the gatekeeper of the Cowley Road, has relinquished its position high on the wall outside the Pub, spirited away to appear somewhere else in the world as an ashtray or a key ring. The hostelry itself has emerged from behind scaffolding in new, tasteful colours and to everyone's surprise has reverted to its ancient title of the Cape of Good Hope. It is a strange sensation; the starting point of my journey has disappeared as if a ladder had been drawn up behind me. The graveyard at St Mary and St John now boasts freshly painted notices about its wildlife and the location of historically interesting graves. As part of a countywide exercise, gravestones that are leaning beyond a certain angle are marked with red-and-white tape, so that their dangerous asymmetry can be corrected at a later date and the dead marshalled into better order. The congregation of drinkers still meet beneath the trees, seemingly unfazed by the changes taking place in their back garden or the signage forbidding them from consuming alcohol. In a distressing incident, one of their number dies while being arrested by the police; the graveyard is sealed off and a tent erected on the spot where the struggle took place, flood-lit twenty-four hours a day while an investigation takes place trying to establish the cause of death. Within a few days it is gone, and the dead man's erstwhile companions are back, raising a can to his memory perhaps.

The Russian Fairytale supermarket has changed hands to reemerge as the Baltic Food Centre, as its former proprietor pursues her dream to become a travel agent. Blackwell Publishers have moved their offices, along with the literary ghosts that haunted them, to a new industrial estate near the BMW factory. Nile Vallie Fast Food has disappeared, replaced by an upmarket café-bar, its fittings designed to attract the young professionals who have moved into the area. As one business fails, another opens. I am walking down the Cowley Road one day in the pouring rain when my eye is attracted by a new bright yellow shop-front on the site of a long-closed confectioner's. 'Jordan's Fish House and Tropical Grocery,' its signage reads. I cross over the road to peer through the window; the door opens and a young Ghanaian man pops his head out of the door. 'Come in! Come in!' he calls to me. 'This is a new shop! Have a look! We just opened yesterday.' Inside he shows me his selection of fresh fish laid out on a bed of ice on a small table; barracuda, herring, sardines, red snapper, tilapia, fresh tuna. Around the walls are baskets of plantains, yams, cassava, and sweet potatoes, and the shelves bear other delicacies: palm oil, fufu flour, white sifted maize meal, and bottles of Alafia Bitters, Baba Roots Herbal Drink, and Sweet and Dandy Mauby Syrup. With enthusiasm he explains his vision for the new business. 'I am a chef, actually. If the public allows, I will give people advice on how to cook the fish, even season the fish for them so they can just take it home and grill it. This will be good for the students because I hear they don't like to cook too much. They can pop it on the barbecue! I have been to Tesco and the covered market to check the prices and see what is available.'

Elsewhere on the road, halal fast-food outlets with names like Chicken Cottage, King Kebbabish, and the Kebab Kid have appeared, replacing restaurants serving more complex cuisine, changing the street's olfactory map for those who navigate by their noses (the reek of hot oil replacing the pungent odours of cardamom and coriander); the stark white fluorescence of their interiors generates pools of intense activity on the late-night pavements. The pavements themselves have changed, thanks to the redevelopment programme, from undulating tarmac the colour of spilt Guinness, to pale orange paving, punctuated with wooden posts outside the flood-lit temple that is Tesco. Set into their surface at intervals, the brass ingots proposed by artist Liam Curtin gleam, unnoticed by many, but leading those who choose to follow on a trail through the neighborhood. The images upon them have been selected by local people and refer to the history and character of the area. Controversially, the symbol chosen for the ingot placed at the entrance to the graveyard was a hypodermic syringe. Overnight and without consultation, it was removed by council workers acting under orders from above, provoking an intense debate about public art and democracy.

For the whole of one summer, construction works tip the road into constant snarling gridlock before it can emerge in its new dandified clothes, the end result of all the discussions and protests, the meetings and the stand-offs that have taken place during the consultation process. At various points the thoroughfare has been narrowed, forcing the traffic into single file. Bus drivers have been instructed not to try and overtake cyclists at these points; on occasion they still draw up close behind those on two wheels, breathing hot diesel breath on the back of their necks, jerking forward threateningly with a hissing of air brakes and the occasional frustrated blast on the horn. All the changes have not made the road feel much safer; the new twenty-mile-an-hour speed limit and the reprogramming of the traffic signals means that the BMWs with blacked-out windows, vibrating with self-importance, lurch pointlessly from light to light, puffing smoke. The original character of the road as a pathway through a marsh reasserts itself after heavy rainfall, despite all the cosmetic changes that have taken place at surface level; water accumulates in barely discernible inclines, and the enhanced pedestrianised space outside Tesco becomes a murky pool. Meanwhile, the pinkish light reflected from the new paving changes the ambience in a way that is almost subliminal, but not quite, creating a rose-tinted glow at ankle level reminiscent of a thousand pedestrianised city centres up and down the land.

It is perfectly true that many, including those with a far greater stake in the road than I, who run businesses along its length welcome these changes. It is hard to set oneself against the economic imperative, when those on the other side of the argument can claim that their jobs and livelihood depend upon it. However, economic regeneration projects do not always directly benefit those who are already trading in the location affected. Sometimes outmoded businesses have to be cleared out of the way and new ones attracted to the remodelled neighbourhood before money begins to flow. It is notable that some of those most vociferous in their support when such schemes are first mooted subsequently find themselves in opposition when rents rise and they discover that they are being priced out, not part of the master plan, after all.

I recognise that the shifts in the neighbourhood's visual character that I have chronicled, which seem so dramatic to a relatively recent arrival such as myself, are just another stage in an ongoing process. There is no more logic in freezing the frame now, or at a point six months ago, than there would have been thirty years past, when the city end of the street was dominated by junk shops and the old workhouse buildings still stood in their final incarnation as a geriatric hospital, their bleak profile attracting film-makers seeking locations to stand in for an Eastern European city-scape. My worry is that the changes, gradual at first and now moving at an extraordinary speed, have reached a tipping point. As Claude Lévi-Strauss wrote in *Tristes Tropiques*, 'Humanity has taken to monoculture, once and for all, and is preparing to produce civilisation in bulk, as if it were sugar-beet. The same dish is to be served to us every day.' The melancholy that afflicted the French anthropologist as he travelled the world searching for a people untouched by Western civilisation, returning, as he put it, with just a handful of ashes, can afflict the traveller in his own country, observing the rolling out of 'retail concepts' that suffocate the earth with an impermeable skin of similitude. The buildings that surround us are not so much frozen music, as somebody once said, but frozen thought; and the thought on display in the malls and arcades that form the labyrinth of contemporary urban experience is of such devastating banality as to constitute an assault on the psyche.

I have often asked myself on my journey, when I became mired in arguments about seemingly insignificant details in the appearance of the local environment, the question that might also have been nagging at my reader: Does it really matter? Are these things worth worrying about when my country is at war and the world is being torn apart by rapacious greed and ancient historical antipathies? Gradually I have come to think that these conflicts are not unconnected. In the days following the American invasion of Iraq, I heard an interview on the radio with a US Marine sergeant. When he was asked about the apparent (and unexpected) hostility of Iraqi citizens to the arrival of the liberating army, his answer was to keep repeating: 'We're gonna show them a better way of life; we're gonna show them a better way of life.' His firm belief was that with time, the glories of American culture would be sufficient to melt all opposition; that Coke, cars, Hollywood, and consumer desire would achieve what the tanks could not. Once Iraqis were eating the same food, watching the same movies, wearing the same trainers, and living surrounded by the same shopping malls as Americans, peace would reign in the global hegemony one writer misguidedly termed 'the end of history.'

With unholy synchronicity, as the wraps come off the newly buffed streetscape, news of rent rises arrive on the mats of the road's small businesses, many of whom claim they will be forced out of business if they do not manage to win a reprieve. They advertise their plight with posters in the windows of their shops and stage a protest march to the city centre. A prominent city councillor goes on record in the press with his reaction. 'I find it odd traders should be asking for a reduction in rent when they have got themselves a greatly improved road,' he tells reporters. 'The whole point about roads is that from time to time we have got to repair them. The idea we should reduce their rents because of disruption I find laughable.' Meanwhile, an informant tells me that a well-known American food chain has made an enquiry about the empty offices of Blackwell Publishers, their interest a sign that the changes in the neighbourhood are having the expected effect.

I am reminded of the illustration that the artist Robert Smithson employed to demonstrate the concept of entropy. Imagine a sandpit half-filled with white sand and half-filled with black sand, he suggested. Get some children to run around it in a clockwise direction and the sand will begin to turn grey. If you then ask them to run anti-clockwise, the sand will not separate out again into its distinct colours but become more mixed than before. You are stuck with grey. Grey is what you get when the chains move in, however bright their window displays or deep their discounts. The drunks and derelicts that still make the street their home in the face of these advances begin to look like heroes. Like the Arctic polar bear, they find their natural territory melting beneath their feet; as their habitat is eroded and they are forced to move from their traditional hunting grounds onto space usually occupied by others, their behaviour becomes more erratic and unpredictable. I do not wish to glorify their situation. Alcoholism, mental illness, and drug addiction are vicious afflictions; furthermore, it is no fun taking your child to the park to find the climbing frame occupied by slumbering boozers and the swings splashed with vomit. Still, even ugliness can be beautiful when it is the last bastion of defence against mediocrity's encroaching tide.

The built environment is not the only thing subject to change. My Pakistani neighbour has decided that enough is enough, and after four or so decades he is taking his family back to Kashmir to live. They make one exploratory visit and are in Kashmir at the time of the earthquake, much to our concern, as we watch news footage of the devastation in England. Their village is virtually unscathed; a minaret collapses, resulting in a mere three deaths. On their return, they bring news from another world; the earthquake, they suggest, was probably the result of the fast of Ramadan being announced at the wrong time. The date of the beginning of the fast is determined by the visibility of the full moon at Mecca, and imams in Kashmir have issued the wrong instructions, resulting in divine wrath. What is more, the calamity was foretold. They recount a story printed in the newspaper in the region of Kashmir to which they are returning to live. A woman in a rural village, it reports, gave birth to a creature that was neither human nor animal, an abomination so strange that its parents decided to kill it. Just as the father was about to strike the fatal blow, the creature spoke, asking him to stay his hand and prophesying the disasters that would befall Pakistan unless her people returned to the path of true Islam. This and other stories – related in a local accent by a teenage girl whose kohl-ringed eyes are enormous with drama, as her mother and little brother listen, nodding their heads – seem to open up a gulf between us that will become physically embodied once they fly to their new home.

My copy of the *Anatomy*, a reprint published by William Tegg and Company of Cheapside in 1857 and printed by McCorquodale and Company, announces it has come to the end of its journey by splitting apart down the spine from top to bottom, somewhere around the middle of the Second Partition. The binding comes away, revealing the recycled pages from another book that have been used in its manufacture. Idly I piece together the fragments of paper, guessing at the missing words, summoning up a few foreshortened lines from this vanished work. I shouldn't have been surprised to find that even here there was no escape from the themes that have possessed me over the preceding months. 'It is both interesting and disgusting to observe the penitents arrive [at their] destination,' the unknown author has written, apparently observing pilgrims at a shrine to the Madonna del Arco. 'Crawling along on their hands and knees, screaming forth their importunate supplications [that] are rendered almost inarticulate by the swollen and inflamed state of their tongues and their throats, their [faces] hideously masked by dirt and dust. But this is one side of the picture; all the realities of life have [taught me that] the gloomy-minded dwell in the shade, the gay-hearted in the bright sunshine.'

This book began as a record of a pilgrimage. Somewhere along the line I got diverted, drawn into local wars I came across on the way. It is not the first time this has happened to a pilgrim. Wes had told me that while the pilgrimage texts he studied start out by being about the journey itself, once narrated they swiftly become something else. The stages of the journey, he explained, the encounters one has on the way, all become part of an initiatory process in the account that pilgrims make of their travels. Like Wes's sixteenth-century mendicant friars, I met a man carrying an axe in the forest; while his shape remained indefinite, his intentions were clear, and in some small way, perhaps my friends and I helped to thwart them. Our resistance, though disorganised and intermittent, seems to have held back the tide, at least temporarily. Whatever the other changes that have taken place, no gateways have yet been built to the Cowley Road.

And what about the pilgrim himself? Have I been changed by my journey, the observer acted on by the observed, in the reverse of the usual dictum? Or to put it another way, has the initiation taken effect? It is true I feel more connected with the place in which I live. Marcus Aurelius in his *Meditations* compared the isolated man to a severed hand or foot, or a head lying apart from the body. 'Yet here is the beautiful thought,' he writes; 'that it still lies in your own power to reunite yourself. No other part

of creation has been so favoured by God with permission
to come together again, after once being sundered and
divided.' Having been behind the façade of its shop-
fronts and businesses, visited its places of worship, and
floated in its waters, I will never view the road in the same
way again. The voices I collected, the details of the lives,
beliefs, and personal endeavours the people of Cowley
Road have been generous enough to share, have given
me a glimpse of the complexity of the plural society that
surrounds us, built up from elements of many cultures.
To put it simply, this is what I love about the moment
in history I inhabit. I remain confident that from it will
flow – despite the problems we currently face – new
literature, poetry, music, wisdom, and commerce, as well
as a whole stream of difficult questions and challenges
to be addressed in the new century.

The travelling companions who have accompanied
me on my journey – both living and dead, in the flesh
and on the page – have been built into the fabric of my
life. My frequent departures have made me appreciate
returning all the more. After all, unlike the refugees
who cry out in the night, gripped by nightmares on the
Cowley Road, I have a place of safety to return to. Wes
told me that the pilgrimage narratives he studied rarely
included an account of the pilgrim's homecoming. In
the rare exceptions to this rule, the question explored
was whether the pilgrims would be recognised by those
they'd left behind, so changed were they by their journey

– emaciated, bearded, with a look in their eye that set them apart from their fellows. I, in contrast, was never gone for long. My family was forced to live the journey with me, sharing in its highs and lows, its moments of elation and frustration. As Lucretius wrote in words both unsentimental and profound, words that never found their way into the *Anatomy* despite Burton's many citations from the Roman author, and that by their very absence give a clue perhaps as to why he never managed to wholly escape the clutches of the black humour: 'Over and above this, love is built up bit by bit by mere usage. Nothing can resist the continually repeated impact of a blow, however light, as you see drops of water falling on one spot at long last wear through a stone.'

Given the pace of change the neighbourhood is now subject to, I have not rushed to correct the misinformation that time has implanted in my text. In a sense, I am pleased that it prevents a too literal reading of its geographies. The account of what I discovered on my wanderings has never pretended to be an objective one. I expect readers who know the area well to exclaim, 'That is not *my* Cowley Road!' To which I can only reply, 'You are right; it is not.' Another traveller would have difficulty following the traces of what is as much an allegorical as a physical journey. All pilgrims plot their own course, even when they tread in the footsteps of another. The thing to do is find a starting point. Perhaps for you, as for me, it lies outside your front door.

The God Delusion
Richard Dawkins

A TIMELY, IMPASSIONED AND BRILLIANTLY
ARGUED POLEMIC ON ATHEISM.

'A very important book, especially in these times . . . a magnificent
book, lucid and wise, truly magisterial'
Ian McEwan

'An entertaining, wildly informative, splendidly written polemic . . .
we are elegantly cajoled, cleverly harangued into shedding
ourselves of this superstitious nonsense that has bedevilled
us since our first visit to Sunday School'
Rod Liddle, SUNDAY TIMES

'A spirited and exhilarating read . . . Dawkins comes roaring
forth in the full vigour of his powerful arguments'
Joan Bakewell, GUARDIAN

'Passionate, clever, funny, uplifting and above all, desperately needed'
DAILY EXPRESS

'A wonderful book . . . joyous, elegant, fair, engaging, and
often very funny . . . informed throughout by an exhilarating
breadth of reference and clarity of thought'
Michael Frayn

'Everyone should read it. Atheists will love Mr Dawkins's
incisive logic and rapier wit'
ECONOMIST

'Richard Dawkins's The God Delusion should be read by everyone
from atheist to monk. If its merciless rationalism doesn't enrage
you at some point, you probably aren't alive'
Julian Barnes

'There is not a dull page in Richard Dawkins's The God Delusion,
a book that makes me want to cheer its clarity,
intelligence and truth-telling'
Claire Tomalin

9780552773317

The Spiders of Allah
James Hider

WINNER OF THE
WHITBREAD BOOK OF THE YEAR AWARD

*'Hider's voice is incisive and rich in the human details that only
first-hand experience bestows. An essential work for anyone
wishing to understand the swirling machinations of Iraq'*
Anthony Loyd, AUTHOR OF *MY WAR GONE BY, I MISS IT SO*

THE BLOODSHED perpetrated in the names of religion in the world
today is nowhere more obvious than in the Middle East. Whether
we are talking about hardcore Zionist settlers still fighting ancient
Biblical battles in the hills of the West Bank or Shiite death squads
roaming the lawless streets of Iraq in the aftermath of Saddam;
whether it's the misappropriation and martyrdom of Mickey
Mouse by Gaza's Islamists, or a US president acting on God's
orders. James Hider sees the hallucinatory effect of what he calls
the 'crack cocaine of fanatical fundamentalism' all around him.

He's not the kind of journalist to shy away from danger, so as he
travels around the Middle East, from Israel to Gaza, to Iraq – the
birthplace of myth that spawned so many faiths – and then back
to Jerusalem, he takes his doubts about religious beliefs to the
very heart of the world's holy wars. He meets terrorists and their
victims, soldiers and clerics, ordinary people and extraordinary
people. The question in the back of his mind is: how can people
not only believe in all this madness, but die and kill for it too?

This extraordinary and timely book takes the *God Delusion* debate
onto the streets of the Middle East. It casts an unflinching yet
compassionate eye on the very very worst and most violent crimes
committed in the name of religion and asks questions that the
world needs to answer if we are to stand a chance of facing our
own worst demons.

9780385615549

Brick Lane
Monica Ali

'Written with a wisdom and skill that few authors attain in a lifetime'
SUNDAY TIMES

AT THE tender age of eighteen, Nazneen's life is turned upside down. After an arranged marriage to a man twenty years her elder she exchanges her Bangladeshi village for a block of flats in London's East End. In this new world, where poor people can be fat and even dogs go on diets, she struggles to make sense of her existence – and to do her duty to her husband. A man of inflated ideas (and stomach), he sorely tests her compliance.

But Nazneen submits, as she must, to Fate and devotes her life to raising her family and slapping down her demons of discontent. Until she becomes aware of a young radical, Karim.

Against a background of escalating racial and gang conflict, they embark on an affair that finally forces Nazneen to take control of her life . . .

*'Brick Lane has everything: richly complex characters,
a gripping story and it's funny too'*
OBSERVER

*'The joy of this book is its marriage of a wonderful writer with
a fresh, rich and hidden world. Her achievement is huge. This is
a book writen with love and compassion'*
EVENING STANDARD

*'The kind of novel that surprises one with its depth and dash;
it is a novel that will last'*
GUARDIAN

*'I was totally gripped by Brick Lane. A brilliant evocation
of sensuality which might occur anywhere'*
DAILY TELEGRAPH

*'A wonderful first novel. Ali's writing is stunning, almost poetic at
times, and she has a beautifully inventive turn of phrase'*
MAIL ON SUNDAY

NOW A MAJOR FILM

9780552774451

The Mystery of Capital
Hernando de Soto

'One of the few new and genuinely promising approaches to overcoming poverty to come along in a long time'
Frances Fukuyma, AUTHOR OF *THE END OF HISTORY*

WHY DOES capitalism triumph in the West but fail almost everywhere else? Elegantly, and with rare clarity, Hernando de Soto revolutionizes our understanding of what capital is and why it does not benefit five-sixths of mankind. He also proposes a solution: enabling the poor to turn the vast assets they possess into wealth.

'A revolutionary book . . . if the criterion is a capacity not only to change permanently the way we look at the world, but also to change the world itself, then there are good grounds for thinking that this book is surely a contender . . . thrillingly subversive'
Donald Macintyre, INDEPENDENT

'Few people in Britain have heard of Hernando de Soto . . . but The Mystery of Capital has already led the cognoscenti to put him in the pantheon of great progressive intellectuals of our age'
EVENING STANDARD

'Astonishing . . . makes a bold, new argument about property'
Matt Ridley, DAILY TELEGRAPH

'A very great book . . . powerful and completely convincing'
Ronald Coase, NOBEL LAUREATE IN ECONOMICS

'A crucial contribution. A new proposal for change that is valid for the whole world'
United Nations

9780552999236

There was a young mom called Hass
Who liked to be in Paris
He stayed in his rooms
When they said: Get a broom
He said - I love my room
That silly old man named
Hass

There was a young uncle called Day
Whose hair was exceptionally grey
When they said: Please don't slump
He let out a great hump
And swept up the meat & the
All over the potatoes & gravy.